Managing Health Education and Promotion Programs

Leadership Skills for the 21st Century
SECOND EDITION

James A. Johnson, PhD, MPA, MS
Professor
Central Michigan University
Mt. Pleasant, Michigan

Donald J. Breckon, PhD, MPH, MA
Past-President
Park College
Parkville, Missouri

JONES AND BARTLETT PUBLISHERS
Sudbury, Massachusetts
BOSTON   TORONTO   LONDON   SINGAPORE

World Headquarters

Jones and Bartlett Publishers
40 Tall Pine Drive
Sudbury, MA 01776
978-443-5000
info@jbpub.com
www.jbpub.com

Jones and Bartlett Publishers
Canada
6339 Ormindale Way
Mississauga, ON L5V IJ2
CANADA

Jones and Bartlett Publishers
International
Barb House, Barb Mews
London W6 7PA
UK

Jones and Bartlett's books and products are available through most bookstores and online booksellers. To contact Jones and Bartlett Publishers directly, call 800-832-0034, fax 978-443-8000, or visit our website, www.jbpub.com.

Substantial discounts on bulk quantities of Jones and Bartlett's publications are available to corporations, professional associations, and other qualified organizations. For details and specific discount information, contact the special sales department at Jones and Bartlett via the above contact information or send an email to specialsales@jbpub.com.

This publication is designed to provide accurate and authoritative information in regard to the subject matter covered. It is sold with the understanding that the publisher is not engaged in rendering legal, accounting, or other professional service. If legal advice or other expert assistance is required, the service of a competent professional person should be sought.

Library of Congress Cataloging-in-Publication Data
Johnson, James A., 1954-
  Managing health education and promotion programs : leadership
  skills for the 21st century / James A. Johnson, Donald J. Breckon.
  -- 2nd ed.
      p. ; cm.
  Rev. ed. of: Managing health promotion programs / Donald J.
Breckon. 1997.
  Includes bibliographical references.
  ISBN-13: 978-0-7637-4237-9
  ISBN-10: 0-7637-4237-6
  1. Health promotion. 2. Preventive health services--Administra-
tion.   I. Breckon, Donald J. Managing health promotion programs.
II. Title.
  [DNLM: 1. Health Promotion--organization & administration.
2. Leadership.   WA 590 J67m 2006]
  RA427.8.B74 2006
  613.068--dc22

                                2006022681

6048

Production Credits

Publisher: Michael Brown
Production Director: Amy Rose
Associate Editor: Kylah Goodfellow McNeill
Associate Production Editor: Daniel Stone
Marketing Manager: Sophie Fleck

Cover Design: Kristin E. Ohlin
Composition: Shawn Girsberger
Printing and Binding: Malloy, Inc.
Cover Printing: Malloy, Inc.

Printed in the United States of America
10 09 08 07 06   10 9 8 7 6 5 4 3 2 1

This book is dedicated to six beautiful Breckon grandchildren, Rachel, Joshua, Kyrstin, Victoria, Maddison, and Andrew and their grandmother. Additionally the three wonderful children of the Johnson family, Allen, Adam, and Elizabeth. Individually and collectively, they are our source of strength and energy. We hope that this book, in some small way, helps to make the world of the twenty-first century a healthier and happier place for them and all the children of the world.

Table of Contents

Foreword

How do you get ahead? When do mangers move beyond merely running an organization to form their own style of leadership? As health organizations become more complex, the tools and skill sets of administrators also need to advance. Financing and funding resources are a battleground in healthcare that only the strong today will survive. *Managing Health Promotion Programs: Leadership Skills for the 21st Century* is a book that will enhance your vision and perception of a successful roadmap to follow. Written by two of the foremost authors in the field of health promotion management (Dr. Donald Breckon and Dr. James Johnson), their careers span a wide variety of both research and practical based expertise.

I wrote this forward for a number of reasons. My background as a past agency director, university grants director, health promotion and program management supervisor, and finally faculty member, give me the practitioner/scholar experiences well suited for this book (as you may also fill one of these or similar roles). During my thirty years of experience in the field of health promotion and administration, I have written five books and over 30 professional journal and magazine articles.

Another unique piece is my close relationship with both authors over the years.

The author of the first edition of this book, Dr. Donald J. Breckon, is past president of Park College in Parkville, Missouri. Dr. Breckon was my mentor while I was a student at Central Michigan University (CMU) during the 1970's. He was also my supervisor when I returned to CMU in the 1980's as a grants center director and feel he was the greatest professional motivator in my life. While I was a young scholar he told me, "Why just read the scientific literature when you can create it?"

In his many roles at CMU he inspired me to move my own career forward. As an author of approximately 150 articles, numerous book chapters/monographs and two nationally used textbooks he carved the path to my own research. Dr. Breckon and I still stay in touch now on a more personal level.

My first introduction to Dr. James Johnson was reviewing his extensive resume when he was recruited to join the faculty at CMU. His publications and professional experience was so exemplary I felt like a rookie. With 13 books and over 100 articles you can see why I felt this way. His previous administrative experience at the Medical University of South Carolina gives him an excellent viewpoint of higher education systems and health organizations. Every summer Dr. Johnson shares his international work with students by taking them to the World Health Organization in Geneva, Switzerland. When he was hired at CMU he was considered what is termed a "super prof."

While these author's bios are most impressive, they are not meant to overwhelm you, but to engage you to reach great heights in health promotion, education, and program management. When you want to learn to accomplish almost anything you emulate the best in the field. Catch a rising star and as it soars so will you. The many principles shared in this book will help you transcend and achieve your potential in managing health promotion programs. I know their guidance and wisdom has served me well over the years.

So here is a book that can serve both as a textbook or personal training guide. Included are in-basket assignments, case studies, comprehensive bibliography, action based concepts and discussion questions. It provides a full range of field studies to assist the reader answer questions in their own working environment.

Management and leadership principles cross many disciplines and this book shares a broad cross section of research. When I was in my master of public administration program we had students and research presented from a wide variety of content areas. Here the authors share their extensive experiences and knowledge for you to contemplate.

Now it is time for you to become the expert. Armed with the tools found in this book you can step out to find your own creative niche and successful path. Great personal and professional gain can result from being considered an expert in your given area of study. I believe this book will help you on your way to both a better understanding of health programs and insight to try new endeavors.

Mark J. Minelli, M.A., M.P.A., Ph.D.
Professor & Chair, School of Health Sciences
Central Michigan University

Preface

Managers are not born, they are made. A few are self-made, having learned what they know mostly from their experiences—by doing and by thinking about what they have done. Undeniably, this system works sometimes, as trial and error works for some, but it is terribly inefficient as an approach to developing managerial skills. Indeed, there are far better ways to learn to be an effective manager. While managers can and should learn from their own mistakes, they also can and should learn from the mistakes (and successes) of others.

Some managers are born into families where management issues are discussed at the dinner table, and they are prepared at a very young age to assume important positions in the family business. For these individuals, management is both "taught and caught" in relatively informal settings and through a series of jobs or positions. A few leaders in the health education and promotion field have a financial or management education and have learned health promotion applications on the job. An even smaller number have completed a master's in business administration as part of their continuing education. However, the authors impressions are that most people in the field have a public health or health care background and are largely untrained for leadership roles. Several college preparatory programs do have introductory courses in administration of various health programs. One projected use for this book is as a required text for such courses.

The process of becoming a manager in the health education and promotion field is typically as follows. There are administrative tasks in most jobs. An educator that does them well naturally migrates to a position that is basically managerial in nature. Unfortunately, the individual, no matter how talented, can be woefully unprepared for the main tasks that make up the job. And of course the individual lacks sufficient time to complete another degree—the learning curve is too steep.

Educators who move into a management role usually develop a self-directed learning program of varying intensity and length. This book is designed to facilitate self-directed management development. It can be used as either an overview of the field or a reference work. Even experienced managers get involved with new issues, and learning what others know about these issues can be a tremendous benefit.

The level of the discussion and the issues considered are appropriate for those who are inexperienced or untrained in the field. Although the book is intended to be wide ranging, not all issues that arise can be addressed in a single book. Most issues that administrators will face, however, are at least introduced.

The book has content, in-basket assignments, and case studies suitable for undergraduate or graduate courses in areas such as public health administration or management of health promotion programs. A bibliography is provided for those who want more detailed discussions of the topics presented.

A key element consists of the Action-Based Concepts found in most chapters and reprinted in Appendix A. These concepts are management principles that emerge from the discussions. They constitute, as suggested by the initials of the term, the ABCs of management. They are present in each chapter, but are also summarized in an appendix, so as to facilitate search and use strategies and review strategies.

The subjects covered by this book are not unique to the health education and promotion field. They are the same subjects found in most introductory college management courses. Moreover, the principles presented are not especially applicable to the administrative tasks that an educator has to perform. They are principles that a full-time manager who used to be an educator or that anyone who aspires to be a manager rather than an educator needs to know.[1]

This book is not about learning to become a better educator.[2] It is about learning to become a better manager or administrator or leader.[3] While some topics are addressed in both types of books, the perspective is different. In this book we seek to integrate our understanding of these topics in ways that are most beneficial to the student and to the practicing manager.

Good wishes go to all who read this book, along with the hope that your college course; continuing education program; or personal development plan is successful and prepares you to excel as a manager and leader in the field of health education and promotion.

NOTES

1. A.O. Kilpatrick and J.A. Johnson, Handbook of Health Administration and Policy. (New York: Marcel Dekker, 1999). This extensive handbook contains over a thousand pages of information that every manager of health programs and organizations should have on their desk.

2. D.J. Breckon, J.R. Harvey, and B. Lancaster, Community Health Education: Setting Roles and Skills for the Twenty-First Century, 3d ed. (Gaithersburg, MD: Aspen Publishers, 1994). This book, an introduction to health education, is an example of the kind of text that can assist anyone who wants to become a better educator.

3. B.J. Fried, M.D. Fottler, and J.A. Johnson, Human Resources in Healthcare: Managing for Success, 2nd ed. (Chicago: Health Administration Press, 2005). This book is an invaluable resource for any manager in the health professions who wants to more effectively manage people in organizations.

Acknowledgments

The authors would like to thank all those who assisted Dr. Breckon in the development of the First Edition and Aamna Qamar for her invaluable assistance to Dr. Johnson with the revisions for the Second Edition. Both authors would like to acknowledge their families for the kind support and encouragement that provided the foundation for this book.

CHAPTER 1

Evolution of Health Education, Health Promotion, and Wellness Programs

EARLY ORIGINS

A search for the origins of health promotion leads to the earliest civilizations. Certainly the fundamental needs of shelter, food, water, and safety are health related, and the writings of the Babylonians, Egyptians, and Old Testament Israelites indicate that various health promotion techniques were utilized.

For example, there were community systems to collect rain water or otherwise provide safe drinking water. There were various sewage disposal methods, including the use of earth closets. Personal cleanliness was advocated. Intoxication was recognized as troublesome. Disease, though not understood, was known to be contagious and various forms of quarantine were used, as were herbal medicines. Days of rest were prescribed and sexual conduct was regulated. Dietary restrictions were numerous, and various sanitary restrictions governed the supply and preparation of food. Regulations regarding menstruation, pregnancy, and childbirth evolved. Exercise was advocated. In some places building regulations were set, and street cleaning and garbage removal began to occur regularly. Mental health and spiritual health (e.g., a sense of harmony) were advocated.

As more was learned about disease transmission, more methods to help control and prevent disease were instituted, such as immunization. Various health care facilities and public health systems were developed to provide better treatment and prevention services. In most early civilizations, health and religion overlapped. Organized religion sponsored many of the earliest health care facilities and practitioners of the healing arts. At various times peoples have portrayed God as visiting disease and destruction on sinful people, as well as being the source of healing for righteous people. In some civilizations, the first temples were also the first hospitals. Medical missionaries have been common to many religions and societies. Regardless of the motivation, religious practitioners' desire to improve the health and well-being of others has been a powerful force in the history of medicine, health education, and health promotion.

Among the positive contributions of religion has been its influence on government institutions and on those who govern. The impact of religion and government on health promotion and wellness programs cannot be fully separated, because many people tend to express their religious commitment through government involvement. Further, the tremendous impact of religion and government on these programs is matched only by the impact of science and technology.

The roots of today's health promotion and wellness programs lie in the Industrial Revolution. The creation of large factories meant that thousands of people were brought together in congested, unsafe worksites located in congested, unsafe cities. The inhumane conditions gave rise to numerous labor laws and worksite programs, not to mention labor unions demanding that the perspective of workers be considered.

Labor union negotiations resulted in various insurance programs that changed medical facility and service utilization patterns. Insurance programs became more accepted by society and more pervasive, and they eventually evolved into nationalized systems that encompassed prevention as well. Economics have always been at the center of such negotiations, and cost reduction or cost shifting was frequently among the most important issues that arose.

Science and technology have had a significant impact on prevention by providing an understanding of the causative roles of pathogens and how to immunize people. Similarly, discovery of the effects of diet, exercise, and substance abuse on chronic disease led to the evolution and elevation of prevention programs. However, science and technology have contributed more to the curative side of disease and disorder through the assortment of disease-specific miracle drugs, therapies, and surgeries they have made available. Of course, the ascendance of technology in health care caused costs to escalate rapidly and making health care accessible and affordable to all became an important goal of providers and third-party payers.

CONTEMPORARY MILESTONES

There are numerous possible starting points from which to choose when discussing the contemporary focus on health promotion and wellness. According to a widely quoted definition, health promotion is "the combination of educational and environmental supports for actions and conditions of living conducive to health."[1] This definition provides a useful framework for describing the contemporary situation.

Health education has traditionally been used to refer to educational interventions. Over time this term has become more inclusive (and coincidentally such interventions have become more effective). The basic approach evolved from the moralistic ("Don't do it because God or the church doesn't want you to.") to the legalistic ("Don't do it because it's against the law."). With this shift, educational programs began to focus on possible harmful effects of certain substances or behaviors and why they were illegal. Of course, one objective was to explain what would happen to lawbreakers if caught. Another was to urge legislators and others to engage in social engineering, such as passing laws mandating safety-related provisions, such as the use of air bags.

The educational process has changed as well. The original models were cognitive (presenting the facts), but they were replaced by affective models (changing attitudes), peer-counseling and peer support models, decision-making models, alternative models, and, most recently, behavioral models. For a discussion of these models and how health education and health promotion have evolved, see *Community Health Education: Setting Roles and Skills for the Twenty-First Century*.[2]

This paradigm shift in the profession did not just happen. It was made to happen by practicing professionals and college professors whose research and writing focused on finding ways to increase the effectiveness of the programs they advocated.

As data accumulated and the profession matured, more leadership efforts were devoted to institutionalizing health education, health promotion, and wellness programming, primarily through government mandates and through focusing on economic issues in business and industry. The creation of the President's Committee on Health Education in 1973 was an important early event. This committee, among other things, legitimized a nationwide emphasis on health education and an expanded role for government in developing model programs and providing seed money for their implementation. It recommended, for example, creation of a National Center for Health Education, which occurred in 1975. The Center successfully pushed for expanded worksite programming as well as nationwide programming, professional credentialing, and comprehensive school health education programs.

Two seminal works that influenced the profession were the 1979 Surgeon General's report on health promotion entitled *Healthy People*, and the 1980 report entitled *Promoting Health, Preventing Disease: Objectives for the Nation*. In 1980, the U.S. Government also created a separate Department of Education in the Department of Health and Human Services and gave it responsibility for supporting health education, health promotion, and wellness programming. In 1981, *Objectives for the Nation in Disease Prevention and Health Promotion* was adopted as policy in the United States and again in 2001 with new goals established.

As the profession gained in national prominence, certifying health education and health promotion specialists and upgrading and standardizing college prepa-

ams at both the undergraduate and graduate levels became important
.ification standards and procedures were finalized in 1988 and national
.ing began in 1990. Finally, the following year, 1991, saw the publication ᴏᴄ *Healthy People 2000: National Health Promotion and Disease Prevention
Objectives* and *Healthy Communities 2000: Model Standards*. Subsequently *Healthy
People 2010* was published and is helping to shift public policy toward prevention
through health education and health promotion programming in communities.

The documents, consultation, and seed money pegged to these initiatives were
intended to facilitate the meeting of the *Healthy People* and *Healthy Communities*
standards by the year 2000 and the newer goals by 2010. Local units of government were charged with taking the lead in this effort:

> Government is "residual guarantor" of health services, whether they
> are provided directly or through community agencies. Every locale and
> population should be served by a unit of government that takes a lead-
> ership role in assuring the public's health. This concept has become
> known as "a governmental presence at the local level.[3]

Each local unit of government was given the responsibility of coordinating
planning and ensuring that local standards would be established and programming
devised to ensure they are met:

> The government at the local level has the responsibility for ensuring that
> a health problem is monitored and that services to correct that problem
> are available. The state government must monitor the effectiveness of
> local efforts to control health problems and act as a residual guarantor
> of services when community resources are inadequate, recognizing of
> course that state resources are also limited.[4]

As the *Healthy Communities 2000* and *Healthy Communities 2010* documents
noted, communities will always need multiple interventions and overlapping programs. The problems and opportunities are too great to be left to government alone:

> Many of the activities . . . go beyond the activities customarily carried
> out by state and local governmental agencies. Even in those areas where
> health agencies are extensively involved, prevention is a shared respon-
> sibility of the public and private sector.[5]

In *Healthy People 2010* there are two overarching goals:

1. Increase quality and years of healthy life.
2. Eliminate health disparities.[6]

As we move further into the twenty-first century, the United States is placing
a greater emphasis on health, health education, health promotion, and wellness

programming than ever before in its history, and several other nations are undergoing the same shift in priorities. The World Health Organization has become much more active in disease management, mitigation, and now, prevention. Goals are being set, public and private sector efforts are being coordinated, seed money is being provided, and results are being monitored. Some of the results here in the United States—increased highway safety and reductions in alcohol misuse and tobacco use—are heartening. The results, of course, are mixed, and motivations vary over time. Hospitals have done much more prevention programming in spite of budget restrictions. Health care reorganization and managed care have been redefining the roles of hospitals. Some states have initiated comprehensive school-based health education programs. Many corporations have provided employee wellness programs, desiring to increase production and employee longevity and reduce absenteeism and employee turnover.

Government regulations and worksite policies are forcing people to engage in healthier behavior. Yet as longevity increases, more disease among the elderly occurs and more dollars are spent caring for this growing segment of society. One thing is certain: there are more opportunities for health education, health promotion, and wellness specialists than ever before, as well as more agencies providing related services. It follows that more and better skilled managers, administrators, and leaders are needed in such agencies.

ACTION-BASED CONCEPT

Managers should read about and be able to discuss historical milestones relevant to their profession and their agency. An understanding of history is always important, because it is the only means of fully understanding the present and anticipating the future.

TRENDS

A review of the history of health promotion programming reveals its roots in the earlier civilizations. After all, health is integrally related to length and quality of life. Religion has also consistently played a role in health promotion. Most religions have advocated maintaining personal health and accepting responsibility for improving the health of others. Likewise, governments typically have acted to improve the collective health of the people being governed. Over the centuries, they have regulated activities that negatively impact health. Their focus has been on promoting the quality of life more than the length of life, although the two cannot be fully separated.

Business and industry have also been major players in health education and health promotion programming since the Industrial Revolution, admittedly prodded into action by labor unions. Early efforts to improve safety and eliminate inhumane working conditions have evolved into comprehensive employee wellness programs.

Science and technology are implicated in the spread of certain health problems as well as in the improvement of health. Discovery of the etiology and epidemiology of various diseases and disorders has made numerous prevention and early intervention actions possible, some of which government has mandated (e.g., the addition of iodine to salt and of fluoride to drinking water). In the last few decades, the science of health education and health promotion has matured and has demonstrated the ability to produce significant results. Major gains have been made in extending the length of life and improving the quality of life, and the practitioners have become recognized as constituting a profession. The improved effectiveness of programs and the recognition of the profession have jointly led to institutionalization.

Philosophically, one can always ask how much programming is enough and, similarly, how much government is too much. All people will ultimately die, and the prevention of health problems, by extending life, gives rise to other problems associated with old age. Health professionals must continue to focus on the quality of life and the prevention of premature death and must accept that death and its antecedent diseases and disorders cannot be postponed forever. Increasingly, it is being recognized that death with dignity is desirable.

Nonetheless, health education and promotion specialists must always remember that they deal with matters of life and death and with quality of life issues. They are often in a position to prevent disease and premature death and concurrently improve the quality of life. Such responsibility is sobering—even awesome—and requires a commitment to act in accordance with the standards of their profession. This can include providing the best possible leadership for a health education, health promotion, or wellness program.

ACTION-BASED CONCEPT

Managers must generally take quality improvement into account. Quality improvement should be an important element of virtually every decision made, whether it be improvement of the quality of life of clients, the quality of services or programs provided, the quality of staff, or the quality of decision-making processes.

The purpose of this textbook is to provide an introduction to the fundamental concepts of management, administration, and leadership and to demonstrate their application in a variety of health education, health promotion, and wellness programs. It is the authors' sincere desire that this book stimulates interest in the management and administration of such programs and improves the practice of those who have migrated from education to management and administration. The profession must have competent leaders, administrators, and managers if it is to warrant the trust placed in it and justify the dollars spent on health promotion. Can the profession do less than adequately prepare leaders, administrators, and managers for the programs they have helped to create?

CONCLUSION

Improving the health of individuals and communities was a concern of the earliest civilizations and it remains a concern today. Indeed, health education and promotion has evolved into a profession, and certification indicating adequacy of training and competence is now available.

Health promotion programming is pervasive in the private and public sectors of most industrialized societies, and it has even been suggested that we are in a "golden age" of health education and promotion. Yet the question remains whether the profession will continue to flourish (because its practice has improved) or whether it will begin to decline (because it has not lived up to its potential). The answer to this question is largely in the hands of today's practitioners.

IN-BASKET ASSIGNMENTS

TO: Health Education and Health Promotion Specialists
FROM: The Director
RE: Terminology and Titles

I don't really understand the difference between health education and health promotion. Please provide me with a written summary, including definitions, examples, and areas of overlap. Should we be using one term or the other, or both?

I would like this information by the first of the month for a discussion at our staff meeting. A page or two will probably be sufficient.

Thanks!

* * * *

TO: Health Education and Health Promotion Specialists
FROM: The Director
RE: Grant Application

    We are working on a grant application, and I need two or three paragraphs that describe the Healthy People 2000 and the Healthy Communities 2000 projects so that I can tie our health promotion proposal to them.

    I need the paragraphs by Monday. Please expedite!

MANAGEMENT CASE STUDY

Setting

    A state health department was preparing to hire a health promotion specialist to stimulate and coordinate activities throughout the state. The position was approved and budgeted.

Problem

    The individuals who needed to approve the job description objected to the requirement that applicants be graduates of a Society of Public Health Education/ American Alliance of Health Education (SoPHE/AAHE)—approved program or be a certified health education specialist. It was argued that this would unnecessarily restrict the applicant pool.

Alternatives Considered

    One alternative considered was to include the phrase "or equivalent work experience" so as not to close the door on nurses and other health care providers who might apply.

    Another was to state "CHES preferred or completion of CHES certification within the first year of employment." Yet a third alternative was not to have a certification requirement at all.

Action Taken

    The job description was approved so as to include "CHES certification preferred or to be obtained within the first year of employment." The rationale given was that CHES certification would ensure that the leader of this state initiative would have appropriate breadth and depth of understanding of professional issues. However, it was accepted that work study and self study were alternative ways to get to the desired point and should not be prohibited.

OUTCOME

A certified health education specialist was among the applicants. She was hired, and the state health department has made good progress toward meeting its goals.

DISCUSSION QUESTIONS

1. How important is the CHES certification? What are the certification criteria? How does one become certified?

2. After reviewing the criteria, explain why CHES certification should or should not be included in a job description. Is there a clear-cut decision that is always right?

3. How might one respond to the claim that requiring CHES certification unnecessarily limits the applicant pool?

4. Should graduating from a Society of Public Health Education- or American Alliance of Health Education-approved baccalaureate program or obtaining a CEPH-approved graduate degree give a candidate an advantage over someone who has migrated to the profession from a related health care field?

5. Are there other strategies that could have been used to ensure an experienced and competent individual was hired for the position?

NOTES

1. L. Green and M. Kreuter, *Health Promotion Planning: An Educational and Environmental Approach* (Mountain View, CA: Mayfield Publishing, 1993): 17.

2. D.J. Breckon, J.R. Harvey, and B. Lancaster, *Community Health Education: Setting Roles and Skills for the Twenty-First Century,* 3rd ed. (Gaithersburg, MD: Aspen Publishers, 1994).

3. *Healthy Communities 2000: Model Standards* (Washington, DC: American Public Health Association, 1991): xvii.

4. *Healthy Communities 2000:* 443.

5. *Healthy Communities 2000:* 443.

6. *Healthy People 2010* (Washington, DC: U.S. Department of Health and Human Services, 2001).

CHAPTER 2

Evolution of Management, Administrative, and Leadership Theories

HISTORICAL PERSPECTIVE

As long as there have been human endeavors, there have been people willing to take charge—people willing to plan, organize, staff, and control the work.[1] One might say that nature abhors a vacuum and thus someone will always step forward to fill a leadership void.

Probably the natural emergence of leadership grew out of our instinct for survival. In the hostile world of early humankind, food, shelter, and safety needs usually required cooperative efforts, and cooperative efforts required some form of leadership. Certainly leadership was vested in the heads of early families via the patriarchal system. The oldest member of the family was the most experienced and was presumed to be the wisest member of the family and thus was the natural leader.

As families grew into tribes and tribes evolved into nations, more complex forms of leadership were required and did evolve. Division of labor and supervision practices are recorded on the earliest written record, the clay tablets of the Sumerians. In Sumerian society, as in many others since, the wisest and best leaders were thought to be the priests and other religious leaders.

Likewise, the ancient Babylonian cities developed very strict codes, such as the code of Hammurabi. King Nebuchadnezzar used color codes to control production of the hanging gardens, and there were weekly and annual reports, norms for productivity, and rewards for piecework.

The Egyptians organized their people and their slaves to build their cities and pyramids. Construction of one pyramid, around 5000 BC., required the labor of 100,000 people working for approximately 20 years. Planning, organizing, and controlling were essential elements of that and other feats, many of them long term. The ancient Egyptian Pharaohs had long-term planners and advisors, as did their contemporaries in China. China perfected military organization based on line and staff principles and used these same principles in the early Chinese dynasties. Confucius wrote parables that offered practical suggestions for public administration.

In the Old Testament, Moses led a group of Jewish slaves out of Egypt and then organized them into a nation. Exodus, Chapter 18, describes how Moses "chose able men out of all Israel and made them heads over the people, and differentiated between rulers of thousands, rulers of hundreds, rulers of fifties and rulers of tens." A system of judges also evolved, with only the hard cases coming to Moses.

The city-states of Greece were commonwealths, with councils, courts, administrative officials, and boards of generals. Socrates talked about management as a skill separate from technical knowledge and experience. Plato wrote about specialization and proposed notions of a healthy republic.

The Roman Empire is thought by many to have been so successful because of the Romans' great ability to organize the military and conquer new lands. Those sent to govern the far-flung parts of the empire were effective administrators and were able to maintain relationships with leaders from other provinces and across the empire as a whole.

There are numerous other ancient leaders who were skillful organizers, at least as indicated by their accomplishments, such as Hannibal, who shepherded an army across the Alps, and the first emperor of China, who built the Great Wall. Many of the practices employed today in leading, managing, and administering modern organizations have their origins in antiquity.

Many concepts of authority developed in a religious context. One example is the Roman Catholic Church with its efficient formal organization and management techniques. The chain of command or path of authority, including the concept of specialization, was a most important contribution to management theory.

Machiavelli also wrote about authority, stressing that it comes from the consent of the masses. However, the ideas Machiavelli expressed in *The Prince* are more often viewed as mainly concerned with leadership and communication.

Much management theory has military origins, probably because efficiency and effectiveness are essential for success in warfare. The concepts of unity of command, line of command, staff advisors, and division of work all can be traced back at least to Alexander the Great, or even earlier, to Lao Tzu.

ACTION-BASED CONCEPT

Specialization, division of work, path of authority, and chain of command are all important elements of management.

The Industrial Revolution created a need for new thinking and the refinement of old thinking. Time and motion studies intensified the division of work, as did centralized production and research and development.

Modern management theory is discussed in the next section. The preceding historical review indicates that thinking about management and leadership is in large part situational and that practices evolved to deal with new situations that arose. It also indicates that yesterday's principles and theories are surprisingly contemporary and surprisingly sophisticated. Some overlap occurs, of course, and some gaps. Today's theorists have attempted to fill in the gaps and adapt the theories to current situations. Yet, like in other areas of thought, not much is of recent origin in the field of management theory.

CURRENT MANAGEMENT THOUGHT

There are numerous management theories, but they more or less fall into four groups: the scientific approach, the systems approach, the humanistic approach, and the contingency approach.

The Scientific Approach

Not surprisingly, the scientific approach uses the scientific method to achieve maximum output, minimum strain, elimination of waste, and reduction of inefficiency. Automation is encouraged. Where human involvement is required, rules, laws, and formulae replace individual judgment. Individual behavior is recorded and analyzed so that it can become the basis of rules. Scientific research is used to try to discover the best way to do a job. Workers are scientifically selected and trained to ensure that work is done as efficiently as possible. Work is studied so that managers are given the work for which they are best fitted, as are the employees they supervise.

ACTION-BASED CONCEPT

Maximizing output and efficiency and minimizing strain and waste are important elements of management.

An overriding concern is that competence govern the division of labor. This principle leads, of course, to standardization and specialization as well as hierarchy. Written rules determine the work each person performs as well as the promotion of employees into management ranks.

Naturally, the emphasis on written rules led to the formulation of what are now known as the classical principles of management, summarized as follows:

- 'Division of work and specialization should characterize any enterprise, and management should be a separate function. Departmentalization is by process or place.
- Authority should be equal to responsibility, with enough authority granted to ensure success.
- Discipline is required to ensure that the best interests of the organization are served.
- Unity of direction and unity of command are required so that people receive direction from only one supervisor.
- Subordination of individual interests must occur so that the general interest is best served.
- Centralization is desirable, especially centralization of decision making.
- Order is essential for everything, and an orderly process and orderly appearance are required.
- Employees should be adequately and fairly remunerated to reduce employee turnover and increase production.
- The emphasis is on production, and standards and incentive rewards are used to maximize production.

The scientific approach, not surprisingly, gave rise to the systems approach. The two approaches share many features but differ in format.

The Systems Approach

The first task of this approach is to break the whole into logical parts that are interconnected in an orderly fashion. The next task is to study the component parts and strive to understand how they perform in various circumstances. The application of systems analysis techniques to management resulted in identification of seven interconnected systems that could be studied separately or as parts of the whole of management:

1. Planning is the process of specifying goals, establishing priorities, and otherwise identifying and sequencing action steps to accomplish the goals.

2. Organizing is the establishing of a structure or set of relationships so that the plan can be accomplished.

3. Staffing is the assigning of personnel to specific roles or functions so that the organization works as designed.

4. Directing is the making of decisions and the communication of them to the staff who will implement them.

5. Coordinating is the task of directing the various components, and otherwise communicating between the units so that their interrelationships are smooth as is the function of the entire enterprise.

6. Reporting is the transfer of information through conferences, reports, and records to those to whom the manager is accountable.

7. Budgeting is fiscal planning, accounting, and control.

ACTION-BASED CONCEPT

Planning, organizing, staffing, directing, coordinating, reporting, and budgeting are important elements of management.

Certainly modern-day managers plan, organize, staff, direct, coordinate, report, and budget. Other words are sometimes used to identify the functions, but their importance remains the same. Of course, not all managers will have the responsibility to perform all these functions. Yet from a systems theory perspective, they are the common subsystems of management.

The systems approach, however, is also concerned with how each enterprise fits into the larger social, cultural, economic, and political system. Although an organization is itself a social system with subsystems that can be analyzed and focused on production or service, it is still only one of many organizations that make up the larger social system. The importance of interconnectedness can not be under estimated in the world of the 21st century.

The Humanistic Approach

Management gets things done through machines and people, and some theorists speculated that treating people as machines was counterproductive. The work environment began to be studied, as did interpersonal relationships and the formal and informal groups in the workplace. Worker satisfaction and worker attitudes were also investigated. The result was a push toward more worker participation in the management process and better communication. Of course, labor unions played a big role in this trend.

ACTION-BASED CONCEPT

Management gets things done through people, and efforts to improve the working environment and worker satisfaction usually increase productivity.

The Contingency Approach

Each of the three management theories discussed above has many variations, and there are yet other theories that do not fit neatly into any of the major categories. Also, advocates of each of the three theories freely admit that their preferred theory has limitations and that other theories have elements that are useful. Indeed, many argue that the theories are not mutually exclusive and that it is possible to use elements of all three in the same situation. Moreover, most would admit that the best managers incorporate all of the theories in their management style.

The strategy of combining elements of different theories is known as the contingency approach. Theorists who favor this approach argue that the best policy is to go with what works given the particular problems, workers, managers, and setting. They claim that there is no best management theory and certainly none that works well all the time. The most reasonable management strategy is to continuously monitor and analyze the managerial environment and integrate strands of different management theories to arrive at the best combination.

The scientific, systems, humanistic, and contingency approaches all still have numerous advocates. Each one has strengths and weaknesses, and each one has its appropriate uses. Therefore, every manager should be familiar with these theories and be able to apply them effectively in the proper circumstances.

ACTION-BASED CONCEPT

No one theory will fit all situations. Managers must understand the particular circumstances and utilize appropriate elements of each major theory while maintaining flexibility.

MANAGERIAL ROLES

College students reading this book may not be especially interested in management theory; instead, they probably are more concerned to find out what managers do, because such knowledge will help them in their consideration of different career options. Managers, when writing about their major responsibilities, typically assert that they plan, organize, coordinate, and control. Yet how are these responsibilities translated into day-to-day activities? One recent research-based article on management by Henry Mintzberg punctured the idea that managers generally engage in systematic planning.

Folklore: The manager is a reflective, systematic planner.

Fact: Study after study has shown that managers work at an unrelenting pace, that their activities are characterized by brevity, variety, and discontinuity, and that they are strongly oriented to action, and dislike reflective activities.[2]

The work of managing involves a steady stream of meetings, callers, and mail from early morning until late night. Coffee breaks and lunches are often work related, and breakfast and dinner meetings are all too common. Workdays become longer over time, and the tasks expand to fill all available hours, regardless of the amount of delegation or additional staffing. There is the ever present "to do" list, the stack of "get to it later" things to shuffle through frequently, as well as the "must read" stack of journals, reports, and newsletters. Interruptions are the rule, and time to think and plan is the most needed, most precious, most missing ingredient. Is it any wonder that stress is a common problem among today's managers?

ACTION-BASED CONCEPT

Management is action-oriented, and managers need lots of energy, the ability to be decisive, and the ability to cope with stress.

Folklore: The effective manager has no regular duties to perform.

Fact: Managerial work involves performing a number of regular duties, including ritual and ceremonial negotiations, and processing of soft information that links the organization with its environment.[3]

One the biggest problems is that a manager's schedule becomes filled with numerous and often long meetings. Far too many appointments concern complaints or issues that should have been handled by others. Standing meetings with key employees and with key groups of employees take too much time. Preparing for meetings and following up on meetings often occupy more time than the meetings do or than the issues are worth.

The public relations functions become "old" after a while, as does the travel. Then there is the enormous task of sorting through the abundant and sometimes conflicting information and making sense of it—trying to see a path or discover which direction to take without adequate time to think reflectively about the issues that must be faced.

Folklore: The . manager needs aggregated information, which a formal management information system best provides.

Fact: Managers strongly favor verbal media telephone calls and meetings over documents.[4]

Again, the authors' experiences are consistent with this claim. Far more time is spent in oral communication or using faxes or e-mail than reading or preparing written reports. This is not to deny that reading widely can be enormously beneficial. Managers need to search for ideas and news items with potential to impact the organization, mentally or physically file them away, and occasionally forward them to others with the appropriate spans of control. Frequent consultation with other managers has been found to be essential as a way of finding out what they are thinking and feeling, because most of their thoughts do not get written down. It is from the mix of soft information, largely verbally transmitted, that decisions are made.

ACTION-BASED CONCEPT

Extensive reading and informal communication are needed by managers, yet finding the time to read and communicate informally is often the most difficult task.

The Mintzberg article belittled the idea that management is or is quickly becoming a science and a profession.

The managers' programs—to schedule time, process information, make decisions, and so on—remain locked deep inside their brains. Thus, to describe these programs, we rely on words like judgement and intuition, seldom stopping to realize that they are merely labels for our ignorance.[5]

Indeed, rarely does time permit full application of decision-making theory. Decisions are often made on the spot, in the midst of a meeting, on the phone, or while walking and talking. They have to be made quickly and intuitively because others need them to be made. To extend the decision-making period would be to slow others down and increase one's own backlog of work. Yet some decisions must be postponed until the opinions of others are sought or the time to reflect is available.

The manager's world is enormously complicated and difficult. Managers are overburdened with obligations yet cannot easily delegate their tasks. As a result they are driven to overwork and forced to do many tasks superficially. Brevity, fragmentation, and verbal communication characterize their work.[6]

So why do people go into management if what they do is stress filled and ultra demanding? The reasons are many, including increased salary, perks and prestige, personality variables ("I like to be where the action is."), the desire to make a difference, and the issue of "Who else will do it?" There will always be managers—and there will always be managerial turnover as individuals decide they lack the proper temperament or interest, or prove that they are missing the skills demanded by their superiors.

AN OVERVIEW OF LEADERSHIP

Many individuals manage at middle levels of an organization without having much leadership responsibility. They simply do specific management tasks. While admittedly an oversimplification, leadership implies change and influence whereas management can perhaps seem static (e.g., concentrated on controlling existing work processes). Of course, management, as discussed earlier, involves planning, organizing, staffing, directing, and controlling, and planning is future oriented. Long-term planning is a responsibility of top-level administrators, but for many managers, especially mid-level managers, the focus is on making decisions required to keep the organization functioning more or less as it is. Sometimes, lower-level managers simply do what they are authorized to do and must seek permission to do anything different. Planned change is a priority for only a few managers, and these are appropriately called leaders.

The distinction between leadership and management is blurry, yet it is worth noting, because leadership is the single most important ingredient in any organization or community. It is also the ingredient in shortest supply.

ACTION-BASED CONCEPT

Leadership implies change and involves management of planned change. High-level managers will also have leadership responsibilities, and leaders often have management responsibilities.

Little is accomplished without leaders, but followers are also required. Leaders would not be leaders if no one followed. And leaders must always recognize that fact and be grateful to their followers and share the credit whenever possible. The authors of this volume strongly believe that leaders receive too much credit for organizational accomplishments and too much criticism for organizational failure. Teamwork and shared credit are preferable, since both leaders and followers are needed.

What is it that makes one person a leader and another a follower? What characteristics distinguish leaders from followers? And what are the leadership skills that can be developed?

Warren Bennis, a widely respected management consultant and author of leadership books, has specified the characteristics of leaders and compared them with the characteristics of managers. Bennis points to innovation, trust, and a long-range perspective as distinguishing marks of leadership. He indicates that leaders challenge the status quo and often ask "why?" or "why not?" But perhaps the two most important distinctions between managers and leaders are these:

- The manager is the classic good soldier; the leader is his (or her) own person.
- The manager does things right; the leader does the right thing.[7]

ACTION-BASED CONCEPT

Leaders innovate, inspire trust, make long-range plans, and motivate people to change.

Much fruitful thinking can be devoted to Bennis's characteristics of leadership. Certainly innovation and original thinking are key ingredients. Focusing on people and inspiring trust are also critical. Taking a long-range perspective, challenging traditional thinking and the status quo, and being willing to do the right thing and take risks are all part of the leadership process. It is easy to agree with Bennis's thinking, and perhaps his analysis of leadership is sufficient for many.[8] However, for the sake of clarification and emphasis, further discussion is in order.

It is useful to think of leadership in the context of planned change. On January 1, 2001 we began a new year, a new decade, a new century, and a new millennium. That all of these occurred simultaneously was a rare event, and thus, represented an unusually good opportunity to contemplate organizational change.

It is no secret that change occurs whether we want it to or not and that the rate of change is escalating. Some authors who write about trends believe that the winds of change are now reaching hurricane proportion. As one author points out, "Americans experience more technological change in a single year than their parents witnessed in a lifetime."[9] In addition, 90 percent of all information created since the Ice Age was created in the last 30 years, and our entire body of knowledge is now doubling every five years. In fact, the human body replaces every single molecule it is comprised of every seven years. The ancient insight of Heraclitus, that "the only constant change," is even more salient as reinforced by the work of modern scientists such as Albert Einstein.

Change is all around us. Organizations have to change in order to respond effectively to an ever-changing world. A vital question is, will people manage change or will change manage and shape people? Similarly, will people dare to simply react to change or will they take a proactive stance and aggressively plan change? One answer is that managers will simply react to change while leaders will proactively manage change. Peter Drucker hints at this role for leaders by stating that "every organization has to build the management of change into its very structure. Every organization has to prepare for the abandonment of everything it does."[10]

ACTION-BASED CONCEPT

Managers devote their time to solving personnel problems, financial problems, and legal problems, whereas leaders plan and manage change.

Managers deal with personnel issues, financial constraints, and legal problems. Although necessary functions, they are not sufficient for long-term organizational success. A past president of Yale University once stated that financial constraints and budgetary deficits can not justify a deficit in intellectual vision or a response to changes sweeping the world. Another author put the issue this way: reliance on yesterday's successful response in the face of new challenges leads to decline. If managers keep on doing what they have been doing, they will keep on getting the same results, or worse. Managers may settle for more of the same, for continuity and stability, but leaders want better results—more growth and increased efficiency.

People are uncomfortable with change, and leaders have to provide the necessary impetus and guidance. To do this, they must deal with people's fear, arrogance, complacency, and lack of imagination, beginning with their own.[11] Self-analysis is a fruitful place to begin working on leadership skills.

Optimism about the future of society, self-confidence, confidence in the organization and staff, and optimism about the organization's future are essential for effective leadership. Of course, optimism about the future of society and optimism about the organization's future are largely determined by current circumstances, whereas self-confidence is partly a matter of personality and partly a matter of having a history of success at work. Mike Friesen and James Johnson have even gone so far as to say the "new paradigm" of success involves embracing change.[12]

CONCLUSION

In any project or organization, someone has to be in charge in order to ensure that decisions are made in an orderly, timely, efficient manner. That person can be called a manager or a leader.

Management and leadership theories have roots in antiquity. Modern theories, however, have evolved in response to increases in the complexity of the work environment resulting from the Industrial Revolution, the growth in high technology, and the development of global transportation and communication systems. Modern managers tend to focus on short-range issues associated with keeping an organization running smoothly, whereas leaders tend to focus on planned change, both short-range and long-range. Yet most managers perform some leadership functions, and most leaders have some management responsibilities. Opportunities to pursue a career as a manager or a leader are increasing because of the population increase, and either type of career can be rewarding and ultimately satisfying. Management or leadership skills can be learned and enhanced through work experience.

IN-BASKET ASSIGNMENT

TO: Health Education and Health Promotion Specialists
FROM: The Director
RE: Time Management Techniques

I would like a reminder sheet for our department heads on time management techniques. They are all very busy and need to be as efficient as possible.

Please review an article or two and prepare a list of six to a dozen strategies that are recommended.

If there is a book or article that is particularly good, list the reference so staff who wish to can do additional reading.

I would like this material sometime this month, if possible.

Thanks!

MANAGEMENT CASE STUDY

Setting

An AIDS-oriented agency in a midsized metropolitan area was being administered by an AIDS patient with only a modicum of managerial or leadership experience. However, because of the capabilities of its staff fund-raiser, the agency raised enough to cover its $250,000 annual budget.

Problem

The fund-raiser saw the manager as a person without an adequate vision of what the organization could become. The manager seemed content to maintain service to AIDS patients and their families as the primary focus. The fund-raiser saw opportunities for AIDS education and AIDS advocacy in the legislature but was rebuffed by the manager, who stated he did not want the organization to take on more than it could do well. The fund-raiser talked to the board chair about the opportunities and about the need for leadership rather than mere management.

Alternatives Considered

One alternative considered was to establish a board-initiated and -conducted planning task force. Another was to ask the manager to survey six similar agencies in other metropolitan areas as to their size, budget, program emphases, and so on. The third alternative was to replace the director with someone who had stronger leadership skills.

Actions Taken

The board decided to direct the manager to survey six similar agencies and to present a summary of the results to the board. The summary was to be presented at the next board meeting so it could be used by an organizational futures task force to be created by the board.

OUTCOME

The survey indicated that most of the six agencies were doing more and that their larger budgets were being covered. The organizational futures task force decided that the local community would support an increase in the budget and a wider range of activities. The board subsequently developed an expansion plan and directed the manager to implement it. The manager started the process but concurrently began looking for another position more suited to his skills, finding one in six months. The fund-raiser was promoted to manager

DISCUSSION QUESTIONS

1. Is a bigger organization better? Could other organizations have been formed to do the additional tasks? What advantage is there to having one large organization encompass AIDS patient services, education, and advocacy instead of having three separate organizations perform the necessary activities?

2. Can a manager evolve into a leader? How could such an evolution be achieved?

3. How likely is it that the fund-raiser was merely attempting to orchestrate a promotion? How might the manager have responded other than by changing jobs? In what other ways might the board have responded?

NOTES

1. The ideas in this section are adapted from R. Stueart and B. Moran, *Library and Information Center Management* (Englewood, CO: Libraries Unlimited, Inc., 1993): chap. 1.

2. H. Mintzberg, "The Manager's Job: Folklore and Fact," in *Management 96/97*, 4th ed., ed. F.H. Maidment (Sluice Dock, Guilford, CT: Brown & Benchmark Publishers, 1996): 7.

3. Mintzberg, "The Manager's Job": 7, 8.

4. Mintzberg, "The Manager's Job": 8.

5. Mintzberg, "The Manager's Job": 9.

6. Mintzberg, "The Manager's Job": 10.

7. W. Bennis, *On Becoming a Leader* (Reading, MA: Addison-Wesley Publishers, 1989): 45.

8. J. A. Johnson, "Interview with Warren Bennis," *Journal of Healthcare Management* (July/August 1998): 293.

9. R. Hetterick, Jr., "Technological Change and Higher Education Policy," *AGB Priorities 1* (Spring 1994): 1.

10. P. Drucker, *Innovation and Entrepreneurial Practices and Principles* (New York: Harper Business, 1992): 19.

11. L. Miller, *Barbarians to Bureaucrats: Corporate Lifestyle Strategies* (New York: Fawcett, 1989): 178.

12. M. Friesen and J.A. Johnson, *The Success Paradigm* (Westport, CT: Quorum Books, 1995): 33.

CHAPTER 3

Health and Quality of Life in the 21st Century

The first decade of the twenty-first century can serve as a reminder of how much the world has changed and will continue to change. We have recently witnessed a very damaging terrorist attack on a major American city and subsequent attacks elsewhere in the world. There is now an ever present concern that a manmade biological weapon will someday be used. Additionally, pandemics such as HIV/AIDS and emerging possibilities such as Avian Flu remain center stage in public health agencies worldwide. With recent natural disasters, such as Hurricane Katrina and the Indian Ocean Tsunami, we are well reminded how woefully under-prepared we are for disruptions in our daily lives.

Indeed, Alvin Toffler, perhaps the best known futurist in the world and author of *Future Shock*; *The Third Wave*; and *Powershift*, said that the winds of change have reached hurricane proportions. He suggested that change comes in major waves that affect all aspects of life. In his view, there have been three waves of change. The first occurred approximately 10,000 years ago, when small tribes of people wandered from place to place in search of food and water. Because of the development of agriculture, most of these tribes were able to give up their migratory form of life and instead stay in one place and farm the land. The spread of farming changed almost everything—the economy, political system, social structure, and even religion—for most groups of people. Some presumably thought this change would be the end of the world, and they were partially correct: it was the end of the world as they had known it.

Toffler suggests that the second wave occurred when the emphasis changed from agriculture to industry. This wave, known as the Industrial Revolution, also was accompanied by widespread and profound change. Factories were built and cities grew up around them, creating many new problems. Life became standardized, specialized, and centralized. Small families became the rule. There were new forms of communication, transportation, education, defense, entertainment, and religion. Again, people's lifestyles were altered irrevocably.

Toffler contends, and most futurists agree, that the world is currently in the midst of a third wave of change—a transformation from an industrial-based society to a technocratic society. The new era, often called the Information Age, was initiated by the development of computers, and computerization continues to be a dominant feature.

There are now computers in virtually every organization in America, as well as in a large percentage of homes. Most business transactions involve a computer at one or more stages. Increasingly, shopping is done at home, work assignments are done at home, college degrees are earned at home, and even worship services are participated in at home via computer technology. The globalization of the economy is facilitated by computer networks that connect businesses in different parts of the world.

Some Information Age technological developments include an increasingly robust information highway that provides access to a diverse array of on-line databases; standard digital formats that allow for the distribution of movies, music, and books to media such as CDs and DVDs and to hand-held devices; Wi-Fi wireless technology and interactive video conferencing that facilitate intra-organizational communications; and advances in robotics and nanotechnology that continue to revolutionize manufacturing and other fields.

CURRENT DEVELOPMENTS IN HEALTH CARE

On the world health scene, AIDS continues to be a costly disease, while diseases such as smallpox and polio largely have been eradicated. The mid-1990s saw death rates from heart disease and automobile accidents continue to decline in the U.S. Tobacco use has also gone down in the U.S. but continues to rise in developing countries. Food supplies are better labeled to promote healthier choices, based on calorie content, fat content, sodium content, and nutrient enrichment, yet being overweight is still a major causative factor of chronic disease and disability in the developed world.

The 1988 Institute of Medicine study on the future of public health contributed to a number of changes in health care.[1] The study identified three core functions of public health: assessment, policy development, and assurance. The needs assessment function involves determining what the major health-related problems are, the policy development function involves planning how to respond to these problems, and the assurance function involves monitoring public health efforts to ensure that results are consistent with the goals set during the planning stage. Needless to say, the study focused on the relationship between health care providers and local and state public health agencies and was written from a "managed care" perspective.

In 2004 the Institute of Medicine held its first annual summit, *A Focus on Communities*, aimed at moving the nation closer to a vision of a twenty-first century health care system. The reports from this and subsequent summits synthesize many strategies and action plans proposed to improve health care.[2]

Health care is in such rapid flux it is hard to even describe it. Diagnostic work formerly done on an inpatient basis is now being done in community clinics or even in the home. More treatments are also provided in the home, and hospital stays have been dramatically shortened. Computers have made laser surgery, magnetic resonance imaging, ultrasound diagnosis, and a whole host of other medical interventions possible. Long-term care of the growing segment of aged and infirmed people is a major concern of the "sandwich generation," who attempt to cope with the care of both their children and their parents while working. The gap between the health status of the rich and the poor is greater than in the past and is getting larger, and the size of both groups is getting larger as the middle class continues to shrink. (Increasingly, a college degree is what separates those in the high-income bracket from those in the low-income bracket.)

Hospitals are getting bigger and nicer, a smaller percentage of people are going to them, and lengths of stay are generally shorter. However, inner-city emergency rooms are more crowded and understaffed. HMOs and PPOs have become commonplace, routinely providing office visits and prevention services at a relatively low cost for insured members, but unemployment and other factors have resulted in an increase in the number of people without insurance. Meanwhile, the entire nation is attempting to reduce health care expenditures and poverty programs, and real fears exist that a generation of children will be severely adversely affected by the reductions.

What does this mean for this new century? Specifically, what health issues must be addressed by those living and working in the first decades of the new millennium?

ACTION-BASED CONCEPT

Managers need to think in terms of trends, recent changes, current shifts, and emerging issues, and read materials on trend analysis.

EMERGING ISSUES

The conditions that provide the context for a quality lifestyle must receive increasing attention. The public health issues of the disposal of toxic waste, the pollution of our great bodies of water, the destruction of the world's tropical forests, the supply of potable water to large population centers, the distribution of food to developing nations and to the poor in economically advanced nations, and the provision of affordable and accessible care for a rapidly aging population will become increasingly important. Redistribution of the health care dollar must continue to be discussed as a priority issue, because most health care expenditures are currently being used to prolong the life of terminally ill patients and relatively little is being spent on prevention. As noted earlier, the rich are getting richer and the poor are getting poorer, and history shows that the rich will dominate policy decisions. The expenditure of dollars to keep terminally ill people alive longer is understandably not viewed as a priority by the poor. Wealth usually carries with it power and influence, so it is reasonable to ask what educated, wealthy, influential policy makers want or need.

A FOURTH WAVE OF CHANGE: THE GROWING EMPHASIS ON QUALITY OF LIFE

Using Toffler's notion of waves of change, might we not ask whether a fourth wave of change is already in evidence? We believe, in fact, that the recent emphasis on the quality of life as opposed to the mere length of life may grow to have the kind of impact that would qualify it as a bona fide wave of change.

Quality of life advocates look at the consequences of an action and weigh the pluses and minuses. If the "plus" consequences predominate, the action is seen as good. Of course, a social perspective is also possible. For example, one can ask the question "Will the action result in the greatest good for the greatest number of people?"

Quality of life ethicists have developed criteria to evaluate individual behavior. According to Winifred Pinch, "These criteria range from quite minimal qualities, such as ability to maintain basic physiological functioning, . . . to the complex ability of self-actualization as described in Maslow's Theory of Human Development."[3] Possible criteria within this scope include "intellectual level, optimal personality development, social usefulness or dire need of health care."[4]

The World Health Organization's definition of health, dating back to 1947, is still just as salient today: "Health is a state of complete physical, mental, and social well-being and not merely the absence of disease and infirmity".[5]

Many different individual actions and social policies can be evaluated by considering their consequences for individuals' quality of life, and thus their health. Indeed, with regard to any action or policy, it is possible to ask the following questions:

- Will it increase the ability of individuals to achieve self-actualization?
- Will it increase the intellectual level, personality development, and social effectiveness of individuals?

- Will it improve human relationships?
- Will it increase the ability of individuals to express concerned caring and actions supportive of others?
- Will it increase individuals' social worth and thereby increase their personal well-being and happiness?
- Will it increase the quality of life in society and the world as a whole?

Although these questions may not seem immediately relevant to health education and health promotion, it is important to remember that health promotion seeks to improve the conditions of living and to enhance not only physical, but also mental, emotional, and spiritual well-being. Moreover, social health has become a priority, especially given the Healthy People 2010 agenda set by the federal government.

Preventing or treating chronic diseases such as AIDS, coronary artery disease, diabetes, and cancer usually contributes significantly to the quality of life of the individuals treated and the community. Similarly, promoting prenatal, infant, and child health has major quality of life ramifications for children, their parents, and society.

Even though the genetic potential for human life is estimated to be as high as 120 years, many people are not interested in efforts to extend life indefinitely. The right to die with dignity when a decent quality of life is no longer possible is more widely accepted than ever before. Paradoxically, society continues to spend most of its health care dollars on the terminally ill. This raises the question, does spending most of our health care dollars on the terminally ill do more for the quality of life of society as a whole than would spending them on prevention programs? This question will permeate many discussions throughout the twenty-first century.

CURRENT QUALITY OF LIFE INDEXES

Hopefully, many health educators realize that improving quality of life is a fundamental goal of the Healthy People 2010 national health objectives or that quality of life is currently being measured as part of the Behavioral Risk Factor Surveillance System. According to the Center for Disease Control and Prevention (CDC) in Atlanta, GA:

> Quality of life, not just physical functioning, should guide the design, organization and integration of services. Although quality of life is a subjective concept, valid measures exist for assessing many of its components, including physical, cognitive, psychological and social functioning. By broadening our attention to embrace all these determinants of individual well being, we are more likely to develop service delivery systems that prevent needless impairment and disability.[6]

In fact, the mission of the CDC is "To promote health and quality of life by preventing and controlling disease, injury, and disability."

Health promotion personnel should be encouraged by some recent results. Health status is better. People are living longer and enjoying a better quality of life. Yet the studies say that quality of life is still threatened, albeit by factors other than physical ailments. Nearly one-third of Americans say they suffer from some mental health problem every month. Mental health problems can be just as prevalent and disabling as physical conditions. In fact, in the rapidly developing research in the neurosciences, it is being found that the distinction between mental and physical processes is pretty nebulous.

Stress, depression, anxiety, and other emotional problems are cited frequently, with a wide variety of causative factors. The prevalence of mental health problems has led health promotion experts to explore an ecological model of quality of life (see Table 3–1).

> ### *ACTION-BASED CONCEPT*
>
> *Managers must attend to quality, promoting it and insisting on it, for nothing can replace the impact that quality has on all an agency does.*

AN AGENDA FOR THE FUTURE

As a relatively new profession, health education has not adequately encouraged or funded research. Its neglect of research is ending, however, and the development of a research agenda is becoming a higher priority. The merging of an increased emphasis on prevention programming and quality of life issues suggests that the following areas will grow in importance.

Violence—including child abuse, spouse abuse, rape or other sex abuse, gang conflict, and homicide—is becoming a topic of primary concern. Can the quality of life be very high if people are afraid they will be assaulted? Does not the fear of violence cause stress? Community organization and education theories and experiences can be applied to violence-related problems, yet very little is really known about them outside of sociological studies or pop culture perceptions.

What settings are most effective for health education interventions to combat violence? What methods are appropriate for which populations? People are no longer willing to tolerate violence because of its impact on the quality of life, and health educators must respond to their demand for an end to the prevalence of fear.

Table 3–1 Selected Elements from an Ecological Model of Quality of Life

Level	Physical Environment	Social Environment	Health and Social	Medical Condition	Functional Status	Lifestyle/ Behavior
Societal International National State	Climate Water quality	Peace Justice	Medicare Head Start	Mortality patterns	Active life expectancy	Voting patterns Opinion polls
Large Community Region County City Area	Transportation Housing	Education Employment opportunities	Ambulance service Information centers	Disease outbreaks	Hospital beds Hospital census	Citizen participation
Small Group/ Community Neighborhood Worksite School Church Hospital Jail Residence Family	Walk trails Access for persons with disabilities	Values Social support	Medical care resources Self-help groups	Disease clusters	Family dysfunction profiles	Group behavior patterns Volunteer patterns
Individual Personal space Body	Privacy Prostheses	Leisure time Spirituality	Medical care access Self-care	Symptoms Illness	Disability Emotional function	Physical activity Safety behavior

Source: Reprinted from Workshop on Quality of Life/Health Status Surveillance for States and Communities, Report of a Meeting on December 2–4, 1991, Stone Mountain, GA, Centers for Disease Control and Prevention, Atlanta, GA, 1993

Group-specific interventions to improve quality of life must be studied carefully because not certain interventions work better in some populations than others. For example, how should interventions in a Hispanic-American, largely Catholic, somewhat patriarchal society to prevent cancer or HIV/AIDS differ from interventions in an African-American, largely Protestant, somewhat matriarchal society? The profession knows that age-specific interventions are generally appropriate and that gender-specific interventions are often necessary, not to mention socioeconomic class–specific interventions. A poor, rural mother of six will usually require a different strategy than an upper-income lawyer mother of two, even if the health problem being addressed is the same.

The research base is so small that many of these issues have not been investigated on a group level, let alone on an individual level. For example, there are several methods for helping people to stop smoking, but not enough research exists to allow any one of them to be prescribed with confidence.

Quality of life advocates want effective, efficient interventions at low cost, and the past "one size fits all" answers of the profession will no longer satisfy an empowered minority.

One important quality of life issue is drug abuse. Increasingly, people are demanding drug abuse prevention help for their kids, their spouses, their fellow employees, and neighborhood drug users. Amazing progress has been made in reducing tobacco use through the Smoke Free 2000 programs. The success of these programs has caused many people to demand similar programs for alcohol abuse and illegal drug use. Yet no proven strategy to eliminate alcohol and drug abuse exists, and people are running out of patience with the health profession because of its seeming inability to solve the problem of abuse.

Quality of life issues are bringing churches to the forefront again. Yet only a few health educators are focusing on spiritual health and how to promote other aspects of health in churches. The resurgence of parochial schools, religious family life centers, and church membership provides an opportunity for spiritually-based health education.

The family structure in the U.S. is changing significantly. For one thing, divorce and single-parent families are far more prevalent than they used to be. Unfortunately, health education hasn't done enough for parents who are trying to cope with the real-world problems they and their children face.

Transferability needs more research devoted to it as well, because of the importance of spending every health care dollar wisely. Are there group intervention strategies that impact more than one health risk factor? Are there common methods of increasing resistance to drug use and resistance to risky sexual activity? Where is the largest return on investment, especially with high-risk populations?

Finally, how can the media best be used for health promotion? After all, society depends on the media for news, education, and entertainment. The media is admittedly made up of private, profit-making organizations and so resists control, but many believe that a combination of regulations and incentives can make the media, especially television, an effective health promotion tool. No one disputes that the media affects the quality of life for better and for worse, but the question remains as to how its positive impact can be maximized.

CONCLUSION

The decades ahead are likely to bring a whole new set of problems requiring innovative solutions. Toffler cautions,

> Society needs people who take care of the elderly and who know how to be compassionate and honest. Society needs people who work in hospitals. Society needs all kinds of skill that are not just cognitive; they're emotional, they're affectional. You can't run the society on data and computers alone.[7]

Sadly, in some respects health education and health promotion programs are still using nineteenth-century strategies and twentieth-century thinking. Socioeconomic and educational levels are changing, and many social groups are being empowered. Society is demanding better service, and health educators must provide it if the golden age of health education is to continue. Practitioners and administrators must keep in mind that they are in the life-saving business and that people can be profoundly affected by their efforts. Health, in the final analysis, is a means to an end—a self-actualized, socially responsible, and personally satisfying life.

IN-BASKET ASSIGNMENTS

TO: Health Education and Health Promotion Specialists
FROM: The Executive Director
RE: Long-Range Plan

> I want to create a long-range plan (perhaps with a ten-year time frame) and would like you to do some background work for me. What do you think the critical health issues that could be influenced by health education and health promotion will be in ten years? What critical health issues will be the most controversial? What issues will impact the most people?

> Please prepare a summary and come see me to discuss it.

* * * *

TO: Health Education and Health Promotion Specialists
FROM: The Director
RE: Quality Emphasis

We are reading more and more about quality—quality of life, quality of work, quality of products, quality of programs. I have heard of quality improvement teams in industry.

Why do you think there is so much emphasis on quality?

Increasing quality will obviously drive up price. Is it worth it? What are the payoffs of increasing quality? What are the tradeoffs?

MANAGEMENT CASE STUDY

Setting

The National Tuberculosis Association was a nationally prominent voluntary health agency with state and local chapters. It was one of the oldest of such agencies and one of the best. It emphasized research on treatment and prevention, education of patients and health care personnel, and service to all involved in the battle against TB. Its efforts, when combined with the efforts of government agencies, were spectacularly successful. Tuberculosis was largely eradicated, at least in the United States.

Problem

Financial contributions decreased, as did the number of volunteers willing to work. The organization had an escalating organizational maintenance problem. The National Tuberculosis Association could not readily help others when the organization itself was not healthy.

Alternatives Considered

1. Allow the organization to die in dignity, because its purpose had been accomplished.

2. Change the focus of the agency to another disease, permitting the organization to survive.

Actions Taken

The organization changed its name to the American Lung Association and expanded its scope to include other respiratory diseases, such as lung cancer and emphysema.

OUTCOME

The expanded scope and name change resulted in a major infusion of new dollars, volunteers, energy, and ideas, and the organization has had a major impact on both lung cancer and emphysema.

DISCUSSION QUESTIONS

1. Are there other organizations that "worked themselves out of a job" and either expanded their focus or closed down?

2. What were the results?

3. What factors could have led the National Tuberculosis Association to close down?

4. Are there some health organizations that should close or be closed?

5. What characteristics do they possess that might support a decision to close?

6. What problems of the 1980s and 1990s are close enough to being solved that the agencies devoted to solving them should consider reorienting themselves or closing down?

7. What new problems are emerging that might call for a national voluntary agency?

8. What organizations are especially concerned with the quality of life?

NOTES

1. Institute of Medicine, *Future of Public Health* (Washington, DC: National Academy Press, 1988).

2. Institute of Medicine, *Crossing the Quality Chasm: A Focus on Communities* (Washington, DC: National Academy Press, 2005).

3. W.J. Pinch, "Quality of Life as a Philosophical Position," *Health Values 10*, n. 6 (1986): 41.

4. Pinch, "Quality of Life": 41.

5. J.F. McKenzie, R. Pinger, and J. Kotecki, *An Introduction to Community Health, 5th Ed* (Boston: Jones and Bartlett, 2005): 5.

6. "Quality of Life/Functional Status, 1995 BRFSS Module," Centers for Disease Control and Prevention, Atlanta, GA, 30 May 1995: 2.

7. *Wikipedia: The Free Encyclopedia*, s.v. "A. Toffler," http://en.wikipedia.org/wiki/Alvin_Toffler (accessed March 2006).

CHAPTER 4

Organizational Dynamics

ORGANIZATIONAL CHANGE

It has been aptly stated that "all leaders stand on the shoulders of giants," meaning that much is owed by contemporary leaders of an organization to those who have gone before. These predecessors have usually contributed a great deal, by either "growing the organization" or keeping it together during difficult times.

Growing an organization is not necessarily better than stabilizing or maturing it. An agency that has survived for 25 years and is respected is usually a strong organization. Managers who preside during periods of stability are entitled to feel as proud as managers who preside during periods of explosive growth.

Managers need not be critical of their predecessors, but instead study the preceding era to learn about the issues, the obstacles and opportunities, and the decisions made. Those who fail to learn from an organization's past put the organization's future at risk. Those who criticize their predecessors probably do not understand thoroughly the environment that existed and the constraints that were faced. Contemporary managers cannot know for sure how they would have led the organization in the same situation.

ACTION-BASED CONCEPT

Managers need to study their organization's history to learn about the problems faced, the decisions made, and the accomplishments and failures.

This does not mean the new manager of an agency should be satisfied with the status quo when he or she takes over. A major goal is to expand the agency's impact. Although bigger is not necessarily better, staying the same size while other community organizations are growing can result in a loss of organizational impact, and maximizing the agency's impact on community health problems is the essential task of the organization's leader from a macromanagement perspective. The goal is to become more visible, more respected, and "more of a player" in community decision making.

Developing the capacity of the agency to make a difference becomes more of a central responsibility as one moves up the organizational chart and is the main focus of the Chief Executive Officer (CEO) and other top-level managers. Expanding the impact of the agency on the community will be addressed in the next section, and expanding the impact of a department on the agency, the task of a mid-level manager, will be covered in succeeding sections. These macromanagement issues are often subsumed in discussions of leadership, and hopefully, making them core topics of this chapter will allow the reader to understand them better.

ACTION-BASED CONCEPT

Managers must focus on macro-management as well as micromanagement issues.

ORGANIZATIONAL DEVELOPMENT

Since change is inevitable, it becomes imperative for the manager to engage in planned change efforts and the kind of thinking that goes along with it. Organizational development, as a field and a philosophy, offers a good opportunity to do this effectively. As stated by James Johnson,

> Healthcare organizations are fundamentally dependent on people who have to fill an extensive range of roles to accomplish the institution's tasks and goals. Leading and managing complex institutions, considering the scope and scale of tasks in healthcare delivery, are a complicated undertaking and also entail organizational development.[1]

Processes are designed and decisions are made to improve the ability of an organization to effectively manage changes in its environment while also meeting the needs of its members and clients. Johnson also asserts that leaders and mangers must go beyond a narrow focus on power and control in periods of organizational change. They must create commitment and motivation among various stakeholders to make the change work. The leader creates a sense of direction, a vision, and then nurtures and supports those who can make the organization a success.[2] Organizational development then becomes a vehicle for enhancing the individual, the organization, and the communities served.

EXPANDING ORGANIZATIONAL IMPACT

A critical management function involves acting as a spokesperson and role model for the organization. Little that a manager does is more important than communicating, and he or she needs to be an effective communicator in both formal and informal settings. If the manager is especially good at making formal presentations, then that role should be emphasized, although other types of communication must not be ignored. The manager needs to frequently and consistently articulate what the agency's mission is, what it is doing to better the community, and what it is striving to become. The main message should be succinct and should be repeated frequently and consistently—in speeches, in conversations, and in the media (and should be contained in printed materials that represent the agency).

Communicating this message to internal constituencies is also important. The manager needs to repeat it in staff meetings, in hiring interviews, in performance evaluation sessions, in staff newsletters, on bulletin boards, and on fax cover sheets. The message must permeate the organization, and the manager can be as creative in spreading the word as he or she wants to be. Finally, to ascertain how effective communication of the message has been, the manager needs to determine whether staff members are themselves disseminating the message.

Being a player in community decisions about health issues means being "at the table." The agency must have a presence at every significant meeting. A top-level administrator who can make decisions about levels of organizational involvement usually should be the agency's representative. This requires a commitment on the part of top-level administrators to attend evening meetings (and thus abandon the comfort of a 9 to 5 schedule) and the creation of a budget to support such community initiatives.

ACTION-BASED CONCEPT

Macromanagement requires expanding the organization's impact, which in turn requires ensuring the organization's presence in decision-making settings.

Expanding organizational impact often involves the development of partnerships. If a health fair is slated to be held, a health organization seeking to establish a community presence should offer to take part. If no health fair is scheduled, the organization may want to sponsor one—and hold it in a high traffic area like a shopping mall or a county fair. There are numerous opportunities to create partnerships with senior citizen groups, schools, churches, businesses, retired employees, and so on. Partnerships create legitimacy through association and by ensuring the organization's presence at co-sponsored events. However, being an effective partner requires a budget and a willingness to spend it on joint activities. Most groups involved in a project will welcome a partner with human and fiscal resources.

Organizational development requires the organization to promote its activities, whether by partnership or otherwise. The organization should feel no pride in being the best kept secret in town. To put it in the vernacular, "if you've got it, flaunt it"— within the bounds of good taste, of course. The more often an organization is in the media for its accomplishments, the more likely it is to be viewed as a player.

Media coverage, marketing strategies, paid ads in appropriate publications, co-sponsorship of events, news releases, fliers, booths, and any other opportunities to build a visible presence and to enhance the organization's image should be used. Although marketing and public relations can be delegated, organizational development cannot be. It is the responsibility of top-level managers to enhance the organization's impact and image. Furthermore, the media messages and themes needed to achieve this goal are somewhat different than the messages and themes marketing and media personnel normally develop.

Mailing newsletters to community decision makers can be very helpful if the newsletters are well done and if they go to the right people. A manager need not be in charge of such publications but should have sign-off responsibility for copy and format.

Managerial sign-off authority is critical, because "the view from the top" is different from other views in the organization. Those at the top must maintain a macromanagement image development perspective, a perspective not easy for those in lower levels of the organization to achieve. First impressions of buildings and grounds are critical, as are perceptions of the quality of services and programs. Mixed or inaccurate messages should not be approved by those with sign-off responsibility. (The "sign off" need not be in writing. The point is that any decision that could affect the organization's image in the community should be reviewed and endorsed or rejected by the manager.)

This process of organizational image building requires the participation of many staff members. Adequate staffing of events, neat and clean facilities, correct and consistent resource materials, contemporary signage, an eye-catching logo, health education–related presentations, partnerships with community organizations—all of these are part of image enhancement. One commonly effective method of strengthening community relations is to encourage community groups to use the organization's meeting rooms, which gets the agency's name in the media and allows community members to see the facilities.

Everything that is done to expand the organization's impact must be done well, because the organization's image is at stake. Image building through visible quality programs is an important theme that needs regular emphasis. Quality must be obvious in everything, and budget must not be allowed to dictate poor quality. For example, the budget may not permit a four-color, four-page monthly newsletter, but a two-color, two-page quarterly newsletter can still be a quality publication, both in format and content.

Managers need to be cognizant of the fact that they are "always on stage," that is, they are perceived as representing the organization, whether at the grocery store, a sporting event, or a community forum. Decorum and appearance play an important role in building the organization's image.

Managers should read materials on organizational development periodically and may benefit from attending workshops and seminars on the topic. But their main task is to establish a presence in the community. Demonstrating concern, helping, whenever possible, through partnerships or sponsorships, and providing financial and human resources, all constitute the basis of a good organizational development policy. Being a good listener and a good negotiator is also important, as is looking for "win-win" strategies. Managers must always seek ways to enhance the organization's image, always be on the lookout for promotion opportunities, and always represent the agency in a professional manner.

EXPANDING DEPARTMENTAL INFLUENCE

For mid-level managers of departments, most of what has been said in the preceding section is also relevant. It is especially relevant for a mid-level manager who wants to move up, because by being sensitive to macromanagement issues and by finding ways to enhance the organization's impact in the community, the manager will increase his or her chances of being promoted. Helping a supervisor achieve organizational goals—and giving the supervisor credit for good things and taking the blame for problem areas—is usually a good career move.

Enhancing departmental influence requires a focus on organizational goals and a plan for meeting them. If one organizational goal is to increase the client load, anything the department can do to bring in more clients expands its influence. If the organization desires to increase its visibility, increase outside funding, and increase the use of high technology, then new initiatives by the department that contribute to the achievement of these goals will also expand its influence.

Departmental staff meetings conducted by mid-level managers should include a focus on organizational goals and contain brainstorming sessions to uncover ways the department can contribute to achieving these goals. Doing what is important and doing it well is essential—not only managing operational tasks, but making sure they are done in the most productive and efficient manner possible.

Being image conscious and impact conscious are both important. There are many little things that a mid-level manager can do to enhance the image of the department. These include being on time for meetings, doing background reading, volunteering the department to do tasks that others might not want to do, taking minutes at staff meetings, getting written assignments done on time, returning phone calls promptly, completing tasks and reporting back, offering insightful comments, supporting one's supervisor in a controversial discussion, and calming an irritated employee in a staff meeting.

A department seeking to expand its influence can explore the possibility of increasing its staff and budget. A request for an increase must be well written and explain how the staffing and budget changes will help in meeting the organization's goals or the goals of the Executive Director. Knowing how the staffing and budget process works and submitting the request in a timely manner are essential. It is often beneficial to have others involved in the budget request process to strengthen the justification for the increase. In the reverse case, if an organization has to downsize or cut its budget, the manager who cuts staff or expenses efficiently and without too much complaining will often get the positions or funds restored if that becomes possible.

ACTION-BASED CONCEPT

Macromanagement issues are important for a department manager whose focus includes expanding the department's influence in the organization and the community.

If the impact of possible reductions is put in writing, in non-emotive, factual terms, it will make it easier for the decision makers to avoid the cut or to restore the lost resources at a later point. Many decisions are made uninfluenced by emotions or passion, and putting the impact in writing permits the case against a cut to receive the full attention of the decision makers at the time of the decision.

Executive Directors and CEO's do not like surprises, so it is often helpful to review important proposals with top management before submission. Obviously, this is not always possible in large bureaucracies, but reviewing a proposal with one's supervisor is often good strategy. It is also a good idea to keep the supervisor informed of problems that are developing or new initiatives and, even if the supervisor is merely supportive, to give him or her some credit for helping develop the proposal. (Sharing the credit generally increases the likelihood of adoption.)

Another strategy to gain top management support of a department is to avoid presenting problems for resolution without offering carefully considered possible solutions. Getting top management input on potential solutions is much different than presenting problems without providing a clue as to how to deal with them.

Although the above strategies are important, the fundamental task of a manager seeking to expand a department's intra-organization influence is to maximize the department's impact on the community. Managers ought to know what competitors are doing and be thinking of ways to expand the market niche of the organization. It can also be helpful to know what colleagues in other cities are doing, as they permit implementation of similar projects locally. And it is always essential to understand the organization's objectives (and the supervisor's or director's personal goals) and strategize how the department can help accomplish them. Managers who focus on these matters will find the impact of their unit increasing, not to mention their career opportunities.

CONCLUSION

A major leadership role of managers is organizational development and the enhancement of the effectiveness, image and community impact of the organization or unit. Although most of this book focuses on micromanagement issues, each such issue must be approached with an awareness of how the unit or organization will be affected by the higher-level actions or strategies available to address the issue. Ultimately, the organization must be seen as highly interconnected with its community and within its own structure. At all levels change occurs and must be planned for and managed.

IN-BASKET ASSIGNMENT

TO: Health Education and Health Promotion Specialists
FROM: The Executive Director
RE: Organizational Development

I have been hearing a lot about organizational development lately and confess I don't know much about it. Is it the same as organizational psychology? How is it alike or different? Please check the library or bookstore for a book or two on organizational development or organizational psychology. Dig out a definition or two, along with answers to the above questions. Please send me your findings within a couple of days.

Thanks.

MANAGEMENT CASE STUDY

Setting

A county health department near a large city hired a health educator for the first time. Previously, education on prevention had been restricted to some of its nursing programs.

Problem

The new health educator wanted to quickly establish a presence and to expand the health education program's influence significantly during the first year.

Alternatives Considered

1. The program could serve as a clearinghouse and referral source and focus on coordinating existing resources.
2. It could educate the existing staff about prevention programming opportunities, encouraging them to design and implement at least one prevention program each year and helping them with the necessary tasks.
3. It could do something with high media exposure potential, such as institute a senior screening and education program.

Actions Taken

The health educator in consultation with the CEO decided to implement senior screening and education programs in two existing senior citizen program locations at three-month intervals. They decided to involve as many departments and as many other community agencies as possible. They also planned to maximize community exposure by printing and distributing posters and fliers; advertising the programs in newsletters; arranging for radio, television, and newspaper coverage; and so on.

OUTCOME

Five other agencies agreed to participate. The health educator chaired the coordinating committee, and the marketing function was distributed among the five agencies. The screening and education programs had a relatively modest number of participants, but the extensive publicity created awareness that the health department was in the health education business. Much valuable networking occurred, and a decision was made to "do it again and do it better."

DISCUSSION QUESTIONS

1. What is the downside of focusing a new program on referrals? Is it realistic for a new health educator to jump into the role of coordinating community health agencies?

2. Is a health educator more likely to be successful encouraging other departments to conduct prevention programs or asking them to assist in an organization wide community project?

3. Is a health educator likely to be successful adopting a strategy of promoting existing prevention activities in existing departments through the media? What are the advantages of such an approach?

4. What are the advantages and disadvantages of doing something with high community visibility quickly, as opposed to engaging in a long-range planning process prior to doing programs?

5. Are there other alternatives that the health educator should have considered?

NOTES

1. J.A. Johnson, G. Ledlow. and B.J. Kerr, "Organizational Development, Training, and Knowledge Management", in Human Resources in Healthcare: Managing for Success, 2nd ed. B. Fried, M. Fottler, and J.A. Johnson (Chicago: Health Administration Press, 2005): 205.

2. T. Kent, J.A. Johnson, and D.A. Graber, "Leadership in the Formation of New Healthcare Environments," Healthcare Supervisor, v. 15, n. 2: 28–29.

CHAPTER 5

Board Governance and Responsibility

A MANAGEMENT PERSPECTIVE

Every employee or volunteer reports to or is supervised by someone, unless of course that person is the sole owner of a business. Even the top executive of an organization typically reports to a board and is supervised by the board chair.

Most organizations have a controlling board and many have a variety of advisory boards. Having a board is a requirement for tax-exempt status, which in turn is an essential condition for any organization that wishes to solicit or receive contributions. In order for a gift to count as a tax-exempt contribution, the organization has to submit bylaws and other legal documents and must have a board of directors, trustees, or others appointed or elected to perform a controlling role.

A board is the legally constituted body that guides and directs the organization. Public members are appointed or elected to ensure that the public good will be served by the board's actions.

Boards have a variety of titles, structures, and functions. For example, local health departments usually have a board of health appointed by the elected county board of commissioners. Many, but not all, state health departments also have a board that sets policy for local boards of health, but staff at the local level usually interface with state health department officials rather than the board.

Hospitals typically have a board of directors established in the enabling charter. The board is usually self-perpetuating, which means that terms of office are limited and the board appoints replacements as vacancies occur. Although health promotion personnel do not usually attend board meetings or interact with board members, new programs, program upgrades, or program downsizing will usually require a presentation to and authorization by the board.

Business and industries large enough to have health promotion programs will often have shareholder boards or public director boards. Again, routine health education interaction with such boards is not typical, but on occasions when it does occur, it may be critical.

A voluntary community health agency might have a small board consisting of local city or county representatives. Such a board would be supervised by regional- or state-level staff, who in turn would interact with the state board. Similarly, the board of a national organization sets policy for the boards of state branches, which in turn set policy for the boards of local branches. The American Heart Association, American Lung Association, and American Cancer Society use this organizational structure.

Health promotion personnel also work with local school boards, which typically consist of elected local officials. As in the case of health departments, a state board of education typically sets broad parameters for local school boards. However, owing to the belief that local citizens should control education in their communities, local boards of education are being allowed a greater degree of autonomy.

There are a whole host of local organizations that deal with substance abuse, AIDS, child abuse, violence, and many other health issues. The board of this type of organization is usually created by an enabling charter, which describes its structure and functions.

More and more coalitions and coordinating councils are being created to address community health problems and increase the impact of the members' advocacy activities. The United Way model, in which a board is appointed to represent the interests of a diverse group of member agencies, is commonly used. Coalitions are often involved in assessing, planning, and implementing community health promotion programs, and they can play a critical role in directing funding and focusing public awareness. On the other hand, coalitions are not always desirable. As they grow larger, their focus may become diluted. Organizations may even disappear through coalescence. Regardless, being elected or appointed to a coalition or coordinating council can assist a health educator to favorably influence decisions that will impact his or her own organization.

This overview of types of boards is presented to help readers realize the pervading influence of boards and the necessity of working effectively with them. Although only the top administrators of an organization normally interact directly with the board, all administrative personnel should be aware of board policies and board personnel.

ACTION-BASED CONCEPT

Managers should obtain a copy of the charter, bylaws, and membership of the organization's board, study them carefully, and file them for convenient access.

BOARD MEMBERSHIP

Because the board of an organization typically controls budgets and operating policies, it is helpful to think about who serves on the board and why, especially if attempting to get a person on the board who is favorably disposed toward health education and health promotion programs.

Those who select board members are typically concerned about the public's perception of candidates and their credibility in the community. If one goal is to gain community acceptance for the purpose of fund-raising and increasing program participation, then high name recognition becomes increasingly important. Individuals who are well known and respected in the community usually serve on a variety of boards, and their membership on a board tends to lend credibility to the organization. An adage in fund-raising is that "people give to peers," and it is commonly thought that the most important factor in the request for a donation is who does the asking. Because one role of board members is to solicit gifts, selecting highly respected individuals to serve on the board is essential.

Sometimes a specific type of expertise might be desirable, such as medical, legal, or financial expertise. Physicians, lawyers, and bankers not only can provide expertise but can act as liaisons between the organization and their colleagues. For example, if an agency intends to interface with schools or hospitals, having an educator or doctor on the board can facilitate planning.

Sometimes, individuals are selected because of their fund-raising skills and experience. Similarly, an ability to influence corporate giving may be one of the selection criteria. Constituency representation may also be a criterion. For example, substance abuse prevention agencies may find it desirable to have educators, doctors, and employers involved. Some tax-funded programs are obligated to have at least 50 percent of board membership consist of consumers.

Given the importance of board functions, an organization's health education and promotion programs need advocates at the decision-making level. If a health education advocate is not presently on the board, then the organization should consider how to influence current board members or how to get an advocate appointed to the board.

ACTION-BASED CONCEPT

Analyze who is on each board with whom you interact, why they were selected, what they bring to that board, and what their attitude is toward your program.

ACTION-BASED CONCEPT

Prepare a list of individuals who meet the status and other board selection criteria and would likely be advocates of your program.

ACTION-BASED CONCEPT

Scan the news reports often to ascertain who is on what board and think about what issues they are focused on. Perhaps keep a file folder of potential board members who could act as liaisons between your program and the community if placed on the board.

BOARD STRUCTURE

Boards vary in size and organization, depending on their purpose. Local boards with a modicum of responsibility for day-to-day operations typically meet monthly, while others meet bimonthly or even quarterly. State and national boards typically meet quarterly and have an executive committee that performs needed tasks between meetings.

Board membership tenure is typically for several years and is staggered so that continuity occurs and yet new ideas are continually infused into the board's deliberations. The board's standing committee structure will vary as well, although a finance or budget committee, an education committee, and a public relations committee are typical. Long-range planning committees are also common, but frequently the executive committee serves that function as well as the nominating committee function.

A variety of ad hoc (temporary) committees are created as needed to deal with specific issues that emerge. Generally speaking, the more often the board meets and the larger the number of standing committees, the smaller the number of ad hoc committees needed.

> ## *ACTION-BASED CONCEPT*
>
> *Minimize the use of ad hoc committees and try not to have any board member serving on more than one standing committee. Board members should be aware of all important issues and have the opportunity to be involved in dealing with most of them.*

> ## *ACTION-BASED CONCEPT*
>
> *The CEO should provide the board with an overview of the major issues facing the organization. If the board meets only quarterly, a brief written monthly report should be sent to the board members.*

BOARD MEETINGS

Busy people want well-organized, efficient meetings, not long or boring meetings. Attention should be given to preparing meeting agendas, ensuring the availability of needed backup materials, and providing an oral or written executive summary of each issue. For each agenda item it is helpful to have a summary sheet that lists the item, suggests a recommended action, provides a rationale, and lists alternatives to the suggested action (see Exhibit 5–1).

Board meetings should be educational. One tactic is to bring in program directors to provide an overview and answer questions. Board meetings also need to be enjoyable, and providing refreshments (meals, when appropriate), meeting in different locations, and preparing interesting reports can help make attending the meetings more pleasurable.

> ## *ACTION-BASED CONCEPT*
>
> *Seek feedback from board members on what can be done to make the board meetings more interesting, more enjoyable, and more productive.*

Exhibit 5–1 Agenda Item Worksheet

BOARD OF DIRECTORS WORKSHEET

ITEM:

SPOKESPERSON(S):

ATTACHMENT(S):

Suggested Actions:

Rationale:

Alternatives:

Relationship to Mission Statement, Goals, Objectives:

BOARD FUNCTIONS

An agency's board is typically charged with oversight of the agency. The level of supervision depends on the charter and bylaws, the personality of the board chair, and the experience and ability of the CEO. In some instances, the board must approve all expenditures, all program initiatives, and all personnel transactions, although this level of involvement is rare. Obviously, if the charter or bylaws require it, or if there is a strong board chair or a president who wants that level of control, it is more likely. That said, the board is usually not involved in day-to-day decision making.

Even if the charter or bylaws require approval for almost all decisions, a board that has confidence in the organization's administrative staff can change the bylaws so that a high level of participation is no longer mandated. The procedure for revising the bylaws is normally detailed in the bylaws and nearly always requires advance written notice and opportunity to review the proposed changes. Revising the bylaws should not be done hastily but should involve a slow deliberate process leading eventually to a consensus.

ACTION-BASED CONCEPT

Managers should be familiar with the procedures for changing the bylaws and charter.

In a more common arrangement, the board hires and supervises the CEO and establishes the policy constraints within which the CEO and the organization must work. Stated differently, the board sets policy and does not micromanage the organization. The narrow line between setting policy and interfering with the administration's prerogatives is the most frequent source of tension between board chairs and CEOs. When a dispute over roles occurs, considerable dialogue is needed—between the CEO and the board chair and occasionally between the executive committee and the full board. The goal should be to clarify the roles of the board and the executive committee as expeditiously as possible.

BOARD POLICY MAKING

A general rule of thumb is that boards create policies and administrators implement them. Board members generally only have decision-making authority during board meetings, although exceptions exist in the bylaws of some organizations, especially for the board chair or president. Board members usually do not have the authority to act individually on behalf of the organization, because power is only vested in the board as a whole. For the board to act as a whole, a quorum must be present and bylaws and other legal requirements must be met (such as compliance with the open meetings act).

Administrators need to emphasize the difference between policy making and administration and to work hard to maintain that fine line. Board members should not have any hands-on role in day-to-day operations or program administration.

Maintaining contact with the board is normally the responsibility of the top administrator. No staff member should get in touch with any board member without first consulting with the top administrator. Certainly it is appropriate to keep the board informed and occasionally to consult with the board chair on controversial matters. But when board decisions are required, a meeting of the board should be called so that all members can contribute to the decision making.

Many board bylaws permit mail ballots, and most provide for emergency meetings of the executive committee. Of course, a board will occasionally authorize the CEO and/or the administrator to make pending decisions when needed information is not readily available.

Again, the reason for requiring board decisions to be made by the board as a whole is to protect the public interest and inject a range of inputs into the decision-making process. There will be differing opinions about how the agency should accomplish its mission, and decisions that grow out of group discussion are nearly always better than decisions made by an individual.

Moreover, group decisions help avoid the appearance of conflict of interest. For example, a board member who owns a business may provide services or products at cost, but unless several bids have been obtained and the board selects the best, the board member may be suspected of collusion by competitors.

Conflicts of interest can be especially complicated in small organizations that do not have paid staff. Individuals may have both board roles and staff roles, and care must be taken not to confuse the two roles and to differentiate between policies that affect the organization as a whole and decisions that are within the boundaries of the staff role. If a board member assumes responsibility as a staff member, he or she acts as a volunteer, responsible to the board as a whole.

Table 5–1 summarizes typical board and administrator roles in cases where a paid administrator exists.

ACTION-BASED CONCEPT

All communication between the board and staff should be channeled through the chief administrator. The administrator must maintain day-to-day control of all organizational functions to keep the organization moving toward fulfillment of its mission.

Table 5–1 Board and Administrator Roles

	Board	Administ
Long-term goals	Approves	Recommends, provides guidance
Short-term goals	Monitors	Establishes, carries out
Day-to-day operations	No role	Makes all management decisions
Budget	Approves	Develops, recommends
Capital purchases	Approves	Prepares, requests
Decisions on building, renovation, leasing, etc.	Makes decisions, assumes responsibility	Recommends, signs contracts, if authorized
Supply purchases	Approves budget	Purchases according to policy, maintains audit trail
Major repairs	Approves	Recommends
Minor repairs	Sets policy on amount that can be spent	Authorizes repairs to predetermined amount
Emergency repairs	Works with administrator	Notifies board and acts with board's agreement
Cleaning and maintenance	Oversight	Sets up schedule
Fees	Adopts policy	Develops or sets fees
Billing, credit, collections	Adopts policy	Proposes policy, implements policy
Hiring of staff	No role	Hires or delegates hiring of all staff
Staff assignments	No role	Establishes
Firing of staff	No role	Makes final termination decision
Staff grievances	No role	Handles grievances
Personnel policies	Adopts	Recommends and administers
Staff salaries	Approves budget	Considers staff recommendations, approves salaries
Staff evaluation	Evaluates administrator	Evaluates all other staff

BOARD MEMBER RESPONSIBILITIES

Managers should understand the expectations placed on board members so as not to make unreasonable demands. (Of course, managers often serve on the boards of other community organizations, and it is helpful to know the role-related expectations if appointed or elected to such a role.)

Because an organization's board is the legally constituted body that guides and directs the organization, a board member's first responsibility is to ascertain and do what is in the best interests of the organization, both in the short and long term. It is easy to be swayed by personal interests or public pressures, but the primary obligation of the member is to do what is good for the organization.

At the same time, a public sector organization exists to serve the community and is supported by the community. In a very real sense, board members also represent the community's interests and may have to mold the organization (usually through shaping its mission statement) so that it better meets the needs of the community. There are cases where a small organization is redundant and not cost effective and where the community's interests are best served by advocating a merger with another organization or even facilitating the demise of the organization. Balancing the organization's needs and the community's needs is not easy—but is an important task.

Of course, a primary responsibility of any board is to hire a chief executive officer, whether that person is called a president, directing manager, or administrator. An associated responsibility is to monitor the CEO's performance. This is normally done informally during meetings or by reviewing written communications. The board also does an annual performance review, which encompasses looking at written materials and doing interviews. Again, the board member must balance community needs and organizational needs, which occasionally may necessitate voting to terminate the CEO. Another balancing act involves determining when to support the initiatives of the CEO and when to bow to fellow board members who feel strongly about moving the organization in another direction. What position a member takes and how strongly they take it will partly depend on where his or her past support was directed.

It may be necessary for the board member to serve as a buffer or even to arbitrate disputes between the CEO and another member or between two board members. The role of arbiter is not a comfortable role, but is a much needed one on some boards. No board member should automatically approve administrative proposals. It is essential to ask difficult "what if" questions as well as clarifying questions. On the other hand, board members must avoid the temptation to micromanage and must stay within the realm of policy making, leaving the executive director (ED) or CEO to implement policy.

If the board does not approve most administrative proposals, this is evidence that there is not a good fit between the administration and the board and that the board lacks confidence in the administrator's judgment. A good administrator will always anticipate how each board member will react to any proposal and will to the extent possible accommodate the anticipated reactions. A series of rejected proposals indicates that the administrator has not done enough preliminary work—has not thought through the issues and figured out the probable reactions of the board members.

A good board member will always be thinking long range. While short-range fiscal stability is essential, CEOs, because they can move on to other jobs, sometimes neglect to plan for the long term. Forcing long-range planning that takes into account changing demographics and technological change may be the major contribution a board member can make. Keeping the CEO or ED focused on the need for stability and the need for change is another balancing act.

A board member must interpret the agency to the community and must pay attention to public image and perception. Enhancing the public standing of the agency is an important responsibility. The board member can fulfill this responsibility by ensuring that public relations and marketing programs are adequate, and by personally telling the agency's story to friends and associates or creating opportunities for the CEO to do so.

Finally, board members have the major responsibility of keeping the organization and the ED or CEO out of trouble, both fiscally and legally. Accordingly, they often need to take the conservative path, avoid big risks, and institute preventive measures. Building fiscal operating reserves or avoiding excess debt may thus be a high priority for the board but a low priority for the CEO. Likewise, complying with legal mandates, such as handicap access laws, may seem more important to the board than to the CEO. And having written marketing and business plans, which the administrator, who keeps track of everything mentally, might view as superfluous, will undoubtedly seem essential to board members. Board members have a duty to anticipate the unexpected, such as the administrator's sudden death or departure, and need to ensure the organization's plans will be carried out no matter who is at the helm.

As noted earlier, the above discussion of board member responsibilities will be useful to the CEO who also serves on boards of other community agencies. However, it is mainly intended to help the CEO (and other administrators) understand the role of the board members. With a firm grasp of this role, the CEO will be less likely to develop unreasonable expectations or to overreact when his or her preferences do not receive the board's endorsement.

BOARD DEVELOPMENT

It would be shortsighted to assume boards will be effective simply because they exist. The manager has a responsibility to engage in some level of board development. This involves some type of orientation for new board members; keeping board members well informed of major organizational changes and initiatives; and an annual board retreat for long range planning. The board needs to be seen as a valuable resource to the manager both in its expertise and its political clout. Additionally, board members need to be aware of the changing legal landscape of health care. Under the 2005 legislation of the Sarbanes-Oxley Act, new standards of accountability were introduced. Ultimately, a well developed board will be seen as legitimate and credible. Legitimacy is achieved when stakeholders perceive the board to represent all significant interests and perspectives, whereas credibility occurs when the board appears knowledgeable and fair and the board process, rational.

CONCLUSION

Boards are a fact of life for most administrators, something "out there" that consciously or subconsciously influences the thinking of those who manage. Some administrators deal with boards routinely, and others only occasionally, but the board of any organization must be taken into account by the administrator during decision making. It is imperative for the administrator to work effectively with the organization's own board for organizational success to occur. Of course the administrator serves at the pleasure of the board, and an administrator who cannot work effectively with the board will likely either leave voluntarily or will be asked to leave.

IN-BASKET ASSIGNMENT

TO: Agency Health Education and Health Promotion Specialists
FROM: The Director
RE: Boards

We are preparing to create a board for a new federally funded program we are starting, but we are unsure whether to make it an advisory board or a board of directors. Either will meet federal guidelines. Which do you recommend, and why?

Please check around a little, and inquire about the board of an organization with which you are familiar. How many people are on it? What officers does it have? What committees does it have? Perhaps if each of you look at a board, we will have a cross section of boards to use in ascertaining how to set up ours.

Thanks!

MANAGEMENT CASE STUDY

Setting

A hospital health promotion specialist frequently arranged for former diabetic patients to visit children who were hospitalized with severe diabetes. The purpose of these visits was to provide emotional support and encouragement from someone who had coped with the disease successfully.

The visits were a huge success, with both the adult role models and the children benefiting. Some of the adults wanted to organize an informal group that would meet monthly to "support each other." One woman even wanted to establish a not-for-profit group, elect officers, raise funds, produce materials, and so on.

Problem

The hospital health promotion specialist did not know whether the greater risk was in resisting the idea of organizing a group or supporting it. Further, she did not know which strategy would benefit the hospital or the patients most.

Alternatives Considered

One approach considered by the health promotion specialist was to assist in establishing monthly meetings. The specialist could simply call in staff as needed to talk to the group about specific issues. This approach seemed to maximize staff control while minimizing use of staff time.

Another approach was to let the group run with the project to see where it might go. As noted, one woman seemed particularly interested in developing a formal program. She had high energy and good organizational skills. She was also quite persistent and at times appeared to want to take over the informal program and turn it into her idea of a worthwhile program.

Actions Taken

During consultation with the hospital administrator, the health promotion specialist was told to not let go of control of the program, and to keep it informal and focused. The primary issues cited by the administrator included loss of control, potential litigation, required staff time, and continuity. The administrator pointed out that the woman pushing for formalization of the program could burn out or move away, leaving the specialist with the primary responsibility of making the program work.

OUTCOME

There was immediate resistance and some criticism. The criticism disappeared after several weeks—when the woman in favor of formalizing the group ceased coming. Other volunteers were recruited to fill in, and the program continued to run essentially as it did before the idea of a support group had been raised.

DISCUSSION QUESTIONS

   1. What might have happened had the other alternative been selected?
   2. What organizational structure might have protected the hospital?
   3. Should the hospital attorney be involved in the formative stages of a group like the one described?
   4. What are the general advantages and disadvantages of organizing a group with a board of directors?
   5. Are there other strategies that could have been used to address the main issues?

CHAPTER 6

Organizational Charts

ORGANIZATIONAL DESIGN

Organizational design has long been viewed as an essential foundation for management. As noted in Chapter 2, it is one of the seven traditional components of any management system. An organizational chart is a written, and more often, diagrammed record of the structure of the organization. It has been likened to an x-ray showing the organization's skeleton, an outline of the formal connections between its various units.[1] Every employee has assigned duties and hierarchical relationships that define his or her role, and every employee must therefore have some awareness of the structure. It is normal, however, for employees to be more concerned with organizational design as they move into supervisory roles and climb up the management hierarchy.

The organizational design must fit the size and nature of the organization. If there are only one or two employees, the "design" need only be in the minds of the employees and can be "adjusted on the run." However, if the number of employees grows to even a few, some structure is necessary to determine who will do what. It is essential that the work be done in manageable, logical units and that the workload is more or less equitably divided. (Fairness and employee morale dictate that the workload be more or less equitable or that compensation be adjusted so as to be commensurate with the employees' responsibilities.) Of course, the workload will also vary according to ability and effort, it being recognized that there are employees who will often do less than what is required, employees who will only do what is required, and employees who will usually do more than what is required.

Knowing who does what involves three basic organizational concepts: division of labor, specialization, and lines of authority. Division of labor is one of the oldest management concepts, and specialization is the criterion most often used to

63

divide up the work. It makes sense that, when work assignments are made, people should be assigned to do what they do best—which often means giving them tasks they have had experience doing. As an organization grows, however, logic will gradually replace experience as the basis for assigning work. Job descriptions will be developed that list the tasks that logically go together as well as the skills needed to complete the tasks, and the individuals selected for the positions will be those who have those skills. Job mobility then becomes the vehicle for matching employees with what the employees do best.

An alternative approach to organization has evolved—an approach now commonly used in conjunction with the organizational chart approach. A project team is a temporary group that lasts for the duration of a project, often a year or less. It may include individuals selected because of the vision, experience, or needed skills they bring to the project. The use of project teams supplements, but does not replace, the type of design set out in a formal organizational chart. Project teams, in particular, provide a means of accomplishing high-priority goals in a reasonably short span of time.

Again, as an organization grows in size and complexity, as tasks become more specialized and work is divided in more ways, greater attention must be devoted to coordination and collaboration. Indeed, if the specialized work of individuals is not compatible, overall organizational functioning will be compromised. Individual work assignments have to be coordinated into a meaningful whole so that they jointly contribute to accomplishing the planned goals and objectives. Likewise, it is imperative that all essential tasks are addressed and that something important is not overlooked. Only when coordination of the work of specialized workers occurs can the organization be reasonably assured of achieving its goals. Ideally, the various workers and units should collaborate so that efficiency and effectiveness are maximized.

ACTION-BASED CONCEPT

Always understand how the work is divided and how the specialized functions are coordinated, and look for ways to increase organizational efficiency by refining these factors.

Without coordination and collaboration, there would be not only inefficiency but conflict and disorder. Organizing is the primary means of bringing order out of chaos, establishing an environment suitable for teamwork, and dealing with or removing conflict. Certainly, if conflict exists, someone in authority will need to make decisions (often with input from workers) intended to alter the organizational structure and reduce conflict and disorder. A collaborative effort should be made to design a new organizational format that will most enhance efficiency while at the same time providing a solid foundation for achieving the organizational goals.

It is not surprising that the word *organization*, which can mean "the manner of being organized," is often used interchangeably with the terms *agency, institution,* and *business*. The plan of organization (as reflected by the organizational chart) is critical to the success of any organization and in large measure determines whether organizational goals will be accomplished and the ease with which they will be accomplished. Thus, all managers must understand organizational charts and associated issues, and the top-level managers of any organization must periodically study and revise its organizational chart as a means of increasing efficiency and effectiveness.

As Peter Drucker says, "Organizations exist to make ordinary human beings perform better than they seem capable of, to bring out whatever strength there is in its members, and to use each member's strength to help all other members perform."[2] This is another way of stating the importance of efficiency and effectiveness in accomplishing organizational goals. And because goals and objectives change over time, it is often appropriate to change the organizational structure. Indeed, some health agencies were created to eliminate one problem, such as polio, but upon achieving success shifted to other related problems. In such instances, it is almost essential for organizational structure to change. Yet organizational change is basically a matter of degree. Most organizational structures change somewhat every year or two in reaction to the hiring of new workers, who have their own unique abilities and personalities; the hiring of a new CEO with a new vision of the future; the development of pressing needs, such as the need for budgetary restraint or for downsizing; or subtle changes in the market.

ACTION-BASED CONCEPT

An organizational chart should not be considered fixed or permanent. It should be reviewed periodically to determine if it offers a good foundation for accomplishing the goals of the organization.

ORGANIZING ELEMENTS

Peter Drucker identified three analyses useful for determining the best type of structure necessary for a given organization. The first analysis to be undertake is an activities analysis, because only by thoroughly understanding what activities are occurring can the manager determine what activities belong together. The second is a decision analysis, which is intended to uncover what decisions are being made, where in the organization decision making occurs, and what data are needed for decision making. The third is a relations analysis, which is intended to show which units logically relate to each other, which often work together, which need to collaborate, and which need to report to the same manager.

Drucker suggests using activities, decision making, and relationships to establish work units or departments, but the more traditional set of factors used in business and in the health field consists of function, geography, customer, and process or equipment.

Function

Function is the most frequently used organizing factor in small organizations and is usually used in large organizations as well. For example, in a local health department, public health nurses who serve mothers and children are typically located in a maternal and child health department, while sanitarians, environmentalists, and engineers are usually placed in an environmental health department. Health educators, health promotion specialists, media specialists, and public relations personnel might be in a community health education department, while administrators and budget, human resources, and computer staff might be in an administrative services department. Function and focus are used to form the departments, although overlap occurs and collaboration is required.

Geography

A large organization, such as the American Cancer Society, will likely superimpose geographical considerations on top of functional factors. It might have a national center and regional and local branches, each with functional units that relate to the functional units above and below. Similarly, in health departments, health education and health promotions specialists at the local level will often interact with health education specialists at the state level. Put differently, state health educators often have to implement their state programs by utilizing local health educators in many areas.

There are several advantages to this structure. For instance, it uses the features of the functional system and increases communication between those who must collaborate. It can cut down on travel costs and improve programs and services (area employees generally know the needs of their clients better than employees many miles away).

Customer

Organizations often use a customer-focused organizing scheme to appeal to clearly defined groups. For example, an outpatient clinic might have a senior services department, a worksite department, a teen services department, and a maternal and child health department. The advantage of this structure is that it allows each department to really focus on the multiple needs of its particular group of clients, allows department personnel to get to know the clients personally, and permits the creation of an appealing and warm atmosphere throughout the organization.

Process or Equipment

It is not uncommon for an agency to have a computer department or a media department because of the complexity of equipment to be used and maintained. However, some agencies prefer not to centralize computer and media equipment and personnel and instead distribute them to a variety of units. For example, a hospital might have an administrative services division that includes staff who support the computers used in payroll, billing, and medical records along with as the media equipment used in nursing, staff development, and human resources departments.

HORIZONTAL AND VERTICAL RELATIONSHIPS

Work units must relate to other work units, and all work units must be supervised. Accordingly, an organizational chart displays horizontal relationships between units at the same level of authority and vertical relationships indicating supervisory responsibilities. The horizontal groupings largely influence communication patterns, because each manager usually holds staff meetings of unit heads within his or her span of control. Although a manager should not be directly responsible for too many employees, there is no set number of subordinates that constitutes the ideal span of management. The number can be large, but generally no more than four to eight individuals should report directly to a manager, or else some of them will be under-supervised. Part of the rationale for keeping this number small is that substantial time is required to understand the issues that arise on particular units and to communicate with the unit managers about how to deal with these issues.

The vertical grouping of positions and units provides a channel through which authority flows from the top manager down to and through unit managers. It also creates a mechanism for coordinating the efforts of individuals performing disparate tasks. The flow of decision making and supervisory authority must be clear in any organization. There will normally be someone with ultimate authority at the top of the organization and a similar person in each unit. In a vertical relationship, authority flows from top down. Authority can, and often is, delegated to those below the manager. Thus, inherent in the flow of authority is the chain of supervision. Also inherent in it is the chain of formal communication.

A related management principle is "unity of command," obviously adopted from military theory. This principle dictates that every employee has one supervisor and only one supervisor. The supervisor makes assignments, prioritizes work tasks, monitors progress, provides assistance as needed, and is generally responsible for the performance of the employee. The principle of unity of command entails that ultimate authority resides in one person and that the organizational structure can be diagrammed in such a way that the lines of authority descend to every subordinate position. It also explains why pyramid organization charts are by far the most common; they most clearly display the spans of control, chains of command, and lines of authority that are features of a structure based on unity of command.

Traditional organizational charts are sometimes described as centralized, because decision-making authority is located at a single place—the top. Most organizations are not fully centralized, in that managers can delegate decision-making authority. Some managers delegate nearly all decision-making authority and instead focus on leadership, communication, motivation, and coordination activities. Some managers retain the right to approve unit plans, all hiring, and all major equipment purchasing. The more decision making that is delegated, the more decentralized or participative the organization. Seldom is an organization totally centralized or totally decentralized.

The amount of decentralization is largely determined by the level of organizational complexity and the degree of confidence top administrators have in unit managers. Large organizations that are in a rapid growth mode or are organizing for a major change usually need to be more decentralized, because they must be able to respond to local conditions quickly.

In the last decade or two, there has been a trend toward decentralization. However, that trend may be changing. Technology is seen by many as facilitating centralization because of the information-providing capability of computers. Computers can now quickly produce data on budget projections, usage rates, and other items of interest that formerly would only have been known by mid-level managers in charge of subordinate units. Certainly, organizational charts are being flattened, and many mid-level management positions are being eliminated (see Figures 6–1 and 6–2). This phenomenon reflects both decentralization and centralization. Because of the elimination of mid-level management positions, some decision making is being pushed downward to front-line units and some decision making is being pushed upward. As mentioned in an earlier chapter, technology is changing management in many, many ways.

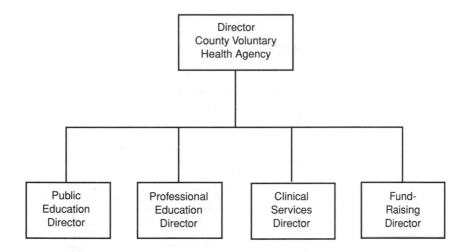

Figure 6-1 Horizontal Organizational Chart

Flatter organizational charts allow decisions to be made more quickly and increase the probability that top management initiatives will be implemented unchanged. The difference between a management initiative as first proposed and the implemented initiative, after the mid-level managers have changed it to accommodate their personal interests and concerns, can be cause for amazement.

People are naturally concerned about organizational structure because it impacts their decision making, flexibility, perks, budget, staff, and prestige. Organizational changes that must filter through several layers in a decentralized organization will commonly be "massaged" as much as possible so as to accommodate the personal needs and interests of the unit managers. In local agencies undergoing organizational change, decision making is often centralized to somewhat neutralize this natural tendency. It is necessary to have one person in charge of change—a national or state leader if the change is of that magnitude, or a local leader if the change is on a local level—to ensure that changes are not inherently contradictory.

LINE AND STAFF POSITIONS

When focusing on lines of authority, the main issue is which administrators report to whom. Left out of the discussion are the myriad support staff positions that are essential for smooth operations. Support staff serve, support, provide advice to, and are responsible to managers in the authority chain of command but have very little decision-making authority, unless it is delegated to them because

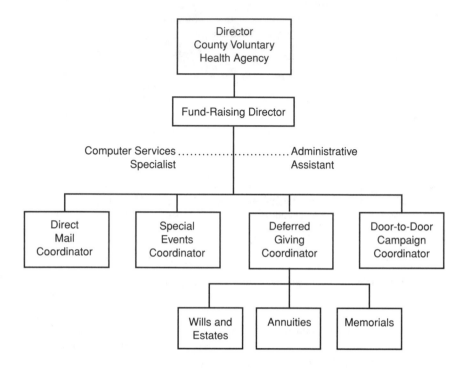

Figure 6-2 Vertical Organizational Chart. A segment of a vertical organizational chart of the same organization diagrammed in Figure 6-1 might look like this.

of their unusual ability. Generally, staff must convince line personnel to adopt their recommendations. Those who are held accountable for results decide which staff recommendations to accept.

What counts as a staff position varies from organization to organization. For instance, the same position can be a staff position in one organization and a line position in another. Secretarial, clerical, and receptionist jobs are obvious examples of staff positions, but computer, public relations, accounting, payroll, and human resources positions can be either line or staff positions. Using human resources as an illustration, the administrator (not the human resources director) decides when to fill a position, what the qualifications are, what the job description is, who is to be interviewed, and who is to be hired. The decision-making authority resides in the administrator. The human resources personnel place ads, handle the applications, answer most mail and phone inquiries, arrange for interviews, and notify unsuccessful candidates. These staff functions are enormously helpful but do not involve much decision making.

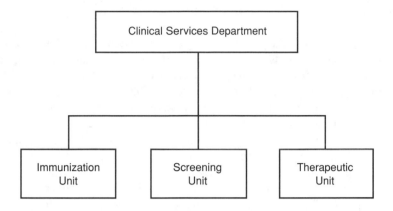

Figure 6-3 Department Organizational Chart

Both line and staff positions are important. Often only line positions appear on an organizational chart. If staff positions are included on an organizational chart, their status as staff positions is indicated by a broken or dotted line, while decision-making authority is indicated by a solid line (see Figure 6–2). The blocks in an organizational chart can represent departments, individuals, or functions. In Figure 6–3, they represent a department and its units. Note that when the words department and unit are dropped, the blocks represent functions. Knowing what the blocks stand for is important when trying to design a chart (or read and understand one someone else has designed).

ACTION-BASED CONCEPT

Managers should ensure that the organization and each unit has an up-to-date organizational chart. The chart should be made available to all staff to help them understand the channels of authority and communication, information flow, status of staff members, and span of control. Because the relationships between staff and managers can change over time, the chart should be reviewed and updated every year or so.

CONCLUSION

There are numerous issues associated with organizational charts. Organizations are dynamic, and the charts that outline their structure should and do change over time. It is generally desirable to keep organizational charts as flat as possible. They should be widely disseminated and discussed periodically at staff meetings. An organizational chart normally indicates supervisory, decision-making, and authority lines; the division of work; the responsibility of each unit; and the degree of specialization. The blocks can represent positions, units, or functions. Organizing is a fundamental management process, and organizational charts are a graphic expression of the outcome of this process. Yet it must always be remembered that organizing is a means to an end, not an end in itself. The focus must be on how organizing can enhance the efficiency and effectiveness of the organization. A clear, beautifully displayed organizational chart will not ensure success, and many successful organizations have outdated or ill-conceived organizational charts that are largely ignored. Organizational charts are tools, and like all tools they can help get tasks accomplished. Yet no tool by itself will get the job done. Managers must understand how to use organizational charts to achieve organizational ends.

IN-BASKET ASSIGNMENT

TO: Health Education and Health Promotion Specialists
FROM: The Director
RE: Organizational Charts

I am preparing to reorganize our agency for the twenty-first century and have been looking at our organizational chart. Other agencies are tending to flatten their organizational charts by delegating more and eliminating mid-level management positions. I'm not sure if we should do this or not.

What are the advantages and disadvantages of flattening our organizational chart? Please prepare a list of three to five advantages and three to five disadvantages.

Thank you.

MANAGEMENT CASE STUDY

Setting

A tri-county health department was preparing to add a health education program and was considering how to incorporate it into the organizational chart.

Problem

A question was raised as to where the new program would most likely flourish given the organization's politics and the personalities of key administrators. One main issue was whether the support and nurturing of the nursing department that would occur if the health education specialist reported to nursing would outweigh the narrower focus that would likely occur. It was recognized that while much of the work would be with nursing, some of the focus should be in other units. Some administrators wondered if work in non-nursing units would be stifled if the program was located in the nursing unit.

Alternatives Considered

The health education program could be organized as a separate unit, with the director on a par with the director of nursing. However, this alternative would drive the cost of the position up beyond what was likely to be available.

Another alternative was to place the program at a level below nursing and to have split reporting lines to other department heads. This was not viewed as desirable because of potential problems due to the multiplicity of supervisors.

A third alternative was to call the health educator's position "Coordinator of Health Education and Health Promotion Programs" and have the position report to the administrator. The job description, however, would require the health educator to coordinate programs within several units.

The final alternative was to create a half-time position in nursing and create another half-time position (occupied by the same person) that would be responsible for programs in other units.

Actions Taken

A separate department of community health promotion was created, and the director was placed at the same level as the director of nursing. Because the nursing director supervised several nurses and the health educator would be a one-person operation, a salary differential could be justified. Moreover, to free additional dollars for salary, the secretarial support position was reduced to half-time for at least the start-up year.

OUTCOME

The health educator had the most support and success in units other than nursing. The personalities and politics were such that nursing preferred to keep doing its own educating rather than work with the new director.

The new director of health education focused time and energy on non-nursing units and developed several highly visible, highly effective programs. While educational services were offered to nursing, it seemed as if the requirements and time frames were always unrealistic.

The administrator was cognizant of the situation and recorded it in the annual performance reviews of the two directors. The director of nursing ultimately decided to change jobs rather than deal with the difficulties. The new director of nursing did not bring political baggage with her to the position and was more cooperative. The health education director and nursing director worked well together, and several major new educational initiatives evolved.

DISCUSSION QUESTIONS

1. Are there other ways the administrator could have handled the creation of a new unit?

2. How might the political tensions have been eased once the decision was made?

3. What strategies can be used when working with difficult people?

4. How should the health educator keep the administrator informed without appearing to be unduly critical of the director of nursing?

5. How might the administrator increase communication and cooperation between the two directors?

6. Are there other strategies that could have been used to address the friction between the two directors?

NOTES

1. J. Greenberg and R.A. Baron, *Behavior in Organizations, 8th ed.* (Saddle River, NJ: Prentice Hall, 2003): 333.

2. P. Drucker, *Management: Tasks, Responsibilities, Practices* (New York: Harper & Row, 1974): 455.

CHAPTER 7

Legal and Ethical Issues

THE LITIGIOUS CLIMATE

Today's society has become increasingly litigious, and in few areas is litigation more prevalent than in health care. Although health promotion programs are less frequently involved in lawsuits than providers of clinical services, they definitely can be the target of litigation.

Any organization is affected by laws. Indeed, the framework of laws provides the context in which nearly all business decisions need to be made. Lawyers will almost always be involved in the creation of an organization (especially a non-profit agency) and in any bankruptcy or other organizational demise, and they often play an important role at many stages of an organization's life cycle. For example, laws govern how employees are hired and fired, how compensation is provided, how marketing for customers occurs, how customers access facilities, how people give approval for services, how billing for services occurs, how much insurance is obtained and what it must cover, and much, much more.

Given how quick people are to sue these days, it is imperative that managers, administrators, and leaders understand the various laws affecting their organizational roles and that they practice preventive law. The higher up the organizational chart a manager rises, the more concern about laws and lawyers he or she must have.

Most health promotion organizations have a working relationship with an attorney. In a small organization, the attorney might be a member of the board, recruited and appointed to give the organization access to free legal services. Sometimes an attorney will be approached to provide legal services on a pro bono basis, which means the services are provided free of charge as a way of contributing to the good of the community. It is not uncommon for firms in a variety of fields (e.g., law, accounting, and marketing) to devote a percentage of total work time to helping needy clients, including nonprofit organizations that require specialized services but often cannot afford them. Legal firms often prefer to provide pro bono services on an item-by-item basis, where their time commitments are apparent, because pro bono assistance has to be worked into their schedule. During a period of peak workload, the answer might be "no" or "not now" because the staff are already overcommitted. Additionally, some cases become extraordinarily complicated because of the complexity of the regulations involved, and it may be difficult to estimate the time required. It is relatively easy for a legal firm to estimate the time needed to be expended on filing papers of incorporation, reviewing a policy and procedures manual for potential liability, or reviewing and executing a contract. In complicated suits, such as a discrimination lawsuit brought by employees of the organization, a legal firm may be persuaded to discount its billing rate or to provide a specific number of hours of service free before charges are applied.

Because legal services are so expensive—as much as a couple hundred dollars per hour depending on the geographic area, the reputation of the firm, and the nature of the case—negotiating a rate could avert a budget crisis. Moreover, employee access to attorneys is usually limited to one or two top-level managers. This means that mid-level managers need to be aware of potential legal problems and practice preventive law (e.g., if a mid-level manager identifies a problem, he or she must brief the appropriate administrator, who will then work with the attorneys).

A cautionary note is in order: it can be more expensive not to use preventive legal services when needed than to pay the high cost of the services during litigation. For example, a review prior to terminating an employee might cost a hundred dollars; whereas defending against an unfair termination suit could easily cost tens of thousands of dollars, plus any settlement awarded to the former employee. A small nonprofit organization might not have to pay quite as large an award as a big for-profit, but most likely it will. Furthermore, if liability coverage has been purchased, the insurance company will probably raise the rates for future coverage, and if it is an uninsured matter, the award may even lead to bankruptcy of the agency. Again, managers must practice preventive law—anticipate the legal consequences of virtually everything they do, act appropriately to avoid litigation, and make sure they have a strong case in the event a defense becomes necessary.

The warning above is not meant to suggest that managers should let fear of litigation dominate their decision making, but to remind them that laws form part of the context in which major decisions are made and that it is not possible to avoid all risk and still run an effective business. Indeed, although firing an incompetent or disruptive employee entails a risk of litigation, the risk resulting from retaining the employee may be even greater. Also, if termination is the option decided on, knowledge of the law can affect when and how the termination occurs. Especially critical in employee cases is the existence of a "paper trail," a series of written performance evaluations or incident reports that document the employee's problematic behavior. This is a good example of what is meant by practicing preventive law—being conscious of potential legal difficulties and acting to reduce the risk.

In other management arenas, the practice of preventive law is just as critical. Clearing an icy sidewalk or replacing a broken sidewalk can be far less expensive than fighting a lawsuit. The decision to repair or replace a torn carpet is a good one from a liability point of view. Hiring an electrician to rewire a room rather than running extension cords every which way can avoid problems with the Occupational Safety and Health Administration. Building a ramp or arranging for disabled persons to be served in an accessible area can be less expensive than violating the Americans with Disabilities Act. Developing and enforcing a sexual harassment policy can be far less expensive than dealing with a sexual harassment claim filed with the Equal Employment Opportunity Commission. The adverse publicity caused by a violation of the Open Meetings Act can be more problematic than complying with the act itself. The list is seemingly endless, but the principles are constant: know the law, seek legal counsel when needed, and practice preventive law.

ACTION-BASED CONCEPT

Managers need to know the laws that can apply to the organization, and emphasize the importance of practicing preventive law.

There are far too many laws that govern for-profit businesses and nonprofit organizations to attempt a comprehensive review. However, the provisions of some of the laws concerning employment are summarized in the following sections.

EMPLOYMENT-RELATED LEGISLATION

The Americans with Disabilities Act (ADA)

The basic purpose of this act is to make discrimination against people with disabilities illegal and to indicate what types of accommodations are necessary. This applies to employment as well as service provision. In hiring and in other employment practices, a person with a disability cannot be discriminated against unless a bona fide occupational qualification can be proven by the organization. For example, a person with AIDS or HIV infection is protected under the ADA. Another fundamental provision of the ADA is that service cannot be denied to individuals because of their disabilities. Programs generally have to be wheelchair accessible, normally through the use of ramps or elevators, and doorways, signage, restrooms, and so on, must accommodate a variety of disabling conditions. If only some of the mandated accommodations are feasible (e.g., curb cuts and a ramp to the first floor but not elevators to the top floor), then alternative provisions must be made to provide services or otherwise serve the needs of people with disabilities in locations that are accessible.

It is generally easier for a nonprofit private organization to meet the alternative provisions portion of the act than it is for tax-supported agencies. But the focus is on services. If accessible space to serve people with disabilities exists on the first floor and other needed services can be brought there, such accommodations will generally suffice.

It must be understood that a wide variety of conditions are now legally considered as disabling, including injuries that are temporarily disabling, such as any that require use of crutches. People who are visually impaired require either braille signage, other services for the blind, or an individual providing oral directions. Increasingly, services may need to be employed for people with a hearing impairment. Hearing amplification systems that meet the ADA guidelines may be necessary—and even the provision of a sign language interpreter in certain circumstances.

A more complex issue is whether mental impairment requires special accommodations, and if so, what conditions and what accommodations. Similarly, do conditions such as dyslexia or other learning disabilities create legal obligations that educational specialists must meet? These issues are currently being hammered out in the courts. One thing seems clear: an agency cannot deny services to clients with disabilities, without some legal and financial risk, simply because the agency lacks the capacity to handle these disabilities. There may not be a crisis until the services have been denied, but then the agency may be forced to provide accessibility or otherwise accommodate the clients and also pay a punitive award.

Again, practicing preventive law means reviewing facilities and programs, discussing how clients with special needs will be handled, and developing a written plan for upgrading facilities and services over time so as to better serve these clients. Having a plan in place, making progress on its implementation, and trying hard to accommodate clients with disabilities prior to full implementation will generally avoid or at least minimize expensive legal problems. It is obviously better to spend money improving facilities or services than to spend it on attorneys hired to help avoid the legal consequences of not making the accommodations. For one thing, any judgment against the agency will probably require the accommodations to be made anyway, but only as part of a final settlement in the case.

Another ADA provision prohibits denying employment to people with disabilities. Obviously, the accessibility issues described above apply to employees as well as clients. However, there are several other provisions that must be considered if a person with a disability applies for work or is employed.

First of all, work standards have to be clear. An employer does not have to lower standards of performance as long as the standards are job related and apply uniformly to others in similar positions. However, if a person with a disability could meet the standards with reasonable accommodations, he or she cannot be denied the job without risk of discrimination charges. A receptionist might need special furniture or answering equipment, or a secretary might need a keyboard at wheelchair height. The requirement does not extend to accommodations that would cause the employer undue hardship, such as building an elevator, but it could dictate changing a traditional office in an inaccessible location for one in an accessible location.

In testing employees (or clients), the organization must generally provide necessary accommodations for a disability. For example, tests must be read to the blind (or be in braille), and appropriate equipment must be provided if needed for other persons with disabilities.

To prevent litigation, managers should examine their employment practices and look for potential problem areas. There are numerous materials published and numerous consultants available. However, the key is to make reasonable accommodations whenever they are necessary. Managers should generally be alert to the existence of situations where accommodations have been provided and begin planning for similar accommodations in their own place of work.

ACTION-BASED CONCEPT

Managers need to focus on reasonable accommodations and be certain that services are provided to all, regardless of ability or disability. Many inexpensive accommodations are available. A written ADA compliance plan that details how the agency will accommodate clients and employees with disabilities is usually needed.

The Occupational Health and Safety Act (OSHA)

Places of employment have to be safe and cannot endanger the health of employees. The Occupational Health and Safety Act covers many work hazards, such as secondhand smoke and other noxious fumes, excessive noise, excessive eyestrain, inadequate lighting, postural problems associated with the structure of the job, and insufficient work breaks. Broken equipment, and defective switches, exit lights, and fire alarms all have to be repaired immediately.

Any item that is perceived to be a problem can precipitate a complaint, typically from a disgruntled present or former employee. OSHA complaints usually result in an inspection, an order to correct the situation, and a fine. It obviously is better to correct the situation before the complaint is filed rather than let it go. For one thing, health promotion agencies should set an example by providing a healthy, safe work environment.

ACTION-BASED CONCEPT

Managers should encourage employees to call unsafe or unhealthy conditions to their attention and must always investigate such conditions immediately. If the conditions are unsafe or unhealthy, they need to be corrected as soon as is reasonable (sometimes within a day or two) because liability increases once a complaint has been filed. Even nuisance complaints should be taken seriously, and written follow-up reports need to be placed in the files.

Equal Employment Opportunity (EEO) Laws

Everyone has the right not to be discriminated against in hiring and promotion. Discrimination cannot occur on the basis of gender, age, race, country of origin, disability, or veteran status. Groups that have been singled out and are generally thought of as protected because of past discrimination include women, the elderly, ethnic minorities, non-native citizens, people with disabilities, and veterans. Hiring, interviewing, testing, training, promoting, appraising, disciplining, and compensating have all been affected by equal opportunity law. Moreover, a complaint filed with the Equal Employment Opportunity Commission (EEOC) can result in legal expenses of tens of thousands of dollars and in a judgment of hundreds of thousands of dollars.

Managers must understand and abide by equal employment opportunity laws. People generally know about these and exhibit a readiness to use them. Ignoring their provisions will almost assuredly result in a complaint being filed by a prospective or present employee. Note that the burden of proof is on the employer; that is to say, the employer has to prove it did not discriminate by documenting that it treated the individual the same as other job applicants or employees. An equal employment opportunity suit can cause the employer to spend hundreds of hours preparing responses, presenting depositions, and so on, and can result in tens of thousands of dollars of legal fees.

Although legal representation is not required, many employers use lawyers because the cost of losing a case can be so great. Moreover, if the agency loses one case, more complaints will likely be filed. Complainants to the EEOC have legal counsel available through the EEOC, and defendants generally obtain it as well, even in so-called nuisance complaints by disgruntled present or former employees.

The EEOC suggests that every agency develop a written equal employment policy and put a management official in charge of monitoring its implementation. (If the agency is tax supported, reports often have to go to the funding agency, and such reports are prepared by the person in this position.) The policy is to be publicized to employees, and recruitment materials should identify it as an equal opportunity employer. None of the protected groups can be adversely affected by recruitment, selection, promotion, compensation, discipline, layoff, recall, termination, or other personnel policies. Individuals in the protected groups have to be treated in a manner consistent with other employees at their level, or the agency is at risk. Moreover, EEOC complaints are frequently used instead of lawsuits, because the EEOC represents the complainant, thus negating the need for the employee to hire an attorney. Moreover, relatively large out-of-court settlements often occur, as defense costs mount.

The risk managers for an organization or insurance company will sometimes negotiate a settlement when the cost of settling a lawsuit is likely to be less than the cost of legal defense during trial. A $20,000 settlement check can be viewed as a better alternative than $20,000 of legal costs and the risk of losing a judgment and paying an additional penalty.

Out-of-court settlements can create a major ethical problem for administrators. Although the most cost effective option may be to forge an out-of-court settlement, the question remains whether it is the right thing to do. Has the settlement simply rewarded the bad behavior of an ineffective employee? Will a settlement encourage other nuisance complaints? Is a settlement the best way to spend that money? These are questions that keep managers awake at night, agonizing over the ramifications of all the alternatives. Of course, equally critical questions to visit and revisit include questions about how the situation could have been avoided and what can be done to prevent similar situations from occurring in the future.

ACTION-BASED CONCEPT

Managers need to be certain that personnel policies and compensation systems are fair and equitably applied to all regardless of race, gender, sexual orientation, religion, veteran status, or disability. Personnel policies must be kept current and be followed explicitly or litigation risk will increase.

Affirmative Action Laws

It is somewhat difficult to write about affirmative action laws because they are in a state of flux. Affirmative action had its origins, like equal employment opportunity, in the Civil Rights Movement of the 1960s. There were many ramifications, but among the most significant was that agencies that received federal tax dollars, either by appropriation or by contract, had to have a written plan to hire additional employees from protected groups in order to remedy the effects of past discrimination. Many states developed similar procedures, and some organizations voluntarily adopted plans to increase the hiring of women, minorities, and members of other protected groups and to develop equitable pay scales for them.

The procedures often brought charges of reverse discrimination, that is, of discrimination against white males. Contrary to popular beliefs, affirmative action does not require quotas, preferential hiring, or employment of unqualified persons. It does, however, require organizations to determine which units have fewer women or minorities than would be expected by their availability and to develop plans to eliminate the under representation in these units.

Many affirmative action efforts by organizations focused on recruiting—how and where it was done. The goal was to ensure that the pool of applicants contained qualified minority candidates from which to select. Internal announcements of job vacancies were scrutinized to be sure that women and minority employees knew of the vacancies in time to become legitimate candidates. The previous custom of choosing a friend or acquaintance for a position, which created a system of close business and political relationships sometimes disparagingly referred to as "the good old boy network," was now considered inappropriate, if not illegal. Although the final decision was still the manager's, there were procedures to follow that increased the likelihood of women and minorities being hired. The threat of losing federal funds or contracts led numerous organizations to establish hiring goals, if not quotas.

Numerous organizations chose to voluntarily hire affirmatively and diversify their work force. If there are business reasons to hire affirmatively, institutions may specify race or gender in hiring announcements. For example, a health service agency that serves a Hispanic population may legitimately wish to hire a Hispanic staff member. Similarly, an organization wishing to increase the enrollment of African Americans may wish to hire an African American. A women's health network might legitimately seek a woman to act as director. The most frequently used means of accomplishing affirmative hiring is to advertise in the media or through agencies that serve the desired population and to use word of mouth, referrals, and other means to ensure qualified minority applicants are included in the pool.

In the 1950s and 1960s, discrimination against women and minorities was rampant, in the workplace and elsewhere. The pendulum of change first guaranteed civil rights, then guaranteed equal opportunity, then facilitated affirmative hiring to address inequities. While there are still many inequities and discriminatory practices, progress has been significant. Now, four decades later, the pendulum seems to be swinging back toward the guaranteeing of equal opportunity and the banning of personnel decisions based on race or gender. It must be noted, however, that while the outcome of this trend is not yet clear, it will still be appropriate to hire members of any group if there are legitimate bona fide reasons to do so.

ACTION-BASED CONCEPT

Effective managers will ascertain if the diversity of an organization's staff approximates the population served and determine the extent to which programs would be enhanced by additional staff diversification. Effective managers know what federal or state laws apply to hiring and always comply with them.

Sexual Harassment Laws

When the number of women in a previously largely male work force increased, the amount of sexual harassment increased. Owing to the resultant publicity, sexual harassment received more attention and was subsequently banned. Sexual harassment is now recognized as a form of sex discrimination. Well-run agencies now have sexual harassment policies, preventive educational programs, and procedures for filing and resolving complaints. Large penalties face organizations and individuals that violate the sexual harassment laws.

In its most fundamental form, sexual harassment involves unwanted sexual attention, with the key word being "unwanted." It is clear that the employee should communicate either verbally or in writing that the actions or words are not wanted and must stop. If then the unwanted behaviors do not stop, a sexual harassment charge can appropriately be filed.

In most cases of sexual harassment, a male harasses a female, but all variations can and have occurred—a female harassing a male, a male harassing a male, and a female harassing a female. Sexual harassment can involve looks, words, gestures, touches, and a variety of other communication methods. Managers must take the lead in developing a sexual harassment policy if one does not exist, educating the work force on whatever policy is in place, and consistently enforcing it. Again, not only is it the right thing to do, it is the law, and not preventing sexual harassment can result in large financial losses.

One common practice used to minimize complaints is to have women staff serve women clients or at least avoid having a male staff member and a female client alone in a room together. In any potentially volatile situation, it is always safer to have two staff members present.

> ## ACTION-BASED CONCEPT
>
> *Effective managers will generally not refer to gender, age, race, sexual orientation or physical capability with other employees in office communications unless it is in ways that will be perceived to be helpful by those whose gender, age, race, sexual orientation or physical capability differ from the manager.*

Collective Bargaining Laws

The right of employees to unionize has been protected for many years, as has their right to engage in collective bargaining. These rights have both positive and negative implications, but the important thing to remember is that they are legally protected.

An area union might approach employees about union representation, or a new or disgruntled employee might advocate for a union. A petition containing the signatures of 30 percent or more of the employees usually requires an election to determine a bargaining representative. Managers have to be careful not to unduly influence this process. If a union is certified as the bargaining agent for a group of employees, management and the union must bargain. If and when an agreement is reached, a contract is signed, which becomes the basis for many personnel decisions. Contract provisions must be followed. Otherwise internal grievances will be filed or lawsuits claiming violation of the labor laws may be brought against the organization.

> ## ACTION-BASED CONCEPT
>
> *Employers in non-union settings should treat their employees equitably and should compensate them fairly. Employees are among the most valuable assets of an organization and should be treated accordingly.*

Many large organizations, like hospitals, have several unions, while most small organizations have none. A union in and of itself is neither good nor bad. A union, of course, will insist that its employees be treated fairly and compensated equitably, but fair treatment and compensation is also the goal of most managers. Following a union contract completely can make it easier for managers, because the process or standards are specified in writing and exceptions cannot be made.

As always, the factor that determines whether unionization facilitates good management is the quality of leadership. If reasonable people are representing management and labor, beneficial compromises can be hammered out. Conversely, if unreasonable, emotional people are on either side, conflict and disorder can result, with long-term negative effects.

Each manager must understand the essence of labor law and should be familiar with the provisions of the contract for each group of unionized employees that work in the manager's unit. Only then can that manager be effective and experience a feeling of equanimity while at work.

ACTION-BASED CONCEPT

Effective managers in an organization that is at least partially unionized will thoroughly understand every contractual provision and will refer to the contract often in order to follow procedures explicitly and prevent grievances.

LIABILITY

The foregoing section focused on laws where compliance is important. Liability insurance coverage is needed regardless of whether the laws are followed. Administrators of community health care agencies generally need to be certain that their employees are adequately protected against liability claims. A million dollar per claim liability policy for all employees is typical, and obtaining such a policy should be explored. Agencies that provide any form of health care should already have such a policy in effect. Individual liability insurance coverage is often available through professional organizations at group rates, and homeowner policies can have riders attached to provide coverage for work-related incidents.

Administrators also need to consider purchasing insurance policies for directors and officers, sometimes referred to as "D and O" policies. Such policies offer expanded coverage to the chief officers and elected or appointed members of the board of directors. An unforeseen event can lead to a multimillion-dollar lawsuit, and the cost of defending against such a suit can easily exceed $100,000. (A key issue is whether the liability insurance policy covers the cost of defending the client and the judgment if the case is lost.) Failure to have D and O insurance might cause influential community members to refuse to serve on the board because of the possibility they might have to defend against frivolous lawsuits.

Agency personnel must be certain that the facilities are safe and in good repair. As noted earlier, neglect of workplace hazards is a common cause of legal difficulties. Likewise, agency personnel must perform their duties in compliance with normal standards. In a suit alleging neglect or incompetence, the burden of proof is on the claimant to prove that the staff member should have done more or should have done it better. Clearly, every staff member must "do no harm," but beyond that the standard is what a reasonably prudent practicing professional would do.

To establish liability, claimants have to show bad judgment or bad practice. Bad practice is hard to defend, if in fact it occurred. Assuming it can be established that someone willfully disobeyed policies or practice standards, then the individual or the agency or both are likely to be found liable for damages. If actions can be shown to be arbitrary, capricious or unreasonable given the circumstances, these actions also can be used to establish liability.

Managers should frequently remind employees of the risk of liability and other types of litigation and emphasize the need for services to meet professional standards. All health care practitioners must be conscious of the possibility of a lawsuit and must always conduct themselves according to the standards of their profession.

ETHICS

Whether an individual or organization is liable for damages depends on the circumstances, and whether a certain behavior is unethical also depends on the circumstances. But ethical issues are even less clear than liability issues.

Ethics involves opinions as to what is good or bad. Determining if a certain action is legal or illegal is usually a straightforward process, whereas ethics, which concerns the beliefs, values, and preferences of individuals or groups, is inherently controversial. What one person considers ethical, another can readily find unethical.

There are several criteria on which to base ethics. One approach commonly used is based on the premise that in any given situation there is no one right or wrong act. Rather, the act that produces impartial justice for the greatest number of people is the best that can be achieved and is therefore ethical. When an act only benefits a few, ethical questions emerge.

Ethical analysis involves examining motives, integrity, trust, exploitation, and results. Professional practice that grows out of helpful motives and has beneficial results will usually be thought to be ethical. Behavior based on mutual trust and free of exploitation is likely to be viewed as ethical. Individuals that meet ethical standards and have good motives for their actions are generally thought to have high levels of integrity.

There will always be ethical issues to discuss and explore, and perhaps some will never be solved. Whether health care personnel are obligated to be role models when it comes to tobacco use or weight control is one example of a difficult issue. Other difficult issues include these: Should ability to pay be a primary criterion for determining the level of health care? Are the rights of smokers currently being adequately protected? Should welfare mothers be counseled into an abortion or conversely be counseled out of an abortion because of the personal beliefs of the provider? There is no end to the ever-growing list of ethical concerns.

CONCLUSION

Working within the framework of the law is imperative. Potential liability for prohibited employment practices is a primary area of concern for most health care administrators. Managers who are not familiar with labor law would do well to read some books on the topic, subscribe to some relevant newsletters, attend seminars on the topic periodically (often offered at conventions), or enroll in a college course on labor law or liability.

IN-BASKET ASSIGNMENT

TO: Agency Health Education and Health Promotion Specialists
FROM: The Director
RE: Accessibility Issues

The next time you are in a community health agency, look at how well they are equipped to handle clients with disabilities. Ask about the accommodations that had to be made. Let me know what you find out so we can see if any of their techniques can be used by our agency.

MANAGEMENT CASE STUDY

Setting

A community teen counseling hot-line program had a minimal budget, used donated facilities, and as is typical, relied heavily on volunteers to staff the phone lines. There were two paid staff members, an administrator, and an office manager–secretary.

Problem

The building used by the program was formerly a home. It contained a telephone center, separate rooms for training, a break room, an office, and a counseling area. Located in an old neighborhood, the building itself was old and in need of considerable work.

The electrical service was inadequate for the range of equipment used in the program's operations. In order to accommodate computers, a fax machine, a photocopy machine, an answering machine, a popcorn popper, a microwave oven, a radio, and a television, several extension cords were needed. If too many pieces of equipment were in use at once, a fuse was blown.

The administrator was concerned that someone might trip over an extension cord or fall in the dark when a fuse was being replaced. She also had a nagging fear that an overload or frayed cord might cause a fire. In addition, the house had creaky front steps, and the sidewalk was damaged in several places. Finally, sometimes late at night only volunteers were in the office, and the administrator was worried about their safety.

Alternatives Considered

One alternative considered was to ignore the safety hazards and make the best of it. The risks could be reduced by using heavy-duty extension cords and posting signs.

Another alternative was to request the landlord to make the requisite changes to make the facility safe.

A third alternative was to implement a modest renovation fund-raising campaign.

Actions Taken

The administrator opted for the third alternative because of the possibility of injury, fire, bad press, and lawsuits. With the landlord's approval of the renovation plan, the administrator approached an electrician to donate the labor for needed rewiring, an electrical supply house to donate the materials, a carpenter to donate repair work on the steps, and a cement contractor to donate replacement of the broken sidewalk. In return, each donor would be listed as a program sponsor for a year.

OUTCOME

The landlord was happy with the repairs and rewiring and offered to donate paint if the volunteers would paint the house. The proposal was accepted.

Press coverage of the donated services was arranged so the donors received a public relations bonus in return for their donations. The agency also gained much needed media exposure. As a result of the coverage, the number of volunteers increased, as did the number of phone calls from teens seeking counseling.

DISCUSSION QUESTIONS

1. What is the worst possible case scenario that could have happened if the renovations had not been made? Why do administrators need to consider worst possible case scenarios?

2. What was the source of the greatest liability exposure: the broken sidewalk, the creaky steps, the overloaded circuits, or the extension cords crossing walk areas?

3. Should the steps have been replaced by a ramp?

4. Is there a significant risk of litigation that results from allowing volunteers to be in a facility after midnight without staff present? What steps could be taken to reduce the liability exposure?

5. Even if the risk of litigation was perceived to be low, is it morally acceptable to place volunteers in potentially unsafe areas? Is any facility completely safe? How much renovation is considered enough to avoid legal problems or moral censure?

6. Can the "first impression" of a facility affect conclusions about the quality of services offered?

7. Are there other strategies that could have been used to address the issue of volunteer safety?

CHAPTER 8

Job Descriptions

OVERVIEW

A position or job is a collection of responsibilities assigned to one person. A position or job description is a written summary of the position that typically includes the position title; rank or grade level of the position; reporting responsibilities; job activities and duties; supervisory responsibilities; educational credential, certification, and experience requirements; and salary range.

Most organizations require written job descriptions, and unless an organization is very new, job descriptions will already exist. In a large organization, such as a hospital or corporation, the job descriptions will be retained on file by the human resources department. In a smaller organization, senior management will retain them. In all cases, the manager of a unit should obtain and frequently review copies of the job descriptions for all employees in the unit. The manager should also report any significant changes in the makeup of tasks performed by employees in the unit and should occasionally do a job activity audit (i.e., make a list of what each employee actually does). Each employee should have a copy of his or her own job description.

Job descriptions should stay relatively stable, primarily because the individuals in the jobs interact with others in the organization and changing one job description can have a significant impact on what others do. For example, giving a health promotion specialist responsibility for coordinating a school health initiative will likely have an impact on the duties of nurses with clinical responsibilities in the schools and could produce conflict. Moreover, job descriptions are intended to provide the basis for equitable pay for equitable work. If job descriptions change too drastically or too rapidly, compensation inequity can occur, unless compensation changes as well.

Of course, it must also be acknowledged that job descriptions should change over time. First, an individual employee or supervisor may emphasize some parts of a job description and de-emphasize others, often because of the skills and interests the employee brings to the position or because of the evolving needs of the organization. Additionally, a job description typically includes a catch-all clause—"other tasks as required or assigned"—that gives the employee and supervisor considerable latitude in customizing the job.

Another reason job descriptions change over time is that employees often desire to grow in their positions and progress up the organizational chart. Individuals who want to be promoted will gradually look for ways to make a greater contribution and to demonstrate they can handle more responsibility and still perform their current tasks well. Supervisors often encourage and reward ambitiousness because they too want the employees to grow and because the employees' progress makes both the organization and the supervisors look good.

A related reason job descriptions change over time is to enrich the jobs and increase employee satisfaction. A job should consist of similar responsibilities that can be accomplished by one person using that person's abilities and training. However, if a job's duties are too alike and too repetitive, the job becomes boring, the employee finds him- or herself unchallenged, and employee turnover may occur. Early authors writing about division of labor extolled the concept of the assembly line and favored a system in which each individual did a few repetitive tasks that he or she was trained to do. More recently, theorists have emphasized job enrichment and advocated redesigning jobs so that they encompass a wider variety of tasks and responsibilities. Job enrichment theory focuses on the psychological nature of the worker and how to minimize dissatisfaction, low morale, and even alienation.

Of course, the higher the educational and skill level of an employee, the more important job enrichment becomes. A job should not be so restrictive that the duties quickly become monotonous and unchallenging. Instead, it should evolve to fit the needs and interests of the employee, who is probably gaining more abilities, an increased understanding of the business, or more education. Job enrichment theory generally encourages variety, employee control over what is done and when it is done, and employee initiative and decision making. Although most tasks in a health service agency have to be done to maintain organizational efficiency, and performance standards have to be met, there is usually enough latitude to allow the employee to grow into the job and the job to grow to fit the employee. Of course, in time many employees will be ready for an internal promotion or a higher position in another agency. Effective supervisors encourage promotion because of genuine concern for the employees and because they realize that unchallenged employees often develop morale problems, which can lead to poor performance.

It is imperative for managers to periodically examine job descriptions in their units, and revise them as appropriate. It is also imperative for them to obtain the necessary reviews and approvals, because mid-level managers seldom have final authority in such matters. If those who supervise employees do not push for job-enriching revisions, the revisions may not occur and performance may suffer.

ACTION-BASED CONCEPT

A manager should obtain a copy of the job description of everyone who reports to him or her and review it periodically to ascertain if what the employee does or what the job description specifies needs to be revised.

JOB DESCRIPTION ELEMENTS

Whether writing new job descriptions for a new agency or for a new position within an existing agency, the first task is to obtain a sample description for a similar position or develop a prototype that will be used throughout the organization. This promotes consistency, order, and equity. A variety of titles and combinations of elements are typically used, but normally the following elements are included (regardless of how the headings are worded).

POSITION TITLE

Titles are important because they indicate status, and, in fact, title upgrades are sometimes given in lieu of raises. Moreover, few things are more debilitating to an employee than to have his or her position or title downgraded. Titles should be consistent among people doing similar tasks, and titles such as director or coordinator should be chosen carefully and only after a review of the responsibilities of others with that title. Position titles often reflect decision-making authority and the number of employees supervised.

Rank or Grade Level

In smaller stand-alone health agencies, specifying rank or grade may not be appropriate, but in larger organizations, it will be mandatory. Equity (and avoidance of discrimination charges) requires that similar positions be at similar levels. Establishing a rank or grade system also helps in establishing wage and salary equity. Moreover, fringe benefits such as vacation time are also often based on the level of the position (e.g., grades 7 and above might receive 3 weeks vacation per year whereas grades 6 and below might receive 2 weeks). Civil service organizations and large bureaucracies nearly always grade positions, often based on an analysis of required education, duties, supervisory responsibilities, and required decision making. Obviously, grading a position independent of the person occupying it helps avoid discrimination. Preparing a chart or table that lists a hierarchy of professional-level jobs is also helpful for ensuring equity and progression. Such a chart will allow a view of the big picture and can aid in identifying problems (see Table 8–1).

Reporting Responsibilities

Every employee reports to or is supervised by someone. While dual reporting sometimes occurs, it is not normally desirable. Lines of authority need to be clear.

Table 8–1 Hierarchy of Organizational Positions

Job Title	Education	Experience	Responsibilities
Director	MS in health education, CHES	5 years, 2 in supervision	Leadership, planning, final decision making
Assistant director	MS or equivalent	3 years, 1 in supervisory role	Budget management, fund-raising
Nutrition specialist	BS in nutrition	None required	Patient counseling
Fitness specialist	BS in health promotion, exercise physiology, physical education, or equivalent; CPR	None required; aerobics experience desirable	Plan and conduct fitness activities; patient counseling and supervision
School health education	BS in school health education or HPER	Teaching experience preferred	Consultation with teachers re curriculum revision, teaching, and in-service education
Community health education specialist	BS in community health education; CHFS desirable	None required; media experience preferred	Public relations, public education campaigns

There should be ultimate authority at the top of the pyramid and clear lines to every subordinate position. Subordinates must know to whom they are responsible, what their decision-making authority is, and what their reporting expectations are. A job description normally indicates the position to which that job is subordinate, and, by implication, the person to whom the employee will report. This is not to suggest that a variety of mechanisms for coordinating with other units are not also required (such mechanisms are sometimes indicated by a dotted line on an organizational chart).

Job Activities and Duties

From two or three to as many as a dozen job activities are typically listed in a job description. Ideally, the tasks should be comparable in the amount of education, experience, and responsibility required, and there should be some rationale for the assigned duties. It is desirable for all tasks to relate to the accomplishment of a single function or to a single program. This is more often feasible for large organizations than it is for small ones. In small organizations, employees often have to be generalists (i.e., do a lot of different tasks). In principle, the number of unrelated tasks assigned to a job should be kept small. As noted earlier, it is typical for a list of duties to end with the phrase "others as assigned," and it is usually good to place unrelated assignments under this classification rather than create an illogical job description.

If changing or upgrading a job description, doing a job analysis is a good starting point. This involves listing all the different tasks that an employee actually does (or having the employee keep a running list) and then comparing it to the job description. Obviously, some similar job activities will be grouped in order to keep the written job description brief, but the overall job analysis can reveal how the position has evolved and can dictate a change in description or a position upgrade.

A job analysis is particularly useful just before an employee leaves a job. It can help create a realistic job description for the person about to occupy the position as well as help smooth the transition.

Supervisory Responsibilities

Just as an employee should know his or her reporting responsibilities, he or she should also understand any relevant supervisory responsibilities . They are important enough to warrant being singled out, and usually they are listed separately in a special section of the job description form or the word "none" is written in that section.

Education, Certification, and Experience Requirements

Again, it is important to think about the position rather than the person when establishing such criteria so as to ensure equity and rationality. Exceptions can be made, and it is very common to hire overqualified individuals. As discussed in a later chapter on hiring, if a candidate is hired who does not meet the educational requirements and yet qualified applicants are still in the applicant pool, the risk of discrimination claims is high. On occasion, degrees can be specified, but adding the phrase "equivalent work experience" obviously gives some flexibility. Health education or promotion degrees can also be required, from SOPHE/ AAHE (Society of Public Health Education/American Association for Health Education)or other approved programs, and they can be used as screening criteria to reduce the applicant pool. Some degrees commonly seen in health education or health administration are listed in Table 8-2. Educational requirements that are not essential for successful job performance may violate labor laws. Often, educational degrees are listed as desirable. For instance, if cardiopulmonary resuscitation certification is needed for a health promotion job, that too (or the willingness to obtain it within a prescribed period of time) must be specified. Likewise, health

---

Table 8-2 Example of Degrees in Health Education, Promotion, and Administration

Undergraduate

B.S. (Bachelor of Science)
B.A. (Bachelor of Arts)
B.S.N. (Bachelor of Science in Nursing-Community Health)
B.Ed. (Bachelor of Education)

Graduate

M.A. (Master of Arts in Health Promotion)
M.S. (Master of Science in Health Promotion or Health Education)
M.Ed. (Master of Education)
M.P.H. (Master of Public Health)
M.P.A. (Master of Public Administration)
M.H.A. (Master of Health Administration
Dr.P.H. (Doctor of Public Health)
D.H.A. (Doctor of Health Administration)
Ed.D. (Doctor of Education)
Ph.D. (Doctor of Philosophy, typically a research degree)

---

education and health promotion specialists can now obtain certification as a certified health education specialist (CHES). Specifying that applicants be graduates of a SOPHE\AAHE-approved baccalaureate degree program or a health education master's degree program certified by CEPH (the Council on Education for Public Health) or that the applicant be a certified health education specialist helps standardize credentials and allows a more precise assessment of educational background. Work experience is also usually specified, especially for supervisory personnel, and again care must be taken not to make the standard too high. The experience specified should be the minimum required to do the job.

ACTION-BASED CONCEPT

Managers should be familiar with the requirements of and the need for certification and if appropriate should lead by example in obtaining it.

Salary Range

Salary ranges will almost always be required in collective bargaining contracts because they promote equivalent pay for equivalent work. Salary is discussed in more detail in a subsequent chapter.

The job description form presented in Exhibit 8–1 does not contain all the sections discussed above, but it is an example of a form in actual use.

CONCLUSION

Job descriptions are important to the organization, to the individuals occupying the positions, and to the individuals charged with supervising the positions. There are also significant legal ramifications involved. Accordingly, job descriptions are formal written documents. Each organization normally uses a single format so as to promote consistency and equity.

Job descriptions normally include the job title; rank or grade; reporting responsibilities; activities or duties; supervisory responsibilities; education, certification, and experience requirements; and salary range; although the headings and sequence of these elements may vary. Moreover, the details of a position change over time, based on the needs of the organization and the ability of the individual. However, job descriptions must first and foremost serve the interests of the organization. Although an individual's needs are important, organizational needs must

Exhibit 8–1 Job Description Form

JOB TITLE:		REVISION DATE:	

LOCATION:	

SUMMARY:	

JOB TASKS:	(*Essential Tasks: Tasks for which job incumbent has primary responsibility; % of Time: Indicates the percentage of time expected to be spent on this responsibility)

REPORTING RELATION- SHIPS:	

POSITION CHARACTER- ISTICS: (How Tasks Are Performed)	

JOB SPECIFICATIONS, QUALIFICATIONS, AND ABILITIES	

All Job Descriptions are subject to revision based upon the changing needs of the college. Employees will be notified if revisions in job description occur.

Courtesy of Park College, Parkville, Mo.

predominate—or charges of discrimination may occur. Managers must always balance the tasks of motivating individual employees, rewarding good performance, and serving the organization in the best way possible.

IN-BASKET ASSIGNMENT

TO: Health Education and Health Promotion Specialists
FROM: The Executive Director
RE: Health Education Specialist Job Description

A friend of mine is starting a worksite health education program. He asked me about a job description. I indicated that our job description was not state of the art but that I would ask you to prepare one.

Please prepare a draft of a job description for a properly credentialed health education specialist who will be employed in an industrial setting.

MANAGEMENT CASE STUDY

Setting

A community education department in a mid-sized hospital had three staff members in addition to an assistant director, who focused on outreach. The director was a nurse with master's level training, some of which was in education. She focused on patient and family teaching.

Problem

The department had been heavily slanted toward patient and family teaching, although some attention was paid to topics of interest to the community, such as weight loss and smoking cessation. The director wanted the department to develop a new emphasis on worksite health promotion programs and considered assigning the assistant director the task of creating these programs. The assistant director did not have any work experience in a union shop, which was viewed as a substantial drawback, because unionized factories in the city were considered logical customers for the new programs.

Alternatives Considered

One alternative considered was to reduce the assistant director's position to half time and hire a worksite specialist as a half-time employee. The director was concerned, however, that a competent worksite specialist would not be willing to accept a half-time position.

The second alternative considered was to assign the new duties to the assistant director. The director's worry here was that the worksite programs would not receive enough attention for an adequate startup.

Actions Taken

The director of the community education department took steps to change the name of the department to the "Community and Worksite Health Promotion Department" to indicate the broadened scope of activities. In addition, she changed her job description so that 25 percent of her time would be devoted to initiating new programs, and she changed her job title to "Director of Community and Worksite Health Promotion."

The director then changed the title of her assistant from "Assistant Director" to "Community, School, and Worksite Health Promotions Specialist." The job responsibilities of the former assistant director were also changed. Now only 25 percent of her time was to be devoted to school health programs and 75 percent was to be devoted to community worksite programs.

The community, school, and worksite health promotion specialist was ordered to spend the summer reading the literature on worksite health promotion programs and to visit at least two well-run hospital-based programs in other cities and at least one good school-based employee wellness program.

The director and the health promotion specialist then started a series of visits to school personnel with whom they had previously worked to explore the development of a cooperative employee wellness program that would become the prototype to be offered to business and industry. Phase two of the initiative was to begin approaching business and industry.

OUTCOME

The results were satisfactory, although the startup was slower than anticipated. Only one school was willing to set up an employee wellness program, and the hospital had to subsidize more of the costs than it anticipated. However, the employee development plan worked well. The health promotion specialist did the readings and site visits and spent three days a week developing contacts and proposing worksite initiatives. Small firms were surprisingly willing to do more in the way of health promotion as a modest employee benefit. When two school district programs and four small business programs were in place, a contract was arranged with a mid-sized unionized firm, and the union, the firm management, and the hospital formed a three-way partnership.

DISCUSSION QUESTIONS

1. Were the visits to other programs an essential element of the assistant director's new job description? How important was the reading assignment?

2. Why was the change in the department title important? What about the changes in the position titles? How might the downgrading of the assistant director's title be handled so as to avoid lowering her morale?

3. How important was it for the director to change the amount of time she devoted to initiating new programs?

4. What scenarios could have caused the director's actions to fail to achieve her objectives?

5. Are there other strategies that might have achieved the director's goals more effectively?

CHAPTER 9

Recruiting and Hiring

A MANAGEMENT PERSPECTIVE

Recruiting and hiring are among the most important tasks of an administrator. An organization and its leaders must depend on employees to get things done. While this is always true, it is especially true in human service organizations, including health promotion agencies. To the average client, the employees with whom the client interacts are the organization. The personality, skills, appearance, judgment, and overall decorum of the employees in a sense join together to become the personality, skills, appearance, judgment, and overall decorum of the entire agency. Gary Filerman observes, "Healthcare, first and foremost, comprises people. It is a labor-intensive enterprise, complicated not only by the number of people involved in delivering health services but also by the number of occupations and the complexity of their relationships."[1]

An organization's success depends on its employees. So does a manager's or a leader's success. As Peter Drucker says, "No organization can do better than the people it has. . . . The yield from the human resources really determines the organization's performance. And that's decided by the basic people decisions: whom we hire and whom we fire and where we place people, and whom we promote."[2] Obviously, those in supervisory roles have the opportunity to motivate employees—and if necessary to replace employees—but changing employees is costly in terms of time, energy, emotional damage, and, of course, dollars. It is critical that good decisions be made the first time.

DETERMINING STAFFING NEEDS

Determining if an employee is needed and what the employee should do is critical. No vacancy caused by resignation, termination, or retirement should be automatically refilled. Much thought and discussion with others on the management team should occur. A vacancy represents an opportunity to re-organize, upgrade the position, downgrade the position, eliminate the position, or combine the position with another—and the decision what to do should consider the current needs and projected needs and plans of the organization. Obviously, if the employee has been in the position a long time, the needs may be significantly different than when the position was last filled. Accordingly, organizational needs ought to be carefully considered and a new job description developed.

For example, essential clerk typist skills may now include word processing and other computer skills. Perhaps voice mail has reduced the need for a telephone receptionist, and the receptionist's duties can be combined with data entry or filing duties to create a new position. Perhaps a wellness center is preparing for a new thrust in cardiac rehabilitation, and cardiopulmonary resuscitation certification is required. Perhaps a program specialist is being replaced, and the new position will include a focus on senior citizens. There are numerous ways in which positions may be changed to reflect current or projected organizational priorities.

ACTION-BASED CONCEPT

Before any vacancy is filled, consider carefully whether the position should be eliminated, upgraded, downgraded, revised, or combined with another to meet shifting organizational priorities, and prepare the appropriate job description. At least as many people and as much time should normally be spent on this task as on the selection process.

PROMOTING FROM WITHIN

Another issue that needs to be carefully considered early on is whether to promote from within or hire an external candidate. Of course, for small organizations promotion may not be an option—there may be no suitable personnel to promote. In large organizations, on the other hand, there may be personnel policies or contractual agreements that mandate internal posting of a position, and if qualified internal candidates exist, they may have to be hired before external candidates are considered. In this era of downsizing, union contracts are increasingly negotiating job security programs that include clauses requiring promotion to be given priority as a method of filling vacancies. Obviously, in large organizations health promotion program administrators will have to work with the personnel or human resources office, and the importance attached to promotion will be one of the issues normally discussed.

Whether required or not, it is still a good administrative practice to consider carefully all current employees who might be qualified for and interested in the position. Publicizing the position is normally achieved by an internal posting of the position or discussion of it at a staff meeting, although in small organizations, contacting qualified employees informally and discussing the prospects for promotion is often preferable.

Depending on organizational policies, the highest priority might be to promote an employee from within the specific program or division, although some organizations require that any employee in any division be considered equally. Also, some organizational policies only permit suspension of the search procedure if a suitable female or minority internal candidate applies. Note that there are inherent discrimination issues involved in applying these types of policies.

Even if organizational policies do not favor internal candidates, it is always possible for internal candidates to apply and to be considered along with external candidates. It is a common practice to announce a position internally and externally at the same time, include both types of applicants in the applicant pool, and evaluate all applicants solely on their merits.

There are several advantages of promoting from within. Perhaps the most significant is that it generally elevates morale. Seeing someone move up in the organization is encouraging to the other employees. They realize it could happen to them and are thus inclined to work harder to increase their own chances of moving up.

Another major advantage is that an internal candidate is a known entity. The candidate's work habits and personal attributes are likely to hold fewer unwanted surprises than those of an external candidate, partly because the skills of an internal candidate are usually underestimated and his or her weaknesses magnified, while with an external candidate the opposite is more typical.

Yet another advantage of promoting from within, when possible, is that internal candidates know the organization, its staff, and its culture. Moreover, they often know some of the clients. The learning curve for the position is always shorter for an internal candidate than for a new employee. Part of the reason for hiring internally is that management can more accurately appraise the suitability of the candidate for the position. Finally, it is cheaper and quicker to promote from within than to institute a full search.

Although there are many advantages to hiring internally, including others not mentioned, there are also numerous reasons to recruit external candidates. The major advantage is that new employees bring with them new insights and perspectives. Also, recruiting and hiring a key leader who is highly respected may make it easier to recruit superior staff members. Organizational inbreeding can be problematic, because employees may only know one way of doing things.

Organizational change becomes more difficult. Or stated positively, organizational change is easier if new people with work experience elsewhere are brought into the organization.

> ## *ACTION-BASED CONCEPT*
>
> *It is generally desirable for organizations to have a carefully developed written internal promotion policy. The best policy is usually to hire capable people at lower levels and promote those who are effective and fully qualified. It is also wise, however, to fill some mid-level and upper-level positions with external candidates to inject new ideas into the organization.*

ATTRACTING APPLICANTS

As described by James Johnson, "Healthcare organizations are fundamentally dependent on people who have to fill an extensive range of roles to accomplish the institution's tasks and goals."[3] So unless an organization is promoting from within, the best tactic is to attract a large, diverse applicant pool so that three or four highly qualified applicants can be chosen for an interview. How big the applicant pool becomes will depend on many factors, such as the title of the position, the responsibilities, the salary, the perks, the advertising budget, and so on.

Applicants are attracted to positions that have impressive titles, especially those that reflect significant responsibility, such as "Director of Substance Abuse Prevention Programming," which is more impressive than "Program Specialist." Titles are viewed as especially important by young, aggressive potential applicants, who like to add impressive titles to their résumés. Therefore, such applicants will apply for a high-sounding position even if the salary is not high. If it is desirable to induce someone with lots of experience to apply, then a good salary is also required. If the salary must be kept low because of budget restraints, it makes sense to minimize the required work experience, whereas if salary is high, extensive experience and education can be required.

Other factors determining the size of the applicant pool include the recruitment plan and the advertising budget. If the object is to recruit locally, announcing the vacancy in local newspapers and employment agencies will likely suffice. Local recruitment is typical for clerical, accounting, and low-level management positions, because the salaries for these positions are not likely to be of sufficient magnitude to induce someone to move from another city. There may be area placement offices associated with colleges, vocational or technical schools, and high schools that can be used, as well as temporary employment agencies. Many locations are now served by agencies that provide workers during peak service periods or when employees get sick or go on vacation. Temporary workers can be utilized until a suitable candidate is found, at which point a permanent job offer can be made.

Specialized or upper-level positions usually require some form of regional or national search that encompasses the use of national journals or placement services or the placement offices of colleges with programs in the required specialization. Exhibit 9–1 displays typical recruitment sources for those seeking health promotion specialists. Once a job announcement is developed, it can simply be sent to any of the sources listed in Exhibit 9–1. However, there are fees for some of the services as well as advertising costs. Paid ad copy is usually much more concise than job announcements sent free through the network because of cost considerations.

Personal networking is also critical. Placing phone calls to people likely to know suitable candidates can often pay big dividends. Many of the best positions are filled in this way, usually with excellent results.

An agency or hospital wishing to hire minority candidates needs to contact organizations that train or place minority personnel. Locating such individuals usually requires some focused recruiting but is feasible. As is the case with all communication efforts, it is important to ascertain where minority candidates are and what communication channels are used most often and then use those channels for recruiting.

Exhibit 9–1 Sources for Recruiting Health Promotion Specialists

- SOPHE job banks associated with various chapters
- Sunday editions of metropolitan area newspapers
- University placement bulletins and bulletin boards
- Health education faculty at colleges that train health educators
- APHA Annual Meeting Placement Service
- *The Nation's Health*
- *The American Journal of Public Health*
- SOPHE chapter newsletter
- Unemployment agencies
- Government job bulletins (civil service)
- Practicing health educators
- Other agencies that hire health educators (health departments, voluntary agencies, HMOs, hospitals, governmental agencies)

SELECTING CANDIDATES TO BE INTERVIEWED

It may seem ironic that after working to increase the applicant pool, the next step is to narrow it. There may be anywhere from two or three applicants to several dozen. If there are only two or three, probably all will be interviewed, but normally not more than three to five candidates are interviewed. Deciding which candidates to interview is critical to ultimate success. The search committee usually reviews the applicant pool for an upper-level position, but an individual may be authorized to hire if the position is lower down in the hierarchy.

Simple job application forms are sometimes used for standard low-level positions, but applications typically include a résumé and cover letter. Sorting through three or four dozen application packets is no small task. Usually a representative from human resources, the manager, or the search committee chair will perform a quick review and weed out unqualified applicants. Sometimes applications will be sorted into "yes," "no," and "maybe" piles. The "yes" applications then are looked at more carefully.

At this point in the process, making a phone call to each promising applicant will often save time and money. After a discussion of the job and the salary, the question "Are you still interested?" should be asked. The answer might narrow the applicant pool, and sometimes the pool shrinks to the point where it is necessary to go into the "maybe" pile.

Usually, however, the phone calls narrow the group of applicants to five or six. From this group two or three are selected to be interviewed. Obviously, a variety of factors can influence the selection, such as credentials, work experience, letters of reference, travel costs, and so on.

APPLICANT TESTING AND BACKGROUND CHECKS

Testing may be a required part of the selection process. Depending on the test and the organization's needs, the testing may be done early in the process, so that the entire applicant pool is tested, or done toward the end. For example, a drug test, if required, might be performed only on the individual chosen for the appointment, whereas a civil service exam minimum score might be required before an application is considered complete. (In the case of many government agencies, would-be employees have to take appropriate civil service exams and meet other qualifications to get on the list of eligible applicants.) Midway between such extremes, a speed and accuracy test might be given on word processing or typing equipment. Some organizations require background checks and security clearance. Some require a psychological profile. Generally, if such requirements exist, personnel in the human resources department are experienced in handling the details, and the appropriate appointments merely need to be scheduled.

Some background checks need to be extensive. Receipt of transcripts directly from the college or university, proof of credentialing when appropriate, and verification of work experience might be required. If the position involves the military or corrections system, a security clearance might be necessary.

It is a good policy to contact former employers to verify that the candidate was indeed an employee and to find out what the candidate's duties or accomplishments were. It may not be necessary to check all listed places of employment, but the most relevant or recent ones should be contacted. It is also appropriate to inquire about the reasons for departure of the employee and whether the employer would rehire the individual. Other questions might also be relevant, but increasingly former supervisors are willing only to verify the length of employment and the nature of the employee's duties, especially if either the employer or employee had any reason to feel dissatisfied.

Individuals that have agreed to serve as references are listed in a résumé or cover letter and are more likely to respond to performance-oriented questions. They are also more likely to provide useful information over the phone instead of in a letter because of the increased risk of litigation if their answers are written down. Note that a great deal can be learned from nonverbal communication, such as a pause in answering the question "Would you hire this individual again?" or the amount of enthusiasm shown while describing the accomplishments or strengths of the applicant.

If an applicant does not list a supervisor from a recent job, it is often worthwhile to contact the supervisor anyhow in order to verify the employment data and to find out whether he or she would rehire the applicant and why.

If an applicant does not list a supervisor from a current job, it may well be that the individual does not wish the current employer to know that he or she is searching for a new position. Professionalism and courtesy dictate in such situations that the applicant be contacted and asked if it is appropriate to talk to the current employer. Normally current employers are contacted only for the final two or three candidates.

ACTION-BASED CONCEPT

Contact former employers any time during the search process, but only contact current employers if the committee has narrowed selection down to one or two finalists and permission has been given by the applicants.

INTERVIEWING APPLICANTS

The initial task of prospective employees is to "make the cut" or "get on the short list," because they can then sell themselves during the interview. Conversely, the individuals doing the search are first focused on narrowing the applicant pool to a group of finalists. For both groups, the crux of the search process is the interview process. During this process, the manager needs to select the best candidate and sell that candidate on the position (it is somewhat debilitating to interview two or three candidates and to have all of them reject job offers). At the same time, the applicants are attempting to learn about the organization and the position to ascertain if they want to make a career move. They may also want to learn about the community or about job mobility within the organization. Obviously, the job interview is a critical step in the attempt to match a candidate with an organization.

Deciding who will interview the candidate and establishing an interview schedule are early tasks in the interview process. Normally, the immediate supervisor will interview candidates for a lower-level position, and members of the search committee will interview candidates for an upper-level position. Depending on the size of the organization, the chief executive officer (CEO) may want to interview the candidate. In a large organization, a vice president rather than the CEO may have final sign-off responsibility for the hire. Few decisions are more important than hiring decisions, so astute managers often want to personally check that the individual is suitable. There often will be an appointment on the interview schedule with someone in the human resources department to discuss insurance, retirement, vacation, and other elements of the fringe benefits package.

If multiple interviewers are used, it sometimes is appropriate to develop a rating form (Exhibit 9–2). Occasionally group interviews are held.

The key to a successful interview is preparation. Of course, holding the interview in a suitable place—one that is comfortable, has refreshments available, and permits interruption-free discussion—is important, but careful reading and perhaps re-reading of the application, along with highlighting material that is significant and noting areas that need exploration, should also be done to ensure the applicant's suitability for the position.

The focus during the interview is on the job and on the candidate's ability to do the job. Antidiscrimination laws prohibit asking about ethnic background, sexual orientation, religion, age, or handicapping condition. Exhibit 9–3 displays legal and illegal inquiries.

Typical interview questions include these: What are your strengths? What are your major weaknesses? Why do you want to leave your present job? What is it about this job that interests you most? What do you see yourself doing 5 years from now? What sort of salary are you looking for? Why have you changed jobs so frequently? Why did you go through a period of unemployment?

Exhibit 9–2 Interview Assessment Form

Name _____ Position _____

Date _____ Name of Interviewer _____

Indicators:
   4 - exceeds expectations
   3 - meets expectations
   2 - partially meets expectations
   1 - does not meet expectations
   N/O - no opinion

It is recommended that this assessment form be completed independently of other interviewers.

		Comments	Score
1.	**Education:** Related to or essential for position		
2.	**Job Knowledge:** Specific experience and/or skills related to position		
3.	**Administrative/Supervisory Capability:** Skills and/or experience		
4.	**Special Skills or Training:**		
5.	**Public Relations:** Ability to deal with students, staff, public		
6.	**Philosophy/Attitude:** Toward education, department and its functions		
7.	**Moral and Ethical Integrity:**		
8.	**Articulation:** Oral communication with and response to interviewers		
9.	**Personality:** Interpersonal skills		
10.	**Physical Appearance/Dress:** Appropriateness for position		
TOTAL SCORE:			

Exhibit 9–3 Legal and Illegal Inquiries on Application Forms and in Interviews

Subject	Lawful Inquiries	Unlawful Inquiries
Name	Full name Have you ever worked for this agency under a different name?	Original name of applicant whose name has been changed by court order
Birthplace		Birthplace of applicant or applicant's parents Requirement that applicant submit birth certificate or naturalization record
Age	Are you 18 years of age or older?	How old are you? What is your date of birth?
Religion or creed		Religion preference Holidays observed
Height or weight		Height or weight
Sex		Ability to reproduce Advocacy of any form of birth control Sexual orientation
Photograph		Requirement that applicant provide a photograph
Family		Marital status (single or married?) Number of children Child-care arrangements Employment of spouse

(continues)

Exhibit 9–3 (continued)

Health	Do you have any impairment that would hinder your ability to do the job for which you have applied?	Do you have a disability or handicap? Have you ever been treated for any of the following diseases?
Citizenship	Are you a citizen of the United States? If not, do you intend to become one? If not, do you have the legal right to remain permanently in the United States?	Of what country are you a cltlzen?
National Origin	Languages applicant speaks and writes fluently	Applicant's ancestry or nationality of parents or spouse
Arrest	Have you ever been convicted of a crime? If so, when, where, and nature of offense? Are any felony charges currently pending?	Arrest record
Relatives	Names of relatives already employed by the agency	Address of any relatives other than parents, spouse, and minor dependent children
Organizations	Organizations applicant belongs to, excluding those that indicate race, color, religion, or ancestry	Requirement that applicant list all clubs, societies, and lodges he or she belongs to

Source: Reprinted with permission from *Marketing Yourself As a Health Educator: Choosing a Setting, Entering the Profession, and Being Mobile*, by D. J. Breckon, Center for Health Related Studies, Central Michigan University, 1985.

THE FINAL SELECTION

It is not unusual for search committee members to have different opinions about who should be hired. Strengths and weaknesses are a matter of perception, and perceptions vary. Therefore, a thorough committee discussion of the candidates is a prerequisite to hiring. This ensures that whoever is charged with making the final decision will have pooled impressions. Typically, the candidates are rank ordered so that if the job offer is rejected by the first choice, it can simply be extended to the second choice.

Once a candidate has been selected and an offer has been made, a written letter of appointment, a contract, or some other form of written agreement needs to be completed. Normally, a signature confirming acceptance of the position is also required before the hire is announced.

It is appropriate to announce the hire to agency staff and usually to the board. It may be appropriate to do a press release if the position has high public visibility. If the individual will work primarily with select clients (hospitals, senior centers, public schools, etc.), sending a courtesy letter to them makes sense.

Finally, when the new employee arrives to begin work, an orientation plan should be in place. The employee will need an orientation to the agency and the community groups with which he or she will have regular contact. Time spent by an administrator making introductions and helping the employee feel comfortable will usually shorten the learning curve and allow the employee to be effective sooner.

CONCLUSION

Recruiting and hiring suitable employees is the foundation of a successful organization. An upper-level employee may earn a million dollars or more during his or her career, and it is important to treat hiring as if it were a million-dollar investment. In addition, hiring mistakes are costly. The consequences include poor performance and rapid turnover, which will mean a quick repetition of the selection process. It is important to do it right the first time.

IN-BASKET ASSIGNMENT

TO: Health Education and Health Promotion Specialists
FROM: The Associate Director
RE: Recruitment Plan

The health promotion specialist position that you requested has been approved. Please develop a recruitment plan.

MANAGEMENT CASE STUDY

Setting

A community substance abuse agency in an urban area decided to create a position to focus on teenage alcohol and drug use. The agency employed a dozen people, although some of them were part time. Included among the staff were recovering addicts and alcoholics.

Problem

Although the job description did not specify minority applicants preferred, the job involved working with inner-city minority teenagers.

The job description did specify a bachelor's degree and work experience preferred in a related field. No candidate for the position had both a bachelor's degree and relevant work experience.

One applicant was a Caucasian recovered alcoholic, and he asserted that because of his experience as an alcoholic and as a member of Alcoholics Anonymous he met the experience criterion.

An African American self-proclaimed youth worker asserted that he met the experience criterion because of his inner-city youth work.

The only candidate with a bachelor's degree was a young unemployed female graduate of a teacher preparation program. She had no familiarity with the inner city or with substance abuse.

Alternatives Considered

One alternative considered was to reduce the level of the position, the title, and the salary and hire the inner-city youth worker. The hope would be that his experience in the neighborhood would more than offset his lack of training.

Another alternative considered was to hire the college educated woman. The idea behind this option was that her ability to learn and her training as a teacher would enable her to become effective over time.

An alternative not considered was the hiring of the Caucasian male alcoholic.

Actions Taken

The decision was made to not hire any of the candidates, to broaden the search, and, if necessary, to increase the salary in order to attract qualified candidates. Specific attention would be given to attracting qualified minority applicants.

OUTCOME

As a result of phone calls and personal inquiries, the agency identified two qualified minority candidates, one of whom it hired.

The decision to reopen the search proved to be a good one. The agency did not have to deal with the problems that could have occurred if it had lowered the job standards, and the candidate hired turned out to be an effective employee.

DISCUSSION QUESTIONS

1. Could the job description have legally specified minority applicants preferred? What criteria would have to be met to justify a hiring preference? What recruiting approaches might have been used?

2. What would the trade-off of listing "bachelor's degree or equivalent experience" have been?

3. Could leaving the position open while a more qualified candidate was located generate enough savings to increase the salary offer? What are the strengths and weaknesses of this line of reasoning?

4. Are there reasonable grounds for a sex discrimination suit by the college educated female candidate? Would it matter if the final candidate hired was male or female?

5. Are there other alternatives that might have had better consequences?

NOTES

1. G. Filerman, "Foreword" in B. Fried, M. Fottler, and J.A. Johnson, *Human Resources in Healthcare: Managing for Success, 2nd ed.* (Chicago: Health Administration Press, 2005): ix.

2. P. Drucker, *Managing The Nonprofit Organization* (New York: Harper Business, 1990): 145.

3. J.A. Johnson, G. Ledlow, and B.J. Kerr, "Organizational Development, Training, and Knowledge Management" in B. Fried, M. Fottler, and J.A. Johnson, *Human Resources in Healthcare: Managing for Success, 2nd ed.* (Chicago: Health Administration Press, 2005): 205.

CHAPTER 10

Compensation

A MANAGEMENT PERSPECTIVE

By far the largest percentage of a human service agency budget is devoted to personnel costs. Paying salaries and wages that are higher than the agency can afford can bankrupt the agency quickly, yet paying salaries and wages that are too low can result in a poor-quality staff. When it is realized that no agency can be better than its employees, that the quality of employees is related to compensation, and that most of a budget goes to salaries, wages, and fringe benefits, it is readily apparent that administrators must understand compensation principles and issues. All administrators occasionally will be involved in discussions about compensation, and for some administrators compensation will be a central focus of their daily activities. A compensation plan or policy that balances individual needs with organizational interests typically includes the following goals:[1]

- Rewarding employee performance
- Achieving equity within the organization
- Remaining competitive in relevant labor markets
- Aligning employee performance with organizational goals
- Attracting and retaining employees
- Maintaining the budget within organizational fiscal constraints
- Abiding by legal guidelines.

THE IMPORTANCE OF COMPENSATION

Acquiring money is a priority for almost everyone, more so at some stages of life than at others. Feeling reasonably compensated for the work that is done and having enough money to enjoy a reasonable lifestyle is important to almost every individual. High wages or salaries are not usually sought as an end in themselves but as a means to good living and as an indicator of worth to others (which affects one's perception of self-worth).

To a degree, a person's level of satisfaction with compensation is a function, not of the exact amount of salary, but the amount relative to how much others are paid, how much the person used to be paid, and how much the person thinks someone in his or her position ought to be paid.

A compensation package for support staff will normally include hourly wages and a fringe benefits package, and for professional staff it will normally include an annual salary and a fringe benefits package. Wages can vary from the minimum wage to $30 or more per hour. The cost of a fringe benefits package to an employer ranges from 15 to 30 percent of the wages or salary paid. Although this percentage may be surprising, remember that a fringe benefits package will likely include health insurance, a retirement program, and unemployment insurance, and possibly even dental, optical, and long-term disability insurance.

The fringe benefits package may be of critical importance to some employees. Understandably, most employees want health insurance and a retirement plan, although these fringe benefits may not be viewed as essential by employees who are covered by a spouse's health insurance and retirement plan. A small organization might find health insurance rates make providing health insurance unfeasible, and even large organizations are intimidated by the rapidly escalating cost and lack of price controls on insurance.

Because sign-ups for health insurance and retirement programs often involve a contribution and subsequent payroll deduction, some employees opt to not participate. Such opting out causes problems for society, as a growing percentage of the nation's employees are without health care insurance and will receive no retirement income other than Social Security.

From a manager's perspective, insurance provisions are expensive, but of most concern is the fact that rates increase by 10 to 20 percent per year, so the trend has been to look for cheaper health insurance plans, such as the various managed care plans. Of course, switching health insurance plans can have a major impact on the coverage of individual employees, because some new insurers will exclude coverage for pre-existing diseases or disorders. Certainly the exclusion of pre-existing conditions discourages individuals from changing health insurance plans (and from changing jobs if the new employer's health insurance will not cover pre-existing conditions). Recent congressional actions largely prohibit insurance companies from the practice of excluding pre-existing conditions.

Some retirement programs mandate participation by most or all eligible employees, and these present a different problem for employers—the problem of justifying the deductions. Some employers provide a specific amount of dollars per employee and a smorgasbord of options. An employee whose spouse has full family health insurance coverage might choose to use dollars not spent on health insurance to pay for life insurance or to increase retirement contributions. While a desirable goal, giving employees the option to do this has the potential to alter the cost of the organization's overall fringe benefits package.

There are also indirect costs of personnel budgets, such as the organization's contribution to Social Security, unemployment insurance (which provides a reduced income for several weeks of unemployment due to layoff or termination), and workers' compensation insurance (which provides a reduced income for several weeks of unemployment due to an injury suffered on the job). These government-mandated insurance programs are often priced as a percentage of wages and salaries paid.

ACTION-BASED CONCEPT

Fringe benefits such as insurance usually involve an employee and an employer contribution. The employee contribution is usually not subject to income tax, which has the effect of increasing the value of the contribution above its face value.

Hourly wages and annual salaries must be viewed as only a percentage of the total cost of employee compensation. Retirement plans, unemployment and health insurance, workers' compensation, and Social Security represent a large chunk of the personnel budget.

Wages, salaries, and fringe benefits packages vary significantly from state to state, area to area, and organization to organization. Important determinants include state laws and union contracts. No matter what factors affect compensation, if an organization is to maintain a competent work force, the wages, salaries, and fringe benefits package must be competitive. Attention must be given to what other organizations in the same market are paying. Employee turnover rates will indicate whether compensation is reasonable.

In the case of support staff positions, the competition usually consists of other employers in the area. Secretaries, clerks, and data entry personnel, for example, do not usually move from state to state to improve the wage they receive, but they may switch to a local company that pays more for the same work. Professional staff, however, may choose to relocate to another state to improve compensation, working conditions, and opportunity for promotion, and therefore their compensation may have to roughly equal what similar professionals are being paid in other similar locales.

> ### ACTION-BASED CONCEPT
>
> *Managers responsible for wages, salaries, and fringe benefits packages will always want to know what other employers are providing for similar employee groups.*

One issue to be considered is what it would cost to replace an employee. Employees who have been with an organization a long while have salaries substantially lower than would have to be paid to replacements. Therefore, it may be less expensive to give an employee a raise than to hire a replacement. (Of course, the cost of recruitment and training needs to be included in the replacement cost.) Many managers do market studies frequently to ascertain if their compensation rates are competitive, and they then make adjustments to get underpaid employees, and sometimes whole groups of employees, up to the market level. There are consultants who will do market studies for large organizations, but a small organization can simply telephone competitors or monitor recruitment ads to determine market rates.

> ### ACTION-BASED CONCEPT
>
> *The employee turnover rate is a good indicator of the adequacy of the compensation package and therefore should be monitored. If the turnover rate is too high, increases in compensation may be used to reduce it.*

UNIONS

Many health promotion agencies do not have to deal with unions, but those associated with a county or city government often have negotiating agents, as do many health promotion programs in hospitals and companies. Of course, managers of employee wellness or other worksite programs will relate to unions daily and must be effective in doing so, often in a partnership role.

Even if a health promotion agency does not have to negotiate with a union, it is still wise to compensate and otherwise treat all employees fairly. Not having to work through a union sometimes allows more flexibility in dealing with matters such as merit pay, fringe benefits packages, and grievances. Also, changes in working conditions can be implemented more quickly, because they do not have to be negotiated. This is not to suggest that management-initiated changes are typically detrimental to workers. For example, a "flex-time" provision to allow working mothers to arrange their work schedules around their child care or their children's school schedules could be offered. Another option would be to institute a "summer hours" program that would give Friday afternoons off in exchange for an earlier start of the workday.

Employee termination may also be different in union and nonunion settings. By charter, unions have to protect the rights of employees and usually play a role in disciplinary or termination situations. Although they do not always oppose the disciplining or termination of employees, they do represent another layer of review that sometimes slows down the process.

Flexibility in administering compensation packages may also be inhibited. Unions are charged with protecting all members and generally want all members treated alike. Unions generally do not favor merit pay provisions, but if such provisions are negotiated, they would typically include restrictions on the amount of money in the merit pay pool and on the method for selecting merit pay recipients.

In addition, union contracts typically require annual raises to cover inflation and specify how much money is to be placed in a "market raise pool." They often cover if and how a market study is to be completed, and what process will be used to decide who gets market equity adjustments. They also often specify a range for employee wages and salaries and require step increases based on seniority.

ACTION-BASED CONCEPT

Managers in a collective bargaining setting should have a copy of the contract and must abide by the requirements exactly.

None of this is to suggest that unions are undesirable. Union contracts, in fact, can make handling of personnel matters easier because they detail the procedures to be used. In nonunion settings, written agency policies can approximate those specified in a union contract, and creating such policies is a good strategy for achieving fairness in personnel matters.

GENDER, RACE, AND SALARY

The fact that women have been paid less than men in similar jobs and with similar responsibilities has caused considerable controversy for some time. Women often entered organizations at lower levels and when promoted, although given significant raises, were offered lower salaries than men in comparable positions. While increasing women's salaries to achieve equity has short-term ramifications, the long-term impact on morale and the risk of cash settlements imposed by the courts can be equally significant.

Note that there can be a major difference in the salaries of employees with similar responsibilities, but if the salaries are different, the reason for the difference cannot be gender or race. It can be years at that rank, number of employees supervised, client load, and so on, but even then each employee's salary must be within the established range for the position.

ACTION-BASED CONCEPT

A salary equity study should be done if a current one does not exist. Care must be taken not to base salaries on gender, ethnicity, age, or disability. However, experience, longevity, education, and duties can legitimately influence salary levels.

If a position normally requires a master's degree and 2 years of experience, a person with a bachelor's degree and 10 years of experience may be able to do the job, and this person may indeed be the best candidate. Yet hiring someone who does meet the stated qualifications instead of a more qualified candidate (on paper, at least) could, and often does, lead to charges of discrimination. If an organization passed over a female or minority applicant with a master's degree and the required experience and hired a Caucasian male with only a bachelor's degree, the risk of a discrimination suit would be high. This example also highlights the importance of not setting education requirements too high. Overqualified persons can be selected with little or no risk, but hiring those who do not meet the criteria when qualified applicants are in the candidate pool can be problematic.

PRIVACY ISSUES

Federal laws prohibit discussing the salary of an individual employee with anyone, even the employee's spouse, unless the employee has given permission.

However, managers should probably assume that employees know more or less what other employees are making.

> ## *ACTION-BASED CONCEPT*
>
> *Only directory information (name, address, phone number) can generally be legally shared without the employee's permission. While there are a few exceptions, employers need to be extraordinarily careful not to divulge restricted information.*

Employees will often share salary levels with each other if they are good friends, if all are unhappy with their salaries, or if favoritism is suspected. However, the salary levels reported to each other may be inaccurately low or high.

Managers should generally discourage the sharing of salary information but should not assume that salary information will be confidential or that the rumor mill will be accurate. The best strategy is to treat all employees in the same category in an equitable manner and to be certain that differences are defensible (i.e., based on differences in responsibility, seniority, education, or work experience).

PERKS

There are a number of other benefits that can be used to help recruit staff. One example is travel money. Some health promotion agencies have no travel budget for out-of-district travel, which means that if an employee wishes to go to a conference in a distant city, he or she could be out two or three thousand dollars in personal expenses. In contrast, some agencies pay the full costs of one state and one national conference per year. Note that money spent on items like travel is not taxable.

Some agencies also pay the membership dues for one or more state or national organizations of the employee's choosing. It is a way of saying to the employee, "We want you to be involved in state and national meetings."

Providing a budget for the employee to use to purchase books and periodicals can be an important way of encouraging the employee to stay up to date. Sometimes the books and journals are eventually retired to the agency library but are ordered and read first by the employee.

Funds for tuition, fees, and textbooks are sometimes provided to employees who wish to obtain additional degrees. Similarly, the expenses involved in obtaining and maintaining additional job-related certification are sometimes covered.

Benefits like these can help convince an individual to accept a position or to remain in one. A nice office and adequate office equipment and support staff should also be viewed as factors that can lure potential employees and reduce employee turnover.

EXECUTIVE COMPENSATION

Leaders should be well compensated, because leadership is essential and agencies tend to get the leadership they pay for. A market study will show what leaders are paid in similar agencies.

Although strong leaders often come in at low salaries, they will move on if their salaries stay low. If a leader does leave, the agency will have to train another leader, which can involve substantial costs. Manager contracts often have performance incentives. For example, bonuses might be tied to past performance, such as increases in clients served or revenue raised.

Whether a performance incentive contract exists or not, the manager may need to build a large salary increase into the budget and then convince the board to award the large raise.

CONCLUSION

Wage, salary, and fringe benefits package issues are important to employees and managers. Compensation can make or break an agency because it affects the budget, the quality of employees, the employee turnover rate, training costs, and morale. Further, inequitable compensation can lead to discrimination complaints and litigation.

Wages, salaries, and fringe benefits should be competitive with those at like agencies. Wage differentials must be defensible and must be based on factors other than gender or race.

IN-BASKET ASSIGNMENT

TO: Health Education and Health Promotion Specialists
FROM: The Director
RE: Salary Study

We are doing a salary study and would like to know what the going rates are for a health educator and a manager of health education programs. Check some of the listings and give me a report.

MANAGEMENT CASE STUDY

Setting

A community agency that specialized in serving runaway, missing, or abducted children was located in a suburb of a large city. It had a paid internship available for college seniors. The stipend was low, but because the intern could also receive internship or practicum credit, the agency did not have difficulty filling the position.

Problem

The current intern was the "best one yet" and clearly demonstrated management potential. A state grant had just been received that included a position for an adolescent health specialist. The position was funded at a low salary and had a low responsibility level. It was offered to the intern, but he rejected the offer.

Alternatives Considered

The intern had stated during the interview that he wanted to get a master's degree soon, so one alternative considered was to provide tuition reimbursement and add flex-time provisions to allow class attendance. The agreement would be that the intern had to stay at the agency 1 year beyond receipt of the master's degree for each year spent earning the degree.

Another alternative was to pay the intern's tuition in exchange for a contract to begin not later than 30 days after the degree was completed.

A third alternative was to do a routine search.

Actions Taken

A compromise was worked out. For the 2 years of graduate study, the intern would receive three-quarters pay for working three-quarters time, plus tuition reimbursement. The other quarter of the salary would be used to hire an additional paid intern who would do assigned tasks so as to cover the workload. The health specialist position would be upgraded to full time when the degree was earned, and the employee would stay for at least three additional years.

OUTCOME

The intern accepted the proposal and earned the degree as a part-time student while employed in a part-time position. Although conflict and stress occurred occasionally, it was generally a satisfactory arrangement.

DISCUSSION QUESTIONS

1. This agency did not have a policy that all vacant positions must be posted internally and advertised externally. What effects on the morale of other employees might occur if someone was handpicked and promoted? How does an administrator decide whether to risk the occurrence of such adverse consequences?

2. What are the possible ramifications of offering tuition reimbursement to one employee and not others?

3. The intern was a Caucasian male. Could this fact expose the agency to any racial discrimination charges? Would the agency have more or less risk if the person recruited through the arrangement was an African American or a Mexican American?

4. In general, what type of employee recruitment plan would expose an agency to the least risk of litigation?

5. Are there other strategies that might have been more effective or had better consequences?

NOTE

1. B. Fried, M. Fottler, and J.A. Johnson, Human Resources in Healthcare: Managing for Success, 2nd ed. (Chicago: Health Administration Press, 2005).

CHAPTER 11

Performance Incentives and Motivation

INTRODUCTION

Given the fact that no agency is better than its employees, it is essential for managers to help employees perform at their maximum level most of the time. Motivation, merit pay, career advancement, and training, and development are effective strategies for increasing performance. Each is discussed in this chapter.

JOB SATISFACTION AND PERFORMANCE FACTORS

Generally speaking, if employees are satisfied with their jobs, like the people they work for and with, and are satisfied with their working conditions and their compensation package, they will be highly productive. Conversely, if employees do not like the work they do, do not like their supervisor or fellow employees, do not think their working conditions are safe or pleasant, and feel they are under-compensated, they will perform below par.

Of course, there are other factors that can influence performance, such as health, age, family problems, or general attitudes toward work. But even if job conditions are challenging and home conditions are relatively normal, productivity will still not be consistently at peak levels. The term *peak performance* itself suggests there will be peaks and valleys. Moreover, people are not normally capable of working at peak levels all day long, let alone day after day. Individual peak performance periods vary as well. Some people tend to be more productive in the early morning, others late at night, and yet others at mid-morning or mid-afternoon.

ACTION-BASED CONCEPT

It is important to monitor the productivity of each employee in both informal and formal ways. If a noticeable drop in productivity occurs, the reason for the drop should be explored informally and, if necessary, in a formal setting to determine if intervention strategies would be appropriate or helpful.

STRESS AND BURNOUT

Stress can affect productivity in both positive and negative ways. The concept of working against deadlines illustrates how stress can be used positively. Monitoring performance and providing periodic feedback also typically increases both the stress and the productivity of employees. Yet if stress levels get too high, performance can be affected adversely, regardless of whether the source of stress is personal or job related.

Chronic high levels of stress can be debilitating and may cause either chronic depression or burnout. These two similar, often overlapping conditions appear to result from an overload of the central nervous system for a long duration and eventually lead to extended periods of lethargy and moodiness. They are sometimes accompanied by fearfulness, lack of initiative, and shortened attention span (sometimes, in extreme cases, an inability to focus on any task), all of which adversely affect productivity.

Formal diagnosis is difficult and self-diagnosis is common. More often, concerned and caring fellow workers or supervisors are the first to notice the symptoms. Medical treatment is commonplace and may involve rest and renewal activities, stress reduction activities, use of antidepressants (or mood elevators), and psychotherapy. The treatment of depression, regardless of whether it is self-treatment or medical treatment, takes a long time to work. Therefore, performance levels can be impaired for several months.

Managers concerned with peak performance should thoroughly understand depression and burnout and be alert for early symptoms, when the downward cycle is most able to be interrupted. Insisting that employees use vacation time is a useful prevention strategy, as is introducing fun activities. For example, monthly staff meetings could be held at a different restaurant each time, and Friday could be marked as a dress-down day. Reassigning, reducing, or rescheduling more challenging work can be useful for interrupting stress cycles. Monitoring workload, bringing in temporary help when needed, limiting overtime, and providing compensatory time off are also useful in many situations. Bringing stress management workshops on site or scheduling the staff to attend a stress management workshop off site is a common strategy.

Similarly, arranging for time management training on or off site is a good way to enhance productivity. Most employees can become more efficient by wasting less time. There are numerous books on time management, and the techniques are easy to implement. They are also easy to forget or ignore, especially when the employees are busiest. For example, handling each piece of mail only once—either answering it, filing it, or discarding it—increases efficiency. Yet it is common for busy employees to skim through the mail, set aside all but the most urgent letters, stack the rest, and then over the following days or weeks spend lots of time sorting through the stack for needed items.

Finally, when considering job satisfaction and performance factors, it is necessary to remember that effort and energy expended do not necessarily correlate with productivity. People may be working long and apparently hard, but if they are not working efficiently, they still may not be near peak performance. Of course, people's metabolism rates and skill levels will produce individual variations in productivity that must be taken into account. Some people do everything quickly, while others do everything more slowly, and certainly skill deficiencies, such as an inability to type fast, can retard productivity. Productivity is also adversely affected by tardiness in arriving at work or in returning from breaks or lunch, absenteeism, accidents, grievances, strikes, and employee turnover. Monitoring and improving job satisfaction can and often does improve productivity by positively impacting all these factors. But it is also imperative to remember that peak performance, not employee happiness, is the goal.

ACTION-BASED CONCEPT

Managers must formally or informally monitor job satisfaction, employee performance, productivity, absenteeism, tardiness, and employee turnover.

MOTIVATIONAL THEORY

Managers usually believe motivating employees is a primary focus of management, because it is usually perceived as a good way to increase productivity and thus increase the managers' likelihood of keeping their jobs or being promoted. Another way to increase productivity used in some organizations is to replace ineffective managers with new and hopefully better managers. Labor laws generally prohibit termination without cause, and marginal employees can do very little other than show up and still avoid providing grounds for termination. It is commonly believed that some employees use less than 30 percent of their ability on the job. The most highly motivated employees use 80 to 90 percent of their ability. Closing the 50-percent gap between unmotivated and highly motivated employees is one way that managers can increase organizational effectiveness.

Yet there are no easy strategies to implement. The personality and managerial style of the manager will be an important factor, as will the personalities of those being supervised, the working conditions, the levels of compensation, and the organizational policies. Even more important are the needs, desires, objectives, and purposes of the employee or employee group that the manager wants to motivate.

A useful framework for understanding workers' needs is Maslow's Hierarchy of Needs. Maslow postulated that the structure of human needs can best be viewed as a pyramid (see Figure 11–1). The most basic needs are physiological needs, the second most basic are safety needs, the third are social needs, the fourth are self-esteem needs, and the highest needs are self-actualization needs.

Employees need to have a job to get money for food and shelter and to take care of other physiological and safety needs. As noted earlier, often very little effort is needed to maintain employment.

Social needs include the need for recognition as a productive employee by other employees. Various forms of peer evaluation of employees, productivity

Figure 11–1 Maslow's Pyramid of Human Needs

review committees, quality review committees, and merit pay committees are used to motivate employees, but usually the recognition occurs informally. Employees normally know who are the most productive and the least productive among their coworkers, and whether the employees accept or tolerate low productivity can be an important variable. Setting group productivity goals is one way to bring the social acceptance aspect of motivation theory to bear on those who are under-producing. Changing supervisors can be motivating, as employees realize that they need to impress a new supervisor. Setting any kind of production goal (if it is not too unreasonable) can also be motivating, as can knowledge that the employee's output is being monitored. Numerous studies have confirmed that the simple act of monitoring productivity enhances productivity because of people's innate need for recognition and social acceptance. Raising group standards will usually raise the individual standards for productivity.

Maslow's esteem needs include pride in one's work. Many people do enough to get by but not nearly enough to feel good about themselves. Helping employees feel that they have done something significant can motivate them to achieve even bigger goals subsequently. Providing work that is challenging, additional responsibilities, or merit pay also fits in this category.

Self-actualization needs include the innate desire to realize one's potential. Training, job rotation, and other enrichment activities; opportunities to train new employees; opportunities to serve on committees, especially in leadership roles; opportunities for community involvement; and opportunities for lateral transfers or promotions are all usually motivational. Selecting employees with the potential for advancement and "fast tracking" them is motivating. A variety of mentoring activities usually enhance the desire to do more and do it better. Encouraging people to go as high as they can in the organization and then offering to provide reference letters and other letters of support as they search for other employment with more opportunity for career development is sometimes motivating.

Employees can be motivated, yet much of the motivation to do more and do it better must come from within. Placing employees in positions where they do what they want to do and can do well is the best form of motivation. When employees believe that they are working for an employer who is fair and provides good working conditions and compensation, that the goals of the organization are admirable, and that they are working near the peak of their ability and are contributing to the organization's effectiveness, then self-motivation largely eliminates the need for managerial motivation. Stated differently, managers who wish to motivate employees need to focus on the organizational and work environment factors that facilitate self-motivation.

> ## ACTION-BASED CONCEPT
>
> *Employees need opportunities for psychological and professional growth, and good managers are sensitive to this need and accommodate it whenever possible.*

MERIT PAY

If merit pay is thought to be attainable, it can be a performance incentive. For example, if a bonus is tied to performance standards that most employees can meet, it can motivate improved performance. However, if only a few employees get merit pay and the rest come to think of it as unattainable, it is obviously not an incentive for most of the employees. In fact, in such circumstances it can become a disincentive because the system will be perceived as unfairly favoring a few at the expense of the majority.

It is also possible to establish a system of corporate bonuses that depends on company production or sales goals being met. With such a system in place, it is in everyone's best interest to work hard and to increase his or her own productivity and that of others. The bonuses do not have to be alike but can be tied to salary (e.g., the bonus for each individual might be a week's pay or 1 percent of salary).

Merit pay and other performance incentives can be useful motivators if handled well. Of course, they can be counterproductive if they are not.

> ## ACTION-BASED CONCEPT
>
> *Employees must be held accountable for productivity and need periodic feedback on their performance.*

CAREER ADVANCEMENT

An organization that promotes from within can use this as a motivator. The knowledge that the organization likes to have those in upper-level positions work their way up through the ranks typically causes good on-the-job behavior. It also is likely to increase longevity, because employees know that they have a chance of moving up when someone above them leaves. Of course, longevity factors built into the pay scale lead people to decide to stay even if they are not promoted. Use of promotion requires some cross-training to cover positions during periods of absence, ascertain employees' interest and effectiveness in other positions, and facilitate promotion decisions.

EDUCATION, TRAINING, AND DEVELOPMENT

For each individual, career advancement depends on additional education, training, and development. Some of the education or training activities can be job related but still contribute to the development of the employee. Computer seminars, as well as the time management and stress management seminars mentioned earlier, are good examples.

Many business organizations encourage their employees to complete college degrees to enhance their likelihood for promotion. Even if an employee leaves after completing the degree, he or she has stayed while working on it. Tuition reimbursement is a viable employee retention tool. Organizations can provide some form of flextime schedule to accommodate coursework and often will pay some of the tuition and fees.

A growing number of large organizations such as hospitals invite colleges and universities to offer entire degree programs on site. Degree programs in computer information systems, management, accounting, and human resource development are commonly offered.

Employees who are working toward an advanced degree are not guaranteed a promotion, and so obviously they have an incentive also to do well on the job. Thus, facilitating degree completion work is one way to get employees to increase efficiency and productivity.

MOTIVATIONAL PRACTICE

Regardless of the motivational theory favored, managers and administrators need to understand and maximize intrinsic and extrinsic motivators. Intrinsic motivators generally come from within the individual or are inherent in the task. For example, if an individual creates a program or significantly improves an existing program, that person will likely experience a sense of achievement and feelings of accomplishment. Simple reinforcing comments from a supervisor, such as, "That was a major project and you've done it well; you should feel really good about it," can strengthen intrinsic motivators. Similarly, the good feelings an employee might have as a result of handling routine problems well or consistently performing well can be maximized by formal or informal management praise. These kinds of motivators are rarely tied to salary but can be very effective performance incentives—and they cost virtually nothing.

Extrinsic motivators may not be related to a specific accomplishment and sometimes are beyond the control of the manager. Yet such items as a bonus, an increased travel allowance, a fringe benefit improvement, a promotion, and formal recognition at an awards ceremony can be performance enhancers. And they need not be expensive. Selecting an "Employee of the Month" and awarding a designated parking space for the month may motivate a lot of employees to do their jobs well.

Managers who wish to motivate employees to perform better should consider using both intrinsic and extrinsic motivators. A combination of the two types is usually better than either type used alone.

CONCLUSION

Some employees will only do enough to just get by, whereas other employees will far exceed the organizational standards. There is a large gap between what most employees actually do and what they can do. Raising the group norm is most readily accomplished by motivating the low achievers.

Low levels of achievement may be temporary, such as in cases of illness, stress, or depression. The combination of time and caring encouragement can have a positive impact on depression and burnout and should often be tried before medical treatment or emotional therapy.

The work environment, the organizational policies, and the personality of the supervisors affect employee productivity. Meeting the daunting challenge of significantly increasing the quantity and quality of work performed is in the best interests of the managers as well as the program or organization being managed.

IN-BASKET ASSIGNMENTS

TO: Agency Health Education and Health Promotion Specialists
FROM: The Director
RE: Stress Management

I think we need a stress management workshop for our employees. Please develop a bibliography on the subject, give me some recommendations for background readings, and develop an outline of topics to be covered.

* * * *

TO: Agency Health Education and Health Promotion Specialists
FROM: The Director
RE: Merit Pay

We are thinking about adding a merit pay provision to our compensation plan. Please give me your recommendations about what it should look like and how it should be administered.

MANAGEMENT CASE STUDY

Setting

A state voluntary health agency employed about 100 people, including a director of public and professional education. The director's job was to work with numerous local units in facilitating community health education and professional staff development. The director, a highly motivated and very productive young man, was responsible for arranging community health fairs in local malls, educational components at fund-raising events, and two annual statewide seminars for professional development, one for doctors and one for nurses. He traveled frequently to the local units and was increasingly in demand as a consultant in other states and as a presenter at state and national meetings.

Problem

The director's stress level was high because of his extensive responsibilities and his frequent acceptance of speaking engagements. He was out of the office and on the road three or four days a week, and when his paperwork mounted, he worked on the weekend to catch up.

The director became a workaholic. He also became cranky, impatient, and somewhat depressed. His feelings of depression increased to the point where they negatively impacted his productivity.

Alternatives Considered

Because the director had been so productive prior to the period of burnout, termination was not among the alternatives considered.

Referral to a counselor for "burnout counseling" was considered, although no one knew an agency or counselor to handle the referral.

The second alternative was for the administrator of the agency to attempt to handle the problem.

Actions Taken

The administrator called the director in for a one-hour appointment. Included in the meeting was a coworker (and personal friend) of the director. The manager expressed concern about stress and decreased effectiveness and voiced a desire to put together a plan that would help. When the expected denial and protestation occurred, the coworker on cue validated the observations of the administrator. The administrator then stated that the decision had already been made and that a plan would be developed and implemented as a condition of continued employment.

According to the plan that was devised, the director would go on leave immediately, using 8 of 18 available sick leave days, and at least 2 and preferably 7 vacation days. A 2- to 3-week rest was mandated, and all appointments and travel assignments would be canceled.

All out-of-state travel would now have to be approved by the administrator, and the director was not to be on the road for more than 2 days a week for the next six months. Fax and phone conversations would have to suffice in some cases.

Attendance at a stress management seminar at some time during the 6 months of restricted travel was mandated. The director was also to do some reading on delegating responsibility. At the end of the 6-month period, another conference would be held to re-evaluate the situation and determine if an additional six-month plan was necessary.

A memo was written detailing the conference and the agreement. It was signed by all three persons who were present.

OUTCOME

The forced sick leave and vacation time helped the employee see what he was allowing the job to do to his health and his family and understand the impact his condition was having on the job. He did the reading and attended the required workshop, and eventually he recovered from his depression to become a productive employee once again.

DISCUSSION QUESTIONS

1. Why was it appropriate for the administrator to have a third person present in the conference? What were the advantages of selecting a coworker friend as opposed to someone else in the administrative chain of command?

2 If the director had not voluntarily agreed to abide by the plan, under what conditions could termination have occurred? What kind of paper trail would be required? What options might exist if a sufficient paper trail did not exist?

3. What other strategies might the administrator have used?

4. What preventive strategies could be put in place to minimize the likelihood that long-term stress and eventual burnout would be experienced by other employees or this employee again?

5. Are there other strategies that could have been used to address this problem?

CHAPTER 12

Performance Appraisals

PERFORMANCE APPRAISAL ISSUES

The previous chapter stressed the importance of performance incentives. Encouraging employees to perform as well as they can is a necessary but not sufficient part of management. Human nature being what it is, not all employees will voluntarily perform at their peak, even if given incentives to do so. Labor studies such as the Hawthorne experiment demonstrated many years ago that productivity increases when people know they are being watched. In particular, most employees will perform closer to their peak for more of the time if they know they are being monitored, although the monitoring need not involve visual supervision. It can be accomplished using activity reports, productivity reports, and other documentation.

Of course, supervision itself may not be enough to stimulate productivity. Perhaps the manager is not demanding and the standards are low and easily met. Perhaps the manager avoids dealing with low activity levels or inefficient or ineffective performance. Employees in such situations could conclude that their performance is good enough and not try to do better. Therein rests the need for formal performance appraisals.

Management of employees, of necessity, involves a type of performance appraisal. However, this type of informal appraisal is less likely to be communicated back to the employee or up to the next level, and it will not be permanently recorded in the employee's personnel file. It thus has a minimal chance of impacting the employee's performance and productivity.

Besides having a greater effect than informal performance appraisals, formal appraisals are more comprehensive and more objective. First, they typically involve the use of checklists and rating scales that cover the basics and provide opportunities for elaboration. Second, they allow comparisons among employees.

Third, the raters are usually required to obtain a sign-off from an employee's supervisor for each performance appraisal, which increases the likelihood that the raters will be fair in assessing the employee's strengths and weaknesses and that the employee's rank vis-à-vis other employees will be an accurate reflection of the employee's relative level of performance.

It has been established that the "halo effect" and the "horns effect" need to be watched for. These two effects reflect a reviewer's tendency to rate people well or poorly based on past performance rather than present performance. Other forms of bias include subconsciously rating employees higher or lower based on their gender, sexual orientation, race, or ethnic background or on whether they have a disability.

It is important that performance appraisals be done properly. The resultant paper trail can be useful for many purposes, but its fairness and consistency must be demonstrable. Many appraisal forms are available (see Exhibit 12–1). Any organization is likely to be able to find at least one that it can adapt to meet its own appraisal needs.

ACTION-BASED CONCEPT

Managers should use a formal performance appraisal system for the employees they supervise. If a system is already being used in the organization, it should be utilized to promote consistency and facilitate comparisons. If a system is not in place, one should be adapted or developed.

PURPOSE AND USE OF PERFORMANCE APPRAISALS

The main purpose of performance appraisals is to enhance performance. Another related purpose is to create a permanent record of performance that is fair and consistent across employee groups.

Performance appraisals can be of enormous help in assessing the need for training programs. If a review of formal performance appraisals reveals a common problem, such as poor employee telephone skills, targeted training may be the obvious solution.

Performance appraisals normally focus on strengths and areas where improvement is needed. Every employee can improve some necessary skill or other, and a performance appraisal can help the employee develop a growth plan. The employee's supervisor, manager, or continuing education staff might be able to suggest a mentor, a book, or a workshop that the employee would not otherwise utilize.

Exhibit 12–1 Performance Evaluation Report

[Confidential]

Name _____ Title _____ Date _____

Length of time in position _____ Department/site _____

Place an X in the box which most clearly indicates the extent to which performance has met, exceeded, or fallen below the standard.

JOB KNOWLEDGE/SKILLS   Consider the functions of the job requiring the demonstration of specific knowledge and/or technical skills.

Below Standard	Meets Standard	Above Standard

ORGANIZATION & TIME MANAGEMENT – Consider the functions of the job requiring the identification of priorities, schedules, deadlines, and the physical organization of work area.

Below Standard	Meets Standard	Above Standard

INITIATIVE – Consider the functions of the job that should be performed on a regular basis by identified priority and/or according to schedule.

Below Standard	Meets Standard	Above Standard

PERCEPTION & JUDGMENT – Consider the functions of the job requiring the evaluation of situations and identification of factors necessary to reach logical, timely, and effective decisions.

Below Standard	Meets Standard	Above Standard

COMMUNICATION – Consider the functions of the job requiring the organization and expression of thoughts in a clear, logical, and concise manner, either orally or in writing.

Below Standard	Meets Standard	Above Standard

ADAPTABILITY & FLEXIBILITY – Consider the functions of the job that require the person to objectively evaluate circumstances and confrontations between self and others and adjust thoughts, attitudes, and behavior accordingly.

Below Standard	Meets Standard	Above Standard

DEPENDABILITY – Consider the adherence to attendance standards and work schedules affecting overall productivity.

Below Standard	Meets Standard	Above Standard

TO BE COMPLETED FOR SUPERVISORY POSITIONS ONLY:

LEADERSHIP – Consider the roles and responsibilities of the job (performance, evaluation, counseling, communication, discipline, equal opportunity, etc.) requiring effective application of supervisory skill to create a positive organizational climate.

Below Standard	Meets Standard	Above Standard

OVERALL EVALUATION: This employee's overall job performance is:

☐ Unsatisfactory   ☐ Marginal   ☐ Good   ☐ Very Good   ☐ Excellent

If the employee is rated as marginal or unsatisfactory, the employee will be re-evaluated on _____ .

(Date)

(continues)

Exhibit 12–1 (continued)

What are your general remarks concerning the employee's performance of present duties?

What suggestions would you make to assist the employee in improving his or her performance?

What is the employee presently doing to improve skills, such as additional schooling, etc.?

Has the employee demonstrated any outstanding accomplishments in his or her job?

EMPLOYEE COMMENTS.   This section is for the employee to record his or her impressions of his or her performance and to state his or her views of the completed evaluation form.

Signature of Rater _____ Date _____

Signature of Reviewer _____ Date _____

Signature of Employee _____ Date _____

Courtesy of Park College, Parkville, Mo.

Identifying growth areas and devising a growth plan can be a useful part of the improvement process.

Discussion of an employee's performance can actually enhance the relationship between the employee and the supervisor doing the evaluation. It can help the supervisor better understand both the employee as a person and the position being supervised. It can also modify the supervisor's expectations or at least clarify for the employee what the supervisor's expectations are, thereby helping the employee to reorder priorities appropriately.

Perhaps the widest use of performance evaluations is to determine what personnel actions are proper, such as pay increases, promotions, transfers, commendations, warnings, and terminations. Fairness and consistency are required to maintain morale and to avoid union grievances, complaints to equal opportunity agencies, and litigation.

LEGAL ISSUES

To be legal, performance appraisals must not be discriminatory. They must be equitable and not be influenced by the gender, age, race, sexual orientation, or religion of the employee. To decrease the risk of sex or other kinds of discrimination, most organizations use some form of rating scale and a review by a third party, primarily looking for bias.

Another way to avoid discrimination is to be certain that all elements being rated and all comments made are job related. The focus must be on the job, not on personal or family issues. For example, if an employee did not attend evening meetings because of child care issues, it is better to note the lack of attendance and document the effect it is having on the employee's work and leave unrecorded the reason attendance did not occur.

ACTION-BASED CONCEPT

All performance appraisals should be limited to factors that directly affect performance. Job-related personal issues should be carefully addressed, and non–job-related personal issues should not be discussed unless brought up by the employee.

The most complex task is to eliminate politics, personalities, and personal bias from evaluations. Extraordinary care must be exercised when evaluating employees who the supervisor really likes and works effectively with and when evaluating employees who the supervisor dislikes or finds too frequently uncooperative or critical. Many forms include sections for "strengths" and "areas that can be improved." All employees have strengths, and it is often useful to think about these when evaluating a difficult employee. Similarly, all employees have areas that can be improved, and identifying these can increase productivity. For example, a good employee may be behind on filing, reticent to learn a new technology, not visible in the community, too verbose in meetings, or spend too much time socializing and thus wasting the time of others. Although such an employee may be more productive than others and more productive than is required, focusing on areas for improvement can enhance the employee's effectiveness.

It is helpful to have performance standards when evaluating employees (e.g., three group presentations per month, four media contacts per month, or attendance at four community events per month). However, an employee might meet all of the standards set and still not be working near peak performance. Thus, including a section in the evaluation form on "suggestions for improvement" or "agreements reached" or "concerns that need to be addressed" can be useful. The choice of what phrase to use as a heading will depend on whether the employee is a valued employee or concerns are significant enough that they may lead to disciplinary action. The point is that all employees can strengthen or improve their performance and most employees will if the performance appraisal includes a section on areas needing improvement.

PERFORMANCE APPRAISAL ELEMENTS

Performance appraisals typically include an assessment of productivity. In some areas of a health promotion program or agency, quantifiable productivity standards are appropriate, but more commonly the assessment of work output or productivity will be subjective. Frequently, the factors that impact productivity are identified, such as attendance, punctuality, time management, attitude, and knowledge of the job. Of course, some identified factors might be very specific, very much job-related. Usually, the identified factors are general work-related behaviors and attitudes, and a section is provided for comments about job-specific factors.

ACTION-BASED CONCEPT

Because so much of performance appraisal is subjective, it is usually appropriate for supervisors to review each performance appraisal with a superior before discussing it with the employee being evaluated to minimize the effect of rater bias.

COMMUNICATION AND FEEDBACK

If a performance appraisal is to be perceived as successful by both the supervisor and the employee, considerable communication needs to occur. Especially if it is a routine annual evaluation, the communication element needs to be carefully planned. There are a variety of methods to maximize the motivational aspects of performance appraisals, and all involve various elements of communication and feedback.

Enough lead time needs to be provided so that planning can occur, a suitable private location can be arranged, and so on. The discussion of the evaluation by the supervisor and employee should not be spontaneous or in a noisy public place.

One approach is to ask the employee to do a self-evaluation and then devote the feedback session to a discussion of the ratings done by the supervisor and the employee. The weakness of this approach is that the employee will not have spent time evaluating other employees and will probably not be able or willing to do any comparative ratings that are important for equity and for objectivity of the entire system.

Another approach is for the supervisor to complete the performance appraisal form and send a copy of it to the employee a few days before the meeting. This tactic eliminates the element of surprise for the employee and lessens the tension between the employee and the supervisor. It also allows the employee to think about his or her performance and to provide additional information if appropriate. (The supervisor may choose to add some of this additional information to the form, or the employee may add some of it in the "Employee Comments" section.)

Perhaps the most critical preliminary task is to think about the tone that should be set. If the evaluation is of a difficult employee who needs to improve significantly, maybe another supervisor should sit in. Having a third party present can prevent emotions from getting out of hand, and the person can act as a witness in case the feedback session leads to termination of the employee and litigation.

ACTION-BASED CONCEPT

Communication and feedback during a performance evaluation session should enhance rapport and respect and be motivational.

One tactic that can be used in feedback sessions is to focus on how much improvement has occurred or on transitioning from one project to another. The main message might be, "You are one of our best and are capable of moving up." Or it might simply be, "Keep up the good work" or "The only concern that we have is . . ." (Note the use of "we." If appropriate, its use can decrease the likelihood of an emotional response.) Feedback sessions should usually start and end on a positive note. Focusing on strengths at the beginning makes subsequent suggestions for improvement more acceptable, and ending with "Thanks for all you do" and appropriate expressions of confidence can help put any criticism into perspective.

The performance appraisal document is important because it stays in the file for use in follow-up and is available for litigation if it occurs. But verbal communication can soften written criticisms and make them easier to accept and respond to constructively.

It is common for raters to rate employees too high when the scales have categories entitled "below average," "average," and "above average." Obviously, not all employees can be above average. Some agencies choose to use titles like "needs improvement," "meets expectations," and "exceeds expectations," whereas others simply use words like "excellent," "good," "fair," and "poor."

No matter what the categories, it is important to begin rating employees low enough that some improvement is possible. The normal tendency is to overrate employees that are liked—and it is possible to like all the employees. Generally, it is easier to start with lower ratings and document improvement in one or more areas over time than to start high and then to lower some ratings.

In an ideal performance evaluation session, strengths and weaknesses as well as major achievements and failures are identified, a plan for improvement is developed, and consensus is reached. Obviously, a commitment on the part of the supervisor and the employee to work as a team, engage in honest inquiry, and communicate openly can help make an evaluation session a reasonably pleasant and effective encounter.

CONCLUSION

In most organizations, informal performance appraisals occur every day. It is human nature to form opinions and a normal part of supervision to form opinions about those who are being supervised. Nonetheless, a formal, structured system is usually needed to provide objective data for future personnel decisions and identify areas where additional growth should occur and the best methods to achieve it. A formal performance appraisal should give the employee a clear understanding of where he or she stands in relation to the supervisor's expectations. Whether rating scales are used or whether the scales are subjective or objective, the supervisor and employee should discuss the job factors being rated and the areas needing improvement. The feedback sessions should generally be handled in such a way that the supervisor and the employee learn more about the job's problems and possibilities and about performance expectations and develop a better working relationship. There should be a written document with room for employee comments and a place for the signatures of the supervisor and the employee. The most successful performance appraisal systems are designed with recognition in mind and are sensitive to these understandings:[1]

- Performance improves most when specific goals are established
- Coaching is needed on a regular basis, not merely once a year
- Mutual goal setting by the employee and the manager improves performance
- Criticism and praise have less effect than participation by the employee.

Finally, the advice in this chapter applies to employees who are at least moderately effective. The next chapter discusses situations where termination may be a reasonable possibility.

IN-BASKET ASSIGNMENTS

TO: Health Education and Health Promotion Specialists
FROM: The Director
RE: Performance Appraisal

It is time to evaluate your performance again. I will be completing the performance appraisal form (Exhibit 12-1), and we will meet to discuss it soon.

Before we meet, I would like you to do a self-appraisal, and in our meeting we will discuss your assessment and mine. Think specifically about what you can do to improve your performance in any areas of concern, and develop a three- or four-step action plan for improvement in these areas.

       * * *

TO: Health Education and Health Promotion Specialists
FROM: The Director
RE: Coaching, Feedback

We are nearing performance appraisal time. I think our biggest deficiency in the process is communicating—that is, it is too often a "telling employees what they need to do," and I think such an approach is resented.

Please do some reading about "coaching" and "providing feedback," and give me a summary sheet of "Helpful Dos and Don'ts" derived from your reading or your personal experience.

Thanks!

MANAGEMENT CASE STUDY

Setting

A family planning agency was located in a large city near a university. Its staff consisted of a director, a secretary-receptionist, a billing clerk–bookkeeper, a community outreach worker, and three nurse-counselors.

The agency was the only one of its kind in that city. While it relied heavily on fees for services rendered, it also received significant community support, primarily through the United Way.

Client counts had largely remained steady after the second year of existence. The clients were mostly students, faculty, and staff from the university. The outreach worker had graduated from the university and was comfortable working in that setting.

Problem

The United Way funding committee regularly asked for a report on how many of the clients served were permanent members of the community as opposed to students located there only while attending college. Although a reduction in funds had not yet been threatened, the director of the agency feared the committee might reduce or eliminate the agency's United Way funds unless the agency was able to increase the percentage of "locals" in the total client population.

Alternatives Considered

One alternative considered was to approach the university's health center about helping to fund the agency because the majority of clients served were from the university.

Another alternative considered was to give the outreach worker responsibility for diversifying the clientele served and to establish appropriate performance goals.

Yet another alternative was to hire another outreach worker, a local with ties to the inner city.

Actions Taken

The second alternative listed above was selected. The director met with the outreach worker to develop an outreach plan that included performance goals. The plan contained the following guidelines. Not more than one day a week would be spent at the university. During the academic year one day would be spent contacting public and parochial school personnel, and during the summer the focus would shift to inner-city summer youth employment programs. One day a week would be spent contacting ministers and church youth workers, one day would be spent contacting youth centers, and the fifth day in the week would be spent contacting neighborhood health centers, working at health fairs, and performing other outreach tasks.

It was agreed that if nonstudents made up 80 percent or more of the clientele and low-income clients made up 50 percent or more, a $2,500 bonus would be given to the outreach worker at the end of the fiscal year. It was further agreed that monthly reports would be developed and discussed.

OUTCOME

The outreach worker did not feel comfortable working with inner-city programs and agencies, and continued to focus on the university. She sent letters to the other constituencies but got little response. When discussing the first month's report, the director stated that letters were not enough and urged her to get into the community. The outreach worker began a telephone campaign and called the various constituencies, but again she had limited success. At the end of the third month, the director insisted that the outreach worker make personal visits. The outreach worker immediately began searching for other work and accepted a position at a university health center in another state.

The director started a search for a new outreach worker and eventually hired a nurse educator with inner-city work experience. The same outreach plan remained in force, and the desired client composition was achieved in 18 months.

DISCUSSION QUESTIONS

1. Does it make sense to shift the focus of an employee's working assignments from a university base to an inner-city base?

2. How important was it for the director to put the performance goals in writing?

3. How important was it for the director to write a written memo to record the outcomes of each month's conference?

4. What strategies might the director have used if the outreach worker did not resign and the reports did not improve?

5. Was the $2,500 bonus an appropriate incentive?

6. Are there other strategies that could have been used to accomplish the same goals?

NOTE

1. L.F. Novick and G.P. Mays, *Public Health Administration* (Boston: Jones and Bartlett, 2005): 409.

CHAPTER 13

The Paper Trail or Electronic Record

THE ROLE OF PERSONNEL FILES

Every employee must have a personnel file. The file is needed for payroll purposes and as a repository for internal documents and for tax forms and other information required by government agencies.

Personnel files can be kept in any of a variety of locations or in more than one location. In small organizations, the files may be stored in the Chief Executive Officer's suite or in the office of the person who handles the budget and payroll. In large organizations, they may be stored in the human resources department and also in the payroll and administrative offices, with copies of documents routinely distributed to all three locations. It is also common to keep tax documents and payroll data in one location and letters of appointment and evaluation reports in another. Sometimes a manager will maintain employee files for thoughts, concerns, and items needing follow-up that may be inappropriate for the formal personnel file.

Personnel files provide the basis for most personnel decisions. They need to be established as soon as employees are hired and to be retained at least for 7 years after separation (in case litigation occurs).

PRIVACY ISSUES

It is mandated by federal law that personnel files must be kept confidential. Employee access to them should be limited to those with a "need to know." Paper files are routinely kept in locked file cabinets in inner offices. Limiting employee access is also required for computerized files. Prevention of illegitimate access is usually accomplished by establishing passwords that are made known only to authorized persons.

Obviously, professional ethics as well as federal laws prohibit a manager from discussing confidential information such as salary, disciplinary actions, or other data with employees who do not have a need to know. Marital status, drug use history, and a whole range of items that may be in the file should never become coffee room topics of conversation.

ACTION-BASED CONCEPT

Supervisors must always avoid inappropriately revealing information about other employees covered by the privacy laws. It is especially important not to discuss other employees in informal conversations with friends.

One sensitive issue concerns access to the files by individuals outside the agency. Of course, courts have access during litigation, upon presentation of a court order. Other than that, data in the file, other than the dates of employment, should normally not be released.

Spouses, children, and parents may sometimes want to discuss an employee's problems, usually with the intent of intervening on the employee's behalf. However, sometimes their intentions are not good, and thus federal privacy laws prevent discussing personnel matters with anyone other than the employee without written authorization unless the employee is present.

Legally, employers can release mailing addresses and phone numbers (directory information), but many have developed internal policies to preclude this, especially if the information is being requested for solicitation purposes.

ACTION-BASED CONCEPT

Other than directory data, information about an employee should not be released to other agencies without the written permission of the employee.

An employee can review his or her own personnel file and read all evaluations, memos, and other contents. This is one reason why managers often maintain their own files on problematic employees. Also, if a personnel file is subpoenaed during litigation, anything in the file must be submitted.

It is common practice for organizations to develop policies governing employee access. Such policies might require a written request, not permit the file to leave the room, not permit photocopying, and require that a senior administrator be present during the review of the file to ensure materials are not destroyed or altered.

ACTION-BASED CONCEPT

Personnel files and all information in them should always be treated with complete confidentiality. Access to a given employee's file should be limited to supervisors with a need to know and the employee.

There are a few other situations where some file data can be legally demanded. The salaries of senior administrators can be requested, for example. The press can also file "right to know" papers, but a court must rule on the validity of such requests. An important management strategy is to be slow to respond to any request for personnel data and, when in doubt, to obtain legal counsel before doing so. Disclosing information about substance abuse or HIV status is a particularly sensitive issue.

ACCURACY AND APPROPRIATENESS OF FILES

Obviously, files must be accurate and up to date. Titles, dates of appointment, salary information, and other such items must be precise and consistent. Any material placed in the files must be considered admissible in court. Therefore, evaluations, confidential memos, and copies of correspondence must be defensible and must be job related. More to the point, there can be no evidence of bias in any of the documents, nor any discriminatory phrases or words.

One important issue is whether to verify information submitted by applicants for a job. An application form or a letter of application and a résumé are normally included, as submitted. If cardiopulmonary resuscitation (CPR) training is required, for example, it is appropriate to include a copy of the CPR certificate. It may be appropriate to include copies of college diplomas or transcripts.

Understandably, people write letters and résumés so as to present themselves in the best possible light. Sometimes degrees that are expected within a few weeks are not ever earned. Sometimes outright fraud occurs, and fake credentials are submitted or unearned credentials are listed on résumés. Diplomas, licenses, and certificates that are necessary for the position should usually be photocopied for the file. If photocopying is done routinely, as a matter of policy, it is less problematic. Verifying credentials is critical in the case of high profile positions—and especially so for agencies that receive significant media coverage. Unfavorable publicity and embarrassment can occur if the media is probing for a story and discovers the existence of fraud. This is not an infrequent occurrence. Placing copies of diplomas, transcripts, work visas, certificates, and licenses in personnel files should be both the policy and the practice of any agency.

USE OF MULTIPLE FILES

As noted, a formal personnel file is required, and indeed that may be the only file that exists. However, it is not unusual to have more than one file on an employee. An employee's formal personnel file can be subpoenaed or, as an intermediate step in a grievance, reviewed by the employee. A written policy normally governs employee access to personnel files. The policy might require a written request, 24-hour advance notification, and examination of the file only in the room the files are stored in and only in the presence of a senior administrator. The policy might also prohibit photocopying of documents.

Obviously, with the employee and the courts both having access to the file, administrators need to be careful what they place in it. Besides the formal record of employment actions, performance appraisals are typically included. These are not usually problematic, because the employee and the supervisor normally both sign and have copies of them.

If there are formal incident reports, written reprimands, or other documents from supervisors, they should be included. Writing and filing incident reports is especially important in the case of problematic employees. Supervisors who do not take the time to file written incident reports will increase their exposure to unfavorable legal rulings. From the court's perspective, a written incident report that is dated, signed, and filed shortly after an incident will have greater impact. Its impact will be increased if the employee receives a copy, because this shows the supervisor was concerned about avoiding a repeat of the incident.

If a supervisor fails to complete incident reports for a given employee, when discharge is considered, there is no paper trail. The file is "clean" simply because the supervisor did not "write up" the employee. Many employee terminations have had to be postponed a year or two so that a paper trail could be built up and the risk of an unfavorable legal judgment in case of litigation could be minimized.

Documenting verbal reprimands is appropriate and can be useful. A one-paragraph memo stating the reason for the verbal reprimand and any consequences that were conveyed will usually suffice. The memo could be as simple as this:

> Today, I verbally reprimanded _____ for rudeness to a client and indicated that if the behavior were repeated it could be grounds for dismissal.

It is preferable if a third party is present during the verbal reprimand and if this person also signs the written report.

Supervisors may also maintain "desk files" on employees. What goes into these files is completely discretionary, whereas what goes into a personnel file is regulated both by law and agency policy. It is typical to have a desk file for a problematic employee and to place in it notes, memos, copies of problematic work, letters from clients (good and bad), notes detailing observations, and so on. Whenever there is a confrontational episode, at least a "Memo for the Desk File" is appropriate, again completed within 24 hours, dated, and signed by more than one person. Although the majority of memos for the file do not end up in court, they can be used as evidence of what was actually said or done (which might not be what the disgruntled employee claims to remember was said or done). Moreover, they can help remind the manager of what happened if called to testify about the event many months later.

Of course, disgruntled employees sometimes keep their own desk files and write their own memos. They also occasionally smuggle in tape recorders in pockets, briefcases, or purses. Thus it is always important to be fair and to keep written records that can be used in case of a lawsuit.

Desk files can be subpoenaed and with increasing frequency *are* being subpoenaed. Their advantage over formal personnel files is that whoever is keeping them has discretion over what goes in or out and when. If there are items that would weaken a case, they can be removed before the case reaches litigation. In addition, the employee does not have access to a supervisor's personal desk file.

It is a good policy to periodically review desk files on problematic employees because they can be subpoenaed. On occasion it may be appropriate to transfer some items to the formal personnel file or to discard some items judged no longer useful.

CONCLUSION

One of the most unpleasant aspects of management is dealing with problematic employees. Maintaining a paper trail is imperative in case of litigation. Lawsuits may stretch over several years, and details may not be remembered clearly. Cross-examination during depositions can cause confusion, as well as conflicting testimony which could be detrimental to the agency's case. A paper trail will help the supervisor reconstruct the details and sequences of events and will give an attorney documentation to use in building the agency's case or refuting the disgruntled employee's case. Other aspects of terminating employees are discussed in the next chapter. However, written documentation is critical. Dismissals can occur successfully without it, but a good paper trail significantly increases the probability that the reasons for dismissal will stand up in court.

IN-BASKET ASSIGNMENT

TO: Health Education and Health Promotion Specialists
FROM: The Director
RE: Privacy Laws

I have to return a phone call to an employee's wife who wants to know about his work record. She believes he has an alcohol problem. What should I tell her?

MANAGEMENT CASE STUDY

Setting

A community neighborhood health center employed approximately 100 people. The African American director made all hiring and firing decisions, albeit in consultation with the human resources director and the appropriate division heads.

Problem

A Caucasian custodian was often late for work. She cited car problems, traffic tie-ups, and the weather. Her absenteeism record was also poor. She cited her children's illnesses, lack of child care, and her own illnesses. In addition, the quality of her work was not consistent. Some days her work met all performance standards; other days it was poorly done. She seemed increasingly to exhibit lethargy and fatigue and needed frequent rests. The director suspected a drug or alcohol problem.

Alternatives Considered

One alternative considered was to place the employee on probation because of her poor work record, including lateness, absenteeism, and low quality of work.

Another alternative was to confront her with the suspicion she might have a drug or alcohol problem.

Another was to terminate her for cause and to do so immediately.

Yet another was to attempt to assist her in improving her performance.

Actions Taken

In reviewing her file, the director noted that there was relatively little in it that indicated her work did not meet agency standards and that she should be discharged.

The director wrote her a letter placing her on probation for 6 months. The letter stated that unless her rate of tardiness and absenteeism decreased and her performance on the job generally improved, she would be terminated.

The director asked for weekly appraisals from the custodian's supervisor (who happened to be Caucasian), and these were kept in a personal desk file. The director also did unannounced walk-throughs and wrote a memo for the desk file each time a problem was noted.

Because there was no direct evidence of alcohol or drug use, this matter was not dealt with, although the concern remained.

At the end of her first month on probation, the employee was called into a meeting with the agency director and her supervisor. The problems that had been noted were discussed, as was the fact that she still was not meeting agency standards.

The custodian was uncooperative, sullen, and uncommunicative. She claimed that her work record was as good as that of the other custodians, and she asked, "Why are you picking on me?" The director's attempt to uncover reasons for her work problems was unsuccessful. A memo for the file was written to record the nature of the meeting, what was discussed, and the custodian's responses.

At the end of the second month, a similar meeting occurred. The situation had not improved, and the custodian seemed unwilling or unable to change or to admit that changes were needed. After conferring with the supervisor, the director decided to terminate the employee immediately for cause.

OUTCOME

The position was filled with a more reliable custodian who was also more attentive to the quality of her work. The replacement custodian was an African American.

The terminated employee immediately filed a race discrimination claim with the Equal Employment Opportunity Commission (EEOC), claiming that she was fired because she was white and the boss wanted to bring in someone who was black.

After 18 months of investigation by the EEOC, the charges were dropped on the basis they were without merit. However, the agency had spent dozens of hours and several thousand dollars defending itself.

DISCUSSION QUESTIONS

1. Why might the director have decided to keep a separate desk file in this case?

2. Why was it important not to deal directly with the drug or alcohol issue?

3. Would an immediate termination have met with the same results? Were the additional written reports an important element in the paper trail?

4. Should the issue have been handled differently because of the racial dimension? How important was the fact that the immediate supervisor was Caucasian?

5. Were there other strategies that might have been effective?

CHAPTER 14

Career Management

JOB CHANGE FREQUENCY

It was once quite common for an individual to get a job, perhaps move up in the hierarchy, and stay with that organization until retirement. That kind of constancy is now rare. It is more typical for an individual to hold seven or eight different positions in several organizations during his or her career.

One of the main reasons for the current high frequency of job changes is the rapid rate of transformation in the job market. For one thing, there is a substantial amount of organizational downsizing, bankruptcy, and restructuring. For another, positions and expertise change in nature, especially if technology related. Finally, individuals naturally want to climb up the organizational ladder. A career-oriented individual with effective work habits can easily move up—if the individual is willing to go where the opportunities are.

A second reason for the increase in job mobility is the growth in the number of two-career families. In a two-career family, either spouse may obtain a good new job that requires a change in location, thus necessitating a change in jobs for the other spouse. The two openings created offer opportunities for two other individuals, often themselves members of two-career families, and the cycle continues.

The increase in job mobility is also related to the broadened geographic scope of many businesses and organizations. A promotion within an organization like the American Cancer Society may require a move from one state to another state. Further, in many organizations employees are transferred from one location to another because of organizational needs.

Job satisfaction is also seemingly more important than it used to be. Today, if someone simply does not enjoy his or her job, he or she will start looking for another. (From a mental health point of view, that is obviously commendable.)

According to projections, individuals in this twenty-first century will change careers at least three times and change positions seven or eight times. The changing of careers is related to the factors identified above: the growth in two-career families, changes in the job market, the globalization of the economy, and the greater importance given to job satisfaction.

Some career changes are due to changes in aspirations; a sharpening of one's view of the job market; and a better understanding of one's skills, work preferences, and opportunities. First careers are frequently determined in college at the time a major is chosen. The selection of a major is often done casually and without much knowledge of the alternatives. Sometimes first careers are determined simply by what jobs were available and attainable at the time of the first job search. A change in career might then occur if one is unable to find employment in the area of one's major or move beyond an entry-level position.

No matter what the reasons for changing careers, individuals can enjoy doing several different kinds of work and can be effective in several roles. Skills are often transferable from setting to setting—especially in education and administration. Second careers are often tied to decisions to pursue a graduate degree (e.g., a degree in administration might be earned to permit a move from education to administration).

Any job change warrants careful consideration and planning. The employee needs to assure the change is consistent with his or her own career goals, aspirations, and personal lifestyle. Employers need to manage job changes while keeping employee turnover and the need for training within reasonable limits. They also need to have the time and resources to prepare others to fill appropriate vacancies.

AN EMPLOYEE PERSPECTIVE

As discussed in previous chapters, employees generally want to maximize feelings of achievement, status, or income. Thus employees will often aspire to obtain the most responsible, highest paid position they qualify for and feel comfortable in. Many employees don't want supervisory responsibilities and would rather remain in direct service or technical support positions. Others want to be sure their job does not interfere too much with non-job-related goals, such as spending time with family or engaging in some hobby or sport.

Generally speaking, in seeking a change of jobs it is good to prepare a résumé that puts relevant education and work experience in the best possible light. But it is also important to build a résumé around career goals. For example, a health promotion specialist aspiring to become an administrator should seek out administrative roles and tasks so that these can be listed on the résumé. Examples include chairing committees and offering to assist administrators. Even if formal opportunities do not exist, it is wise to select a role model and to analyze what that person does, how the person does it, why the person does it, and how it could be done better. This type of exercise can help the individual determine if he or she would really like to do what someone else is doing and would likely be good at it. It also helps prepare the individual to answer possible interview questions at some undetermined future time.

Dress can be an important factor in seeking a new job. Generally speaking, it is wise to dress as people do in the type of position to which one aspires. It is wise to associate with them as much as possible (e.g., at breaks and during lunch hour) and within reason to act like them. It is important to ascertain what issues dominate their thinking and to become conversant with these issues. One way of doing this is to observe what books, journals, and newsletters they are reading—and read them.

Some job change strategists take this a step further and suggest seeking a mentoring relationship. A mentoring relationship can be very informal. The mentee might merely discuss career aspirations with the mentor, ask for advice on what to read, and ask about opportunities for gaining the necessary experience.

There are usually numerous opportunities to gain needed experience in community-based human service organizations. If an individual needs marketing experience to strengthen his or her résumé—or budgeting, planning, or grant writing experience—there are usually places looking for volunteers.

Computer experience can be gained off the job by buying a state-of-the-art personal computer and using it and by taking training courses as necessary to hone computer skills and gain familiarity with technology issues.

ACTION-BASED CONCEPT

Managers are advised to have a career path in mind, with a realistic plan and timetable, and to maintain flexibility in order to deal with opportunities and obstacles that occur.

AN EMPLOYER PERSPECTIVE

Employers, too, want employees to move up the organizational ladder. A major concern of employers is employee turnover, and helping an individual move up usually delays a move to another organization and the resultant recruitment costs. Financially, it is generally better to retain a valuable employee.

Moreover, job satisfaction is usually enhanced when a promotion occurs. The employee is motivated to perform well in the new position and to bring to it new ideas, a new perspective, and new energy. As noted, it is good practice to have each individual performing near the top of his or her ability.

Opportunities for upward mobility may be limited by factors unrelated to performance. For example, the key positions may be filled by individuals who are not mobile. In addition, politics and personalities complicate most personnel decisions. Politics has to do with power—the power to make decisions, to influence decisions, or to lessen the likelihood of a decision being made. In personnel matters, power can be exerted indirectly, by determining who is involved in the selection process or by influencing those individuals' decisions; or more directly, by encouraging or discouraging potential applicants. Of course, politics also involves personalities. A candidate may be acknowledged as capable, but people with power may simply not like the candidate and wonder whether they would want to work with him or her. Conversely, a candidate may be liked, in which case the candidate's strengths may be magnified and his or her weaknesses minimized.

The general tendency is for the weaknesses of internal candidates to be magnified and the strengths of external candidates to be magnified. This is especially true in the case of administrators, who must make difficult decisions. Many decisions are complicated and could be made differently and still work out. Therefore, people will naturally disagree with the decisions made, sometimes strongly. Thus, anyone who has been an administrator for a while will have detractors, sometimes making it difficult to move up from a mid-level position to an upper management position. (Remember the old saying, "Friends come and go, but enemies accumulate.")

Effective administrators, however, do not manage by popular opinion. It is helpful to consider politics and personalities when making a decision, but ultimately the alternative that is best for the organization is the one that should be chosen. Seldom is making the right decision more complicated than when hiring, promoting, or terminating employees.

Administrative ability is a combination of personality, work experience, decision-making ability, informed judgment, integrity, willingness to deal with controversy, attention to deadlines and details, critical thinking, written and oral communication skills, and even personal appearance.

Managers need to be constantly alert for employees who possess administrative ability and for opportunities to promote them. Astute managers will undertake to encourage and support such individuals. Giving them administrative assignments with progressively more responsibility, praising good handling of a situation, arranging training for them, and sending them suggested reading materials are all beneficial. Informal mentoring is commonplace, and it can be formalized by setting up monthly mentoring meetings.

It is sometimes appropriate to identify potential managers and place them on a fast track. One example is when a pending retirement permits moving someone through one or two interim appointments intended to prepare them for the ultimate appointment. Obviously, fast-tracking employees is most prevalent in large organizations where lots of turnover occurs.

A good mentoring strategy is to create administrative internships. These internships can last a few months or a year or more. They are valuable for the employees and their résumés, but they also give the administrator an opportunity to provide appropriate work experience and training and to observe how the employees respond. Such internships are frequently set up to create opportunities for women and minorities in organizations in which they are underrepresented.

Of course, there will be situations where it is appropriate to facilitate an employee's move to another organization (e.g., when intraorganizational opportunities for advancement are lacking). Many administrators will choose to work with a promising employee, by providing work experiences that will strengthen the employee's résumé, offering to write letters of recommendation, and calling appropriate job opportunities to the employee's attention. This approach strengthens the profession—by identifying and training employees with promise and helping them move into responsible positions—but it can also be good for the agency, because such employees are highly motivated to do well while they are working there.

Occasionally an employee will need to make a lateral move to another agency because of a poor "fit." The poor fit may be due to politics or personalities or a change in job requirements. Sometimes the agency and the position outgrow the ability of the person occupying the position.

Such situations are seldom comfortable and need to be handled carefully so as to minimize the negative impact. Usually more than one person should be involved in making the decision to ask an employee to leave a position in order to minimize the appearance of bias.

One approach is to upgrade the position and give it a new title and new duties. An agency's marketing, planning, fund-raising, grant-writing, or technological needs could be used to justify the restructuring of the position and the inclusion of new functions. It is usually appropriate to talk to the person in the current position about the pending change so as to allow the person additional lead time to evaluate options and perhaps search for a position elsewhere within the organization or in another organization.

ACTION-BASED CONCEPT

Managers need to identify employees with potential for promotion and create developmental opportunities and, when appropriate, a "fast track" to move them into the next appropriate position.

FORCED JOB CHANGE ISSUES

It sometimes becomes necessary to demote an individual, ask him or her to resign, or terminate the employment relationship. Downsizing and "rightsizing" often results in terminations and transfers. A forced job change is generally unpleasant and must be handled very carefully so as not to undermine employee morale or incur unnecessary litigation.

The manager should confer with his or her own supervisor and the director of human resources, the personnel director, or whoever handles the personnel function. There are usually several issues that the supervisor will want to discuss:

- Is the decision to demote or terminate in the agency's best interests?
- Has the employee been given an opportunity to improve?
- Is the paper trail sufficiently extensive?
- Have agency personnel policies been followed exactly?
- Is there evidence of bias?
- What is the risk of litigation?

Whether demotion or dismissal of the employee is in the agency's best interests depends on the answers to such questions. It also depends on agency politics; the effect on public relations; and the perceptions of other employees, board members, and major funding or regulatory agencies, among other things. It is good not only to discuss these matters in a meeting but to record the results of the meeting in a signed memo and place it on the employee's file.

ACTION-BASED CONCEPT

When an employee is terminated, the paper trail must be extensive enough to minimize the likelihood of successful litigation. It should include documentation of poor performance or other problems, opportunities for improvement, and the reason the discharge occurred. It should also identify who was consulted or otherwise involved in making the decision.

Determining whether personnel policies have been followed is usually straightforward. The answer is usually yes or no, with little room for doubt. (If it is not an obvious yes, then the answer is generally no.) Personnel policies typically require periodic reviews, written evaluations, opportunities to correct behaviors identified in written performance evaluations, needed training being made available, repeated written warnings, and so on. Note that, in case of a lawsuit, if any requisite step is not documented, the court will likely assume it did not happen, and the agency's case will be attacked and discredited.

The risk of a charge of bias is usually minimized if the decision does not belong to just one person. Even if the administrator makes the final decision, reviewing the case with an administrative council or a supervisor helps identify any bias that exists and spreads the decision-making responsibility. As noted earlier, employment decisions cannot be based on race, national origin, age, gender, or disability. Of course, discrimination will still be present if an individual is simply not treated as other employees would be in a similar situation.

ACTION-BASED CONCEPT

Managers need to consult with others before forcing a job change, and avoid emotional exchanges and exaggerations that might be used by the employees in future litigation.

CONCLUSION

Managers need to manage their careers and encourage employees to do the same. Career management may involve mentoring, education and training, job changes, and salary adjustments. Thus, it warrants periodic attention and careful, reasoned decision making.

IN-BASKET ASSIGNMENT

TO: Health Education and Health Promotion Specialists
FROM: The Director
RE: Career Planning

> Occasionally I receive requests to recommend persons for promotion within the agency or to nominate people for vacancies that occur elsewhere. If you are interested in being considered for such positions, I need to know about it.

It would be helpful for me to have a one-page career plan for each of you that describes where you would like to be in 10 years and what kind of interim appointments would qualify you for the ultimate position you would like to have.

I would like to see a first draft of such a career plan by the end of the month.

MANAGEMENT CASE STUDY

Setting

A worksite-based program had a staff of three: a manager, a program specialist, and a secretary-bookkeeper. The manager was a 50-year-old widow who had been in the position for several years and would likely retire in it. The program specialist had worked successfully in the program for 3 years.

Problem

The program specialist was ready for a career change. He had a family and needed a salary increase. Moreover, he felt he was ready for a promotion. However, the manager had no plans for relocating, and no other vacancy was anticipated in the near future.

Alternatives Considered

One alternative was for the program specialist simply to begin looking for other positions.

Another was to discuss the matter with his supervisor during his annual performance review.

A third was for the program specialist simply to stay put and look for part-time supplemental employment.

Actions Taken

At the annual performance review, the program specialist discussed his desire to move into a management position with the manager, acknowledging that he understood he would probably have to move to achieve this goal. He specifically asked if the manager would be comfortable helping him obtain such a position. The manager and program specialist scheduled a subsequent meeting to develop a suitable plan and discuss how to implement it.

At the meeting, the program specialist admitted that he needed more administrative experience. The manager offered to give him administrative tasks with increasing responsibility over a 2-year period and change his title to assistant manager at the end of 1 year. The program specialist agreed to stay for the 2-year period, and the manager agreed to nominate or otherwise recommend him for a suitable management position at the end of that period.

OUTCOME

During the 2 years, the program specialist gradually became involved in budget decisions, personnel decisions, and long-range planning. He was asked to chair a technology task force and received the title of assistant administrator on schedule. He attended an administrators convention and a board meeting or two and assisted in fund-raising activities. At the end of the second year, he was evaluated as an administrator and received reasonably good ratings. He was now ready to present himself as a serious candidate for a management position.

The assistant administrator applied for five management positions, and the manager wrote letters of nomination or recommendation. He was a finalist for one of the positions but did not receive it. He subsequently applied for three other positions and was hired to fill a mid-level management vacancy in a nearby city, largely based on the recommendation of the manager.

DISCUSSION QUESTIONS

1. What might have happened if the manager had not agreed to serve as a mentor? How important is a mentor?

2. How could the program specialist have gained administrative experience if the manager had declined to provide opportunities to perform relevant tasks?

3. What advantages accrued to the agency and the manager as a result of the management training program?

4. What obligations did the program specialist incur as a result of being mentored?

5. Were there alternative strategies that might also have worked?

CHAPTER 15

Budgeting

IMPORTANCE OF THE BUDGET

For the most part, every health and human service organization has more financial demands than fiscal resources. Often there are a dozen or more places to spend every dollar. Thus, a budget preparation process is needed to ensure that the dollars are allocated to the projects that will most benefit the organization. Similarly, a budget-monitoring process is needed to ensure that accounts are not overspent and money is not wasted. An organization that has a good budget preparation process and good monitoring process will probably be stable. An organization that does not will frequently struggle.

BUDGETING SKILLS

Budgeting skills are obviously essential for good management. The parameters of managing an organization are set by the budget. The budget defines what staffing levels, what projects, what marketing, what technology, and what staff development is possible. To a large degree, it determines what plans can be implemented, although the planning process can focus on budget shifts or budget reductions or, preferably, budget growth.

Most large organizations have a chief financial officer, and smaller organizations will have an accountant or at least a payroll officer. Such individuals should be viewed as critically important employees.

The technical skills needed to accurately perform accounting functions are absolutely essential for an organization. If the organization does not maintain its financial integrity, it will not be deemed worthy of support by the public. A small or new organization may choose to subcontract accounting functions. Hiring a certified public accountant firm to do some or all of the "bookkeeping" and payroll tasks is often cost efficient because the firm will have the expertise and the computer hardware and software to do them accurately and efficiently.

Yet managers dare not leave control of the budget to the "bean counters." The accounting staff is concerned with managing what is, not what ought to be. The latter is a leadership or management function.

ACTION-BASED CONCEPT

Effective managers thoroughly understand the organization's budget and are able to roughly determine the budget status at any future point in the fiscal year. A standing weekly meeting with the fiscal officer, or a thorough reading of budget status and cash flow reports, is an essential foundation of sound management practice.

THE NATURE OF A BUDGET

A budget is a formal statement of the estimated revenues and expenditures for an organization's fiscal year (which is rarely equal to the calendar year). Both revenue and expenditure statements are divided into categories that facilitate planning.

Budgets are stated in monetary terms and are organized by general categories such as personnel, equipment, marketing, office supplies, travel, staff development, and operating reserves. These categories vary from organization to organization, and the level of detail of the reports also varies. For example, a personnel budget may include expense lines for Social Security, company-provided insurance, and other "indirect" personnel expenses, but the summary computer printout might only list "personnel" and give a dollar amount. In another organization, the indirect personnel expenses might be grouped and listed elsewhere as "fringe benefit costs" or under another appropriate title.

Similarly, equipment budgets are defined in various ways, frequently by cost of the equipment. Minor items like staplers or paper punches are listed in "office supplies and expenses," whereas computers, fax machines, office furniture, videotape projectors, and other expensive pieces of equipment are separated. Likewise, a major equipment purchase that might have to be budgeted over 2 to 5 years, like the purchase of a new telephone switchboard or video conferencing equipment, is often placed in a capital equipment account or even a separate capital improvement budget in order to facilitate the development of multiple-year budgets and depreciation schedules.

The point of these remarks is that the managers of an organization must understand the budget and must ask questions until they have mastered "what is located where and why." In addition, managers of nonprofit organizations must be aware of the rules governing nonprofits, and managers of for-profits must understand the rules governing them.

TYPES OF BUDGETS

This is not a financial management textbook, so no attempt will be made to be comprehensive or detailed. Most health agencies, and certainly the smaller ones, have a simple operating budget with the two major categories of income (or revenues) and expenses. Such a budget spells out in detail how much income is anticipated during that fiscal year and where it will likely be spent. Obviously, both the income and expenditure figures are planned amounts that will need to be carefully monitored and may need to be adjusted if revenues are not received at the projected rate. It is the responsibility of the managers to ensure that the organization will always have funds available to cover expenses, especially when shortfalls of revenue occur.

One of the stark realizations new managers face is how little of a budget is discretionary (or, conversely, how much of a budget is in fixed costs). Fixed costs may include a variety of items, such as salaries and fringe benefits, taxes, liability insurance, rent and utilities, debt service, postage, data and video transmission services, equipment leases, or multiyear payment plans for major equipment purchases. Discretionary dollars may in fact constitute an insignificant part of the budget unless a growth in revenue occurs.

The downside of a budget dominated by fixed costs is that, when revenue shortfalls occur, virtually the only option is reduce the work force through layoffs. It is sometimes possible to reduce equipment expenses, and one reason equipment purchases are frequently scheduled at the end of a fiscal year is to maintain a financial reserve. The travel budget might also be reduced during revenue shortfalls, assuming most of the funds have not already been spent (e.g., for travel to an important conference).

One fact critically important to remember is that layoffs late in a fiscal year save very few dollars. For example, if a layoff occurs at the beginning of the fourth quarter, only 25 percent of the annualized salary is saved. Managers monitoring budget shortfalls might choose to layoff one employee or not fill a vacant position during the first quarter of the fiscal year rather than eliminate three positions during the fourth quarter. Either decision could be appropriate, but delaying the decision in effect may make the decision for the manager.

Monitoring budget status is a relatively easy function once the budget and the reports are understood. Computer printouts typically list budgeted amounts, revenues and expenditures during that month or equivalent reporting cycle, year-to-date revenues and expenditures, and projected year-end variations. By scanning the appropriate columns, a manager can usually ascertain what budget lines are above or below projection and what the cumulative effect will be. Of course, if the bottom line or balance remains positive, transfers or other adjustments can often be made. If, however, the bottom line shows a deficit, a reduction in expenditures must occur unless appropriate infusions of cash are anticipated.

Because of the importance of cash flow, managers need to understand cash flow budgets. Cash flow budgets project not only how much revenues will be received but when. For example, an organization receiving United Way disbursements needs to know whether those disbursements will be monthly, quarterly, or annually. Similarly, the time of receipt of clinic revenues can be projected, as can the time of receipt of city, county, state, or federal revenues.

Cash flow budgets also project expenses and identify when payroll, rent, equipment, utility, and other expenditures will be processed. Unless an agency has a large cash flow balance (has far more anticipated revenues than expenditures) or has a large operating reserve, the managers might find themselves in the undesirable position of having to decide which bills to pay on time and which bills to allow to become delinquent.

Worse yet, an organization with cash flow problems may not be able to meet its payroll obligation, and few things affect employee morale more than not getting paid on time (partly because it affects the employees' cash flow).

If sufficient revenues are expected from an imminent government disbursement of funds, a bank might be willing to write a cash flow line of credit. That is, it will grant money to cover the payroll for a few days or a few weeks, charging an interest rate, of course. Such lines of credit, while common, take time to arrange. Developing and monitoring a cash flow budget can aid in projecting what months' revenues will likely not cover expenditures and will facilitate the development of a line of credit to smooth out ripples in the cash flow.

A cash flow budget brings into focus the pattern of cash disbursements and receipts. In a new or struggling organization, few things are more important than cash flow. Weekly and even daily cash flow monitoring sessions can be crucial for an organization's survival.

The balance sheet budget is another type of budget that all managers need to understand. Balance sheets combine all other budgets to project what the organization's financial status will look like at the end of the fiscal year. Financing and lending agencies often focus heavily on balance sheets in analyzing an organization's net worth and its level of indebtedness. Budget sheet analysis is also used by managers in deciding whether to buy an expensive piece of equipment, add a new staff position, or remodel the physical plant. Even if the cash flow permitted a major expenditure, an organization might decide to postpone the expenditure until the balance sheet looked better.

EXTERNAL AUDITS

One of the most important things a manager can do to ensure that fiscal practices are sound is to engage an external auditor, especially if a CPA firm has not been hired to do the organization's accounting. Auditors are sometimes thought of as investigators looking for fraud, embezzlement, or "juggled figures." The prudent manager, however, will use the auditing firm as a management consultant—and as a way of demonstrating to the public that the organization is using sound business practices and standard accounting procedures. The external audit verifies that the agency has accurately prepared its reports and valued its assets and liabilities. It discourages the temptation to use "creative accounting" (and to engage in theft). Equally important, it assures bankers, directors, trustees, and funding agencies that the agency's publicly available and/or privately distributed financial statements are flawless.

The external auditor does not prepare financial statements, but instead audits or verifies that the financial statements prepared by others are correct and complete. The audit takes place at the end of the fiscal year and may involve verifying any aspect of a report in any way necessary.

An auditor will typically provide management notes, often contained in a separate letter, intended to advise the manager about areas of concern or areas that must be handled better next year. Management notes should be discussed thoroughly with both the auditor and the board, and care must be taken to follow through on the important points raised.

Of course, if problems are uncovered, they will be detailed in the auditor's report itself. In addition, if the financial statements are problematic, a qualified report may be issued. In such a report, the ways in which the agency strayed from standard accounting practices will be specified. A qualified auditor's report makes it difficult to obtain loans, lines of credit, grants, and contracts, because it indicates that organizational stability is at risk. A "clean" or unqualified audit, which is routine for most agencies, can usually be obtained by rigorously dealing with the issues cited in the management notes.

ACTION-BASED CONCEPT

Managers must understand auditor reports and respond to the issues cited in the management notes. Few, if any, organizations should try to get by without an annual audit of the books by a qualified firm that prepares auditor reports for other organizations.

THE BUDGETING PROCESS

Developing a budget is an essential part of the planning process. It is a way of implementing the strategic plan, because it ties resources to elements of the plan. It is also a way of planning revenue enhancements and expenditures. Like any other element of the planning process, it must be developed carefully.

Of course, budget parameters must be kept in mind when developing a plan of action. Yet when thinking about long-range goals and objectives, it is important to think about what ought to be rather than what is possible right now. So in a sense the budget determines how much of the plan can be implemented in any given fiscal year, and the plan determines what the budget must be.

The budget is also used to establish priorities among planning elements. Funds can be allocated to ensure some items are accomplished, while other items can be included "if money is available" or "if the contingency fund is unspent at the end of the year."

In any case, the people involved in the planning process and other key decision makers should be involved in developing the budget. It is important that at least one accounting person participate so that items others might miss are included, like increases in payroll taxes associated with new positions, interest add-on, planned purchases, and service agreements.

The budget planning cycle must begin several months before the fiscal year to allow for adequate review and formal approval. In some agencies, approval must occur at several levels (e.g., local, regional, and state). Knowing the deadlines for submission of budget requests is important for estimating when to begin the cycle.

There are numerous strategies for developing a budget. One commonly used approach is to assume a base budget, or a carry-forward budget, and to request and justify changes, especially increases. A contrary approach is zero base budgeting.

Zero base budgeting puts everything up for justification every year. It normally involves an informal or a formal cost-benefit analysis. The purpose of zero base budgeting is to minimize the tendency merely to continue doing what the organization has done. Activities and positions previously important may now be less important as a result of changes in the legal and business environment or changes in the organization's objectives.

True zero base budgeting is not used much anymore because it is time consuming and often demoralizing. However, sometimes specific items, such as equipment purchases, travel budgets, and even staff positions, are detailed with zero-based-budgeting justification.

Another approach to budgeting is "top-down" budgeting. Managers can choose to incorporate position reductions (or increases), equipment purchases, and program elimination (or expansion), and force subordinates to explain why the management plan should not be eliminated. Top-down budgeting processes tend to facilitate change and the accomplishment of organizational goals.

"Bottom-up" budgeting instead requires units to submit budget requests, which are then synthesized, prioritized, and made to balance with projected revenues. "Bottom-up" budgeting focuses on operational goals. Because of its decentralized nature, it tends to lead to the achievement of departmental goals instead of organizational goals and tends to increase the size of the budget. It works best in organizations that are stable or growing.

Organizational change, especially downsizing, is best handled by a top-down budgeting process. On the other hand, the individuals who must implement a budget are less likely to overlook important factors and are more likely to be realistic, which is one reason to favor bottom-up budgeting. Furthermore, morale and satisfaction are usually higher when managers of units participate in developing their own budgets.

ACTION-BASED CONCEPT

Managers must utilize a budgeting approach that is appropriate for the agency—one that takes into account past practices, staff personalities, and agency politics.

CONCLUSION

Regardless of the budgeting process or the type of budget, top management needs to approve the budget. After approval is given, the budget is copied and distributed to account managers to implement.

The budget should be based on clear, unambiguous criteria for funding organizational activities. It should facilitate the coordination of activities and the accomplishment of departmental and organizational goals.

IN-BASKET ASSIGNMENT

TO: Health Education and Health Promotion Specialists
FROM: The Director
RE: Budgeting

I would like to know what sort of budgeting process other community health agencies use (i.e., how their budget is developed and approved). Would some of you contact a community health agency on my behalf and inquire about its budgeting process?

Perhaps if each of you contacted one agency manager and did a phone interview, the workload would not be excessive.

Thanks!

MANAGEMENT CASE STUDY

Setting

A large municipal health department employed approximately 200 people. Forty of the positions were funded by soft money, in this case, block grants. There were seven major divisions within the health department.

Problem

New state guidelines were released requiring block grant recipients to provide health care programs for welfare recipients. Because of political considerations, the city council and the local board of health made the provision of such a program a priority.

However, there was no increase in funding. The cost of providing the program had been shifted from the local government to the health department, which had to find a way to implement the program within its budget.

Alternatives Considered

One alternative considered was to try to establish a partnership with another provider, such as a hospital, a large medical practice, or a health maintenance organization (HMO).

A similar alternative was to look for a corporate partner who would cofund the program.

Another alternative was to approach the city council for supplemental funding for the program.

A final alternative was to reduce costs, eliminate or scale back other programs, and phase in a scaled-down program to meet the new guidelines.

Actions Taken

The health department administrator made a few phone calls to explore the possibility of forming a partnership with a hospital, HMO, or area corporation. She found interest, but no available funding. All of the organizations' budget cycles required at least a year's lead time, so that planning would need to begin immediately in order for assistance with the program to even be considered for the following year.

A call to the mayor's office quickly discouraged the administrator from formally requesting supplemental funding. There were simply too many other priorities—bridge repairs, community policing, and sports arena construction overruns.

The administrator decided that the astute thing to do, given the political climate, was to create the program and reduce expenditures elsewhere to free up funds. The administrator appointed a project team to design a program whose cost would not exceed one million dollars. An outreach worker who had experience dealing with the media was asked to serve as leader of the project team, which included representatives from nursing, health education, and environmental health.

The planned new welfare program was designed as a seven-person operation and had an $800,000 startup cost. The administrator instituted a hiring freeze, and her personal approval was required for the filling of any vacancy. Of the next 12 vacancies, 4 were approved for rehiring and the other 8 were eliminated; this allowed creation of the 7 positions needed for the new program. (Each department that lost staff was asked to submit a plan for reprioritizing and redistributing work to be done.)

A task force was created to revise the budget, and each of the seven divisions was asked to propose budget reductions totaling at least $100,000. The saved funds and new positions formed a reasonable foundation on which to build the new program.

OUTCOME

The program received a great deal of media coverage and was reported nationally as a local government's response to a national problem and mandate.

The administrator discussed the mandate and the plan with the seven division heads. Although their response to the staffing and budget reductions was less than enthusiastic, they understood the need for the reductions and cooperated fully.

As the shifting of workload occurred, there was considerable grumbling among the units that had lost staff, but the discontent dissipated within two months' time.

DISCUSSION QUESTIONS

1. Would you consider the revision process used primarily a top-down or a bottom-up process? How else could the cuts have been made?

2. What were the likely reasons for having the administrator make the personnel cuts? What were the likely reasons for having a task force reduce the budget rather than the administrator?

3. What are the relative advantages and disadvantages of simply transferring people to new positions rather than cutting positions and making new hires?

4. Are there other strategies for creating startup funding that should have been explored?

CHAPTER 16

Fiscal Control and Accountability

THE IMPORTANCE OF FISCAL CONTROL

Few things are more important in an organization than managing the finances. Although managers must do far more than exert financial control, they must succeed in this role to be successful overall. The most serious consequences of lack of fiscal control include deficits, missed payrolls, and bankruptcy. Only slightly less serious are overdue payables, lack of credit, and a poor fiscal reputation. Managers in any health organization must understand and control the budget.

No single method of control has been devised that works for all organizations. There are simply too many variables. A good place to begin in attempting to achieve fiscal control is to learn what the critical problems or pressure points are. Some organizations have difficulty meeting the monthly payroll, while others experience depressions in the revenue cycle, such as during the Christmas holidays or the summer. An organization's pressure points might include the dates when bills for clinical supplies come due and when quarterly payments on long-term debt must be made. Its problem areas might include purchasing and inventory, management of receivables, billing, and theft or fraud.

These and other problems and pressure points can be discovered within a week or two of being on the job simply by asking questions of those in a position to know. Whatever the top two or three problems are, they need regular review—receiving at least monthly, perhaps weekly, and sometimes even daily, attention. In some situations, it is even necessary to check cash flow before paying a large bill or releasing a payroll to be certain funds are there to cover it.

ACTION-BASED CONCEPT

Managers need to know the organization's traditional fiscal pressure points, especially any pressure points that are related to cash flow.

THE WHO AND HOW OF FISCAL MONITORING

The chief executive officer (sometimes called the executive director) is the person ultimately responsible for fiscal control, but he or she often delegates much of the responsibility to account managers or, in large organizations, to the chief financial officer. The account managers are obviously responsible for any accounts they manage. Department heads and other mid-level managers will often receive copies of all the accounts managed by subordinates.

Fiscal reports are usually periodic (weekly or monthly), and each budget status report usually reports actual revenue and expenses for the period, year-to-date actual, and year-to-date variance (see Exhibit 16–1).

A manager would analyze an expanded version of the report shown in Exhibit 16–1. If at 55 percent of the fiscal year, 78 percent of the money in a given account had been expended, the manager would need to consider options. One option would be to reduce expenditures in that account, while another option would be to transfer money from an account that was underutilized. Of course, the key issue would be whether total expenditures (and revenues) were ahead or behind projection.

Exhibit 16–1 Sample Budget Status Report

Date of Printout:	6-11-05
	19:30
Account Number:	10-7742-04
Person Responsible: Smith	

Item Description	Total Expenditure
Month Actual	20,678
Full Year Budget	304,718
Year to Date Actual	168,656
Date Enc.	0
Variance Percentage	55

ACTION-BASED CONCEPT

Managers must fully understand budget printouts and be able to interpret them correctly.

Budget status reports are also usually available on demand (i.e., at any point in time a current report can be displayed on the screen of a computer). This is particularly important for ascertaining if enough cash exists to cover a large expenditure.

An organization needs a system of controls to stop expenditures when budgets have been used up, or, earlier in the year, when expenses are ahead of projections. A controller or a purchasing officer can refuse to authorize expenditures if an account is overdrawn or can call in an account manager to discuss plans for balancing the bottom line.

Other types of fiscal controls are often helpful. For example, requiring approval of out-of-state travel and travel advances and requiring prompt settlement of travel expense accounts helps a manager know what the budget status really is at any point in time. Additionally, approval of equipment purchase requests is usually required so the timing of the payment coincides with the availability of cash. Similarly, buying a large volume of an item (a year's supply instead of a 3-month supply) could be a good decision if cash is available or a poor decision if it is not. Many organizations require that a purchase order be signed before any money is expended. This prevents employees from purchasing large amounts of items and turning in the bills at the end of the fiscal year, when money might not exist in the budget. A related fiscal control issue concerns the availability of company credit cards. Dispensing credit cards to employees allows bills of unknown amounts to accumulate, which can be problematic. Regardless of how payment is rendered, control of purchasing is critical in any agency with a tight budget. Limiting the authority to purchase is critical.

ACTION-BASED CONCEPT

Managers must monitor all the accounts of the individuals they supervise, ensure that fiscal restraint is being used, and ensure that their subordinates fully understand key reports and the need for fiscal controls.

Payables need to be carefully monitored in most organizations. Software exists to project and monitor payables. Although it is not unusual to have payables more than 30 days old, it is usually problematic if they become more than 90 days old. Computer reports showing how many payables are less than 30 days old, how many are 30 to 60 days old, and how many are more than 60 days old are useful. In some agencies, one managerial task is to decide which bills to pay on time and which bills to let sit.

It is similarly important to monitor receivables (e.g., to check who has owed the organization money for more than 30 days and how much money has been owed for more than 60 days). It is advantageous to have clients pay when services are rendered and to set a policy to determine how much credit to extend. Allowing bills to be paid by credit card reduces bad debt, but payment by credit card does involve a service charge. Similarly, determining when to write off bad debts and when to turn bad debts over to a collection agency is critical. A policy of turning all uncollected bills more than 90 days old to a collection agency will reduce receivables but will also alienate clients. It may be that long overdue bills are turned over to a collection agency only when a cash shortfall is expected. Again, denying services to clients or patients with bills more than 60 days old enhances fiscal control but sours client relations. The pros and cons of such policies have to be evaluated in each situation.

ACTION-BASED CONCEPT

Managers need to carefully monitor receivables and payables. Their goal should be to keep receivables from extending beyond a 30-day limit and payables from extending beyond a 60-day limit.

There are numerous other forms of financial control that may be appropriate, such as requiring receipts for all meals instead of setting a low per diem rate and not requiring receipts. High per diem travel reimbursement policies usually mandate collection of receipts because otherwise employees could ask for reimbursement for meals not eaten.

An organization can control what size cars are rented, what flight class employees travel in, what hotels are used, and whether attendance at a conference encompasses paid travel days before and after. Case by case, these may be small matters, but in a large organization they can make or break a budget.

INTERNAL AUDITING

It is typical in a large organization to have an internal auditor, who randomly selects a unit and investigates whether its assets are properly used and its financial records are reliably kept. Because internal audits are used as spot checks, they are only reasonably reliable.

Internal audits may be done in units where problems have occurred. Overuse of petty cash, a decrease in revenues, or an increase in expenditures can be a reason to do an internal audit. The audit might uncover careless bookkeeping, petty theft, or major fraud. For example, a fraudulent bill submitted by a friend of the payables clerk can be paid by that clerk and the money shared by the two conspirators.

Perhaps the primary reason for instituting routine, random-internal audits is that the knowledge that any unit may be audited can deter theft, fraud, and careless reporting mistakes.

ACTION-BASED CONCEPT

Managers cannot assume that employees will be honest or accurate. Accuracy should be checked routinely, and spot checks should occur periodically.

CONCLUSION

Managers are held accountable for staying within the budget, and thus they need some means of fiscal control. Managers must know how to use income statements, cash flow statements, budget status reports, and balance sheets. In dealing with fiscal issues, timeliness is essential. By monitoring fiscal matters and uncovering problems in time to make corrections, managers can achieve a desirable bottom line. A whole range of controlling mechanisms and methods are available to guide the spending behavior of individual employees. These mechanisms, too, must be understood and used as needed.

IN-BASKET ASSIGNMENT

TO: Health Education and Health Promotion Specialists
FROM: The Executive Director
RE: Travel Expenses

The agency's travel costs are rapidly escalating, and we want to study ways to keep costs down without restricting travel. Is it to the agency's advantage to buy cars and have the staff use them or to continue to pay mileage for employees to use their own cars? Which alternative is to the employees' advantage?

Similarly, is it to our advantage to have a maximum reimbursement for each meal or a per diem expense rate? Which alternative would most benefit employees?

MANAGEMENT CASE STUDY

Setting

A county commission became concerned about the fiscal status of an agency that received $1.2 million in funds to provide services to AIDS patients and develop preventive programs. The director of the agency resigned under pressure, and a new director was hired and told that his first responsibility was to establish fiscal control procedures.

The agency employed an accounting clerk, a health services specialist, a disease prevention specialist, and clinicians staffing four separate clinics. All but the accounting clerk had large travel and expense accounts. The health services specialist and the disease prevention specialist also had large program accounts, but the largest accounts were those assigned to the four clinics.

Problem

There was little or no internal auditing. The accounting clerk merely checked the reports for mathematical errors and processed the reports. The new director was not experienced in fiscal management. Fiscal accountability was a prerequisite for regaining the commission's confidence and avoiding a funding loss.

Alternatives Considered

One alternative considered by the new director was to subcontract the fiscal management function to a local accounting firm.

Another was to upgrade the accounting clerk position to a controller position and to let the current clerk become a candidate for the job.

Another was to approach a local certified public accounting (CPA) firm about providing consultation on a pro bono basis.

The final alternative considered was to approach an accounting faculty member about using the agency as the focus of a class project during the next term (which happened to be a summer term).

Actions Taken

The first action taken was to call all account managers together to raise the county commission's concern and discuss each of the above alternatives. The account directors preferred the class project idea and did not want to terminate the accounting clerk.

The director decided that more sophisticated fiscal control was needed and created a controller position anyway. The director believed from the tone of remarks made by the account managers that they did not want a new controller or a CPA firm micromanaging their accounts.

A candidate with a master's in business administration was hired as controller. She was assigned the task of approaching a faculty member about using the agency for a class project. After an initial meeting between the controller and the faculty member and a subsequent meeting that included the agency director, the faculty member agreed to the idea of doing such a project.

The students were organized into three-member teams assigned to examine payables, receivables, cash flow, travel expenses, reporting formats and review, opportunities for dishonesty and embezzlement, and so on.

The agency staff were directed to cooperate fully with the students during the first two weeks of the project, which were to be devoted to information gathering. The students would then discuss the team reports and options, prepare a general report, and send this report to the agency at the end of the sixth week.

OUTCOME

Numerous recommendations were given, and these were reviewed with the account managers. The director decided to implement nearly all the recommendations and directed the new controller to take the necessary steps.

One account manager immediately started looking for other employment and left within 6 months. Her resistance to the changes impeded their implementation in her department.

No fraud was uncovered, but several "sloppy" fiscal accounting procedures were eliminated. A full written report was sent to the county commission, which seemed satisfied with the reform that had occurred.

DISCUSSION QUESTIONS

1. What risks did the new director run by going against staff recommendations and upgrading the accounting clerk position to a controller position? How should the director have communicated the decision to the staff? Should a director ask for advice if not prepared to accept it?

2. How important was it for the director to proceed quickly? Would it have been better for him to proceed slowly—to carefully study the matter, fully discuss each step with the staff, and develop a consensus?

3. What were possible advantages and disadvantages of using the agency for a class project?

4. How might the use of a student project to identify recommendations affect the reputation of the director? How important was the written report in implementing appropriate changes?

5. What other strategies might have been used to deal with the commission's concern about the agency's fiscal status?

CHAPTER 17

Grant Writing

A BUDGETARY PERSPECTIVE

It is common for a staff member to suggest a new project and for the administrator to say, "There isn't any money in the budget for that," thus discouraging the staff member from pursuing that and future projects. Similarly, managers often see good programs conducted by similar agencies in other locations, or even in their own city by competitors, and know that the carry-forward budget does not permit a realistic response to opportunities for expansion or improvement. Moreover, as the agency planning process evolves, the need to identify sources of expansion capital becomes increasingly important. Not surprisingly, thoughts often turn to non-budgeted sources of startup funds, including grants, contracts, and other means of raising funds.

Because there seldom is enough money in any organization's budget to do everything that ought to be done, administrators ought always to be searching for supplementary funding. They need to be continually monitoring what sources are available and what projects are being funded.

In a small organization, the manager will be the grant writer. He or she must develop and improve grant-writing skills through training and experience writing grants and must encourage the staff to do the same. Even in a larger organization where a grant writer is available, the manager must be on the lookout for appropriate opportunities and ask the grant writer to prepare the applications, providing assistance as necessary.

PLANNING FOR FUND-RAISING

Millions of dollars are available through grants and contracts from government agencies and private foundations. Additionally, individuals and corporations give billions of dollars in charitable donations each year. Although religious and other charities are the most popular recipients of such donations, health-related programs usually rank second.

ACTION-BASED CONCEPT

Managers must continually monitor sources of supplementary funding and must periodically spend time and effort preparing applications or encouraging and assisting others to do so.

The dollar amounts fluctuate from year to year, but large sums of available money go unclaimed each year. Grant writers must start with the assumption that the dollars are there and must continue to be optimistic and enthusiastic. Some grant writers chase grants and simply try to get a share of whatever grant money is available. This practice is not recommended, for various reasons. Most important, external funding dictates programming. It affects who the clients of an agency will be and what programs will be developed or emphasized. It affects what the existing staff will do with their time as well as what kind of additional staff are to be acquired. Indeed, the image and nature of an agency can shift perceptibly over time as a direct result of grant acquisition. Although the change may be desirable, it ought to be chosen on the basis that it is desirable, not simply because funds became available to implement it.

Almost any organization has a mission, and related goals and objectives. It also has long-range plans it uses to accomplish its goals and objectives, and fulfill its mission. Potential grants should be reviewed and discussed in this context. (Indeed, in some grant applications, a mission statement is required so that the funding agency can ascertain that the applicant and grant are a good fit.) Most important, grant applications should be prepared only to obtain funds for tasks that the agency would like to undertake even if external money was unavailable.

Rational planning is needed for development of the proposal. Grant reviewers look for a proposal that is stated clearly and convincingly. They look for documentation that a problem exists and for a plan that will help alleviate the problem. They look for measurable objectives that are feasible. They look at the credibility of the agency and the credentials of the staff. They look for the probability of success and the method by which the project will be evaluated.

Stated differently, grant reviewers are concerned that the money they are responsible for disbursing is spent wisely and that full value will be received. Rational planning and sound administrative practices are therefore essential parts of the grant preparation process.

The committee approach is recommended for grant development, although one person usually needs to do the actual writing for the proposal to be coherent. The value of having several people involved in generating ideas and in reviewing drafts cannot be overstated. If a proposal represents the good thinking of several people, it will be better than if it represents the best thinking of only one person. The committee approach to grant development is, admittedly, time consuming. However, passage of time allows complex ideas to form and usually results in a better proposal. Although a grant proposal draft can be written over a weekend, a good proposal takes several months to develop fully. A more rational plan usually results when there is adequate lead time for several people to discuss several drafts.

PROPOSAL DEVELOPMENT

A proposal is a statement setting forth a program, initiative, study, or a set of activities. It describes what one organization, group, or individual intends to do, and since it is presented to another organization, should be tailored to suit that organization.

Most proposals are either research or program proposals. In program proposals what is set forth is a program designed to offer a specific set of services to individuals, families, groups, or communities. The program may be intended to provide training and consultation to agency staff and members of the community, or to provide any number of other direct services. Technical assistance is a feature of many grant applications. A planning proposal details a set of planning and coordinating activities intended to result in a program proposal. Similarly, a research proposal lays out a project designed to study a specific problem, evaluate a service, and so on. Of course, there are also proposals to simply fund the requesting agency's project, with no direct benefit to the funding agency.

Proposals can be solicited or unsolicited. A solicited proposal is prepared in response to a formal, written request for proposal, often simply called an RFP. RFPs are prepared and sent to prospective agencies and operations. Similarly, program announcements and guidelines are described in various publications. *The Catalog of Federal Domestic Assistance* and the *Federal Register* are helpful for locating grant money and are available in most libraries. There are also grant-oriented newsletters, some of which are free. Potential grant applicants need only request that their names be placed on a funding agency mailing list. A number of commercial organizations also prepare and sell subscriptions that describe currently available grant money. Many of the sources are now computerized to make searching much easier. Although subscriptions are expensive, they can pay for themselves quickly in terms of time saved and dollars garnered.

Unsolicited proposals are also received and reviewed regularly. It is important when sending in solicited and unsolicited proposals to ascertain if the project being proposed fits one of the priorities of the funding agency. A telephone call to the agency will usually result in the needed information.

Once one or more potential sources of grant money have been identified, they should be contacted and asked for their guidelines and application forms. Further, prospective grant applicants should telephone or visit a contact person in each agency and describe the essence of what will be proposed. Such first-hand information and advice is readily available, and staff members prefer to provide it before a project is fully developed rather than after. Seeking and using such advice can save a lot of time and energy, but more importantly it can increase the probability of a project being funded.

Each funding agency has its own application forms and guidelines. It is imperative that the forms be filled out completely and accurately. Writing a grant is more complicated than filling in the blanks, but an ability and willingness to follow directions exactly is an important part of the process.

GRANT PROPOSAL ELEMENTS

Grant proposals, despite important dissimilarities, have several common elements. These elements may have different names, be grouped differently, or be in a different sequence, but they should be included in some fashion. In writing unsolicited proposals, for which no formal guidelines or application forms are available, these proposal elements can provide guidance.

ACTION-BASED CONCEPT

Grant writing involves studying application materials and guidelines, using the headings suggested, making the requested material readily apparent, and following all directions carefully and precisely. More than one person should be involved in determining what information is requested in what format and in ascertaining that all directions have been followed.

The exposition of the project need not be long. It is not uncommon for agency guidelines to set a page limitation on the exposition. For example, 10 or 15 pages of double-spaced typing. This kind of limitation causes grant writers to revise the exposition until it is clear and succinct, thus permitting reviewers to evaluate it in a shorter period of time.

Letter of Transmittal

The letter of transmittal, or cover sheet, is the first page of a grant, but it may be the last item to be prepared. It provides, at a minimum, the name and address of the organization submitting the proposal and a concise summary of the problem and the proposed program. As a way of establishing credibility, it often includes a statement of the organization's interest, capability, and experience in the area. It must contain the contact person's name, mailing address, e-mail, and telephone number and an authorized signature from a chief administrative officer. The authorized signature is necessary because the program, if funded, would use agency space, equipment, and staff to do specific tasks. Grant reviewers want to know that the agency is committed to such tasks. If accepted, a proposal has the effect of a contract.

Table of Contents

If the application is large, a table of contents usually follows the letter of transmittal. Use of headings in the body of the proposal facilitates development of a table of contents. Headings also make it easier for reviewers to understand the organization of the proposal and should be used even if a table of contents is not needed.

Introduction

An introductory statement that puts the proposal in context is appropriate. The statement may or may not include a description of the problem (the description could be located in a separate section). In either case, it is important to establish that there is a problem and that it has serious consequences for some group of people. Documentation is usually necessary at this point, and even if it is not necessary, it is helpful.

Applicant Agency Description

Funding agencies need to know if the organization is able to carry out the proposed project. Items to describe include the organizational structure, the organization's past experience, the qualifications of the staff, and the budget.

Target Group

The target group should be described in detail, and their location in the geographical area covered by the program should be indicated. The number and kind of clients expected is valuable information. A description of the group's involvement in the project planning process is also important.

Objectives

The specific objectives should be included in measurable form. Although behavioral objectives are not necessarily required, they lend themselves well to grant application specifications. A timetable for accomplishing the objectives should also be included.

Procedures

The procedures that will be used should be detailed. A logical, sequential timetable for the work plan is helpful. Specific methods and materials should be identified, with emphasis given to the innovative features of the program. If this involves consent forms or internal review (IRB) approvals this should be specified.

Evaluation

A plan for evaluation is often a key part of the proposal. The tools and methodology to be used should be described in enough detail to assure the funding agency that the results of the program will be summarized accurately. Many foundations and government grantors are looking to see measure of outcomes and program sustainability.

Budget

A budget sheet is usually included in the application form. Because budget forms vary from agency to agency, the funding agency form should be used when possible. However, grant proposal budgets do have some commonality. Usually they list salaries by position. The salary schedules of the applicant agency should be used in calculations. Fringe benefit costs are ordinarily figured as a percentage of salary. They include employer contributions to Social Security, health insurance, unemployment compensation, workers' compensation, and so on. The total varies from agency to agency and from year to year but is usually about 25 percent of the total salary cost.

If consultants are needed on technical projects, a realistic per diem fee should be used in a separate section of the budget. Consultants are not entitled to fringe benefits.

Supplies and materials should also be described in a separate section. They should be itemized by major types, such as office supplies, mail, telephone, duplication costs, and printing. Equipment is usually itemized in a separate category. Model numbers, vendors, and other specifics are usually provided in the itemization.

Travel should be categorized as in country/out of country, in state/out of state; it can be divided by personnel or by program function. Reviewers usually want to know how travel allowances are going to be used.

Indirect costs include such items as utilities, space, procurement, and accounting staff. Government funding agencies usually have a maximum allowable indirect rate. The rate is often negotiated; it may approach 50 percent of salaries and wages for the project.

Matching Funds

If matching funds are being used, they should be described. They represent the portion of the project cost that the applicant agency is providing. In some instances, in-kind contributions have been used for this purpose. The applicant agency may agree to provide space, office furniture, and so on, and place a monetary value on that. In other instances, cash contributions are required. In any case, the larger the amount of matching funds or in-kind contributions, the more attractive the application will be.

Assurances

When applying to government agencies, it is necessary to provide compliance assurances. There are a number of such assurances, and they change periodically. They might include assurances of compliance with rules regarding treatment of human subjects, affirmative action, handicapped accessibility, and accounting practices. Again, funding agencies can and will readily provide copies of required assurances, but a simple statement that the applicant agency will comply with all state or federal regulations will often suffice.

Appendixes

As in other written documents, appendixes can be used to include material that, if included in the body of the proposal, would interrupt the flow. Résumés of key personnel involved in the project and supporting letters from other agencies are usually appended. Brochures, flow charts, diagrams, and other supporting materials may be included.

FOUNDATIONS

A foundation is a non-government nonprofit organization. It has funds and programs managed by its own board of directors. Foundations are usually established by wealthy individuals or corporations as an efficient way of dispersing grants to aid a variety of social causes. With few exceptions, they make grants only to other tax-exempt, nonprofit organizations.

A foundation may be interested in a narrow range or a wide range of issues or causes. Small foundations prefer to fund projects in their own geographical locale, whereas large foundations may prefer projects that are state, regional, or national in scope. Whether applying to a small or large foundation, it is essential to ascertain that its interests somewhat match the interests addressed in the proposal.

The Foundation Directory available at http://fdncenter.org is a good reference to use in identifying interested foundations. It describes the purpose and activities of specific foundations, the geographic areas in which they make grants, and the general size of the grants they make.

An important follow-up step is to contact each foundation being considered as a possible source of funds and ask for an annual report or material that describes the major thrust of the foundation. A careful review of such material usually reveals whether the foundation would be interested in funding the project. A program officer's first question usually is, "Is this kind of project consistent with our interests?" The second question is, "Is the kind and amount of support requested within the range of what we usually give?" If the applicant agency can anticipate these questions and submit proposals only to foundations that have a good fit, its chance of success will increase.

Proposals sent to foundations are essentially the same as those sent to state and federal agencies, only smaller. Most foundations do not want a fully developed proposal as their first point of contact. Some small foundations prefer personal contact before any written proposal is submitted, and others prefer a letter and a summary. Large foundations often have their own application forms.

ACTION-BASED CONCEPT

Administrators should identify what foundations with a narrow geographical focus are in the immediate area, and should ascertain what their program priorities are. If it appears there may be a fit, a get-acquainted, exploratory meeting is usually appropriate.

In any case, the grant applicant needs to state the problem clearly, describe the proposed program, articulate the expected accomplishments, and outline a budget. The general principles of proposal development are applicable, but the final submission should be in a condensed format. A five-page concept paper is typical for a first submission to a foundation; a more detailed proposal will be required after the first screening. The first submission should be short, clear, and persuasive. It should state at the outset what is to be accomplished, who expects to accomplish it, how much it will cost, and how long it will take.

ACTION-BASED CONCEPT

Large state or national foundations always prepare annual reports and application guidelines. Any foundation that appears to be a potential source of funding should be contacted for these items, which should be studied carefully.

CONCLUSION

Managers should be able to write grant proposals, because often no one else is available for this task. They also need to encourage and support others who engage in the task of writing proposals. Grants and contracts can provide the initial financing for an expansion or improvement of services. However, agencies that are too heavily dependent on soft money may experience budget and staffing instability. As always, a balance is needed. Of course, achieving that balance means watching out for grant and contract opportunities and selecting the most appropriate opportunities to pursue.

IN-BASKET ASSIGNMENT

TO: Health Education and Health Promotion Specialists
FROM: The Executive Director
RE: Grants and Contracts

I understand that there are publications available that identify grants and contracts for health education and health promotion. Please check the government documents section of the library and do an internet search to see what is available and how I can obtain copies.

Thanks!

MANAGEMENT CASE STUDY

Setting and Problem

A university health promotion department wanted the university to establish a student health promotion program at the health center. The director of the health center and the dean of students agreed to do this if a source of funding could be identified. The faculty member who proposed the idea agreed to conduct a search for funding.

Alternatives Considered

One alternative considered was to have the students petition the administration to appropriate the cost of one office visit (currently $20) per year per student to establish a health promotion program.

Another alternative was to survey other health service–based wellness programs about their funding.

A third alternative was to approach an area hospital about helping to fund such a program as a marketing initiative.

A fourth alternative was to use the various directories, including computer databases, to search for a funding source.

Actions Taken

The faculty member developed a letter of inquiry about funding sources, which she sent to more than three dozen universities.

She also asked the university's librarian to identify all available grant and foundation databases.

She also did an internet search for funding options.

OUTCOME

The survey uncovered the fact that most health service–based programs received their base funding from the universities they were associated with, and they then approached various foundations to get funding for specific programs, such as alcohol abuse prevention programs. It also uncovered the existence of many partnerships between the health service–based programs and health promotion organizations, such as a family planning organization that promoted safe sex, a women's group devoted to preventing sexual assault, and a local branch of a cancer organization.

The faculty member had her students present a plan to the administration that called for $10,000 to finance the hiring of a graduate assistant. This amount would be matched during years 1, 2, and 3 by a grant from the local hospital in return for use of the program for marketing purposes.

The program was adopted and implemented and was successful. It evolved over time to become a well-funded, comprehensive program.

DISCUSSION QUESTIONS

1. How important were the survey results likely to be in convincing the administration to provide some of the startup funds?

2. How important was it for the request for a health promotion program to come directly from students rather than faculty members?

3. How important was it for the hospital to be allowed to use the program for marketing purposes? Who should be involved in negotiating what the format of the marketing would be and how much would occur?

4. What were the relative advantages for the university in hiring a graduate assistant to be the first staff person?

5. What other strategies could have been used if the ones chosen had not been successful?

6. How important to future fund-raising strategies might it be to establish an advisory council with membership from various community health agencies and institutions?

7. Are there other strategies that might have worked?

CHAPTER 18

Planning

THE MANAGEMENT OF CHANGE

Leadership involves movement and change. Although occasionally change just happens, more often it results from careful planning. This is especially true of major change. Sometimes planned change is proactive; that is, steps are taken to make the business environment, the market, and the competition act differently. Sometimes it is reactive; that is, organizational changes are made to accommodate changes in the society, the environment, the market, and the competition.

Change may not be optional in situations that threaten the organization's survival. A major change in funding, a change in laws, or the resignation of a key administrator may force substantial organizational change. So, too, may the creation of new opportunities in the market. A chance to participate in the United Way or to secure a major corporate contract can dictate sudden growth. The demise of a competitor can make expansion into the competitor's old service area more than tempting.

More typical than spurts of rapid growth are the long periods during which an organization evolves in response to environmental change. To maintain a reactive posture, the organization needs to continually analyze the business climate and contemplate how it can become more competitive. Responding to changes in technology is one example. Generally speaking, lean organizations with flat organizational charts, a teamwork ethic, and fast internal communications will be more responsive, more flexible, and more innovative in responding to changes in the environment than the typical organization.

RESISTANCE TO CHANGE

While there are forces that precipitate change in an organization, there are also forces that resist change. These forces are not necessarily bad. In fact, they can be viewed as stabilizing agents that support the status quo and add strength. Programs of planned change are in part directed toward removing or weakening the restraining forces and creating or strengthening the forces that drive change. They also are directed toward identifying and accommodating valid reasons for resistance. It is usually not difficult to identify the forces that resist change. An hour's focused discussion among key administrators will usually suffice. The most commonly identified areas of resistance are the budget, the staff, and the organizational culture.

A change, especially a major change, can be expensive to implement. It may involve the purchase of technology, additional staff, consultants, training programs, and more. That is, of course, one reason why top managers need to be supportive of the change, preferably even leading it. They must be willing to shift funds in the budget, either permanently or at least for several years.

Providing the funds to implement a change is always easiest in a growing organization, where there are new dollars to allocate. However, this luxury is not typical, and even then there will be competing demands for each new dollar. More often, dollars for implementing changes will have to come from the cessation or reduction of certain activities. Budgets can be cut or held constant, or entire programs can be eliminated.

Cuts in a budget may or may not require staff changes. For example, a health department may choose to cut back on clinics and do more with schools. In this case, the change might simply require a reallocation of staff time. In other cases, a position may have to be eliminated in order to hire a qualified school health consultant. The elimination of the particular position might be justified by the planned cutting back of a program or it might be offered as a possibility by the incumbent's resignation or retirement. Financial changes nearly always involve staffing changes because personnel costs constitute a major part of most organizations' budgets—often as much as 80 percent.

Managers have to identify ways to finance change. For example, they can seek grants from organizations that support health promotion if an increase in health promotion services is the change being contemplated. However, they can also direct that dollars spent on health promotion will increase by at least 10 percent per year for 5 successive years. Similarly, they can direct that prevention services will receive 2 of every 10 clinic revenue dollars or that prevention services will increase from 3 percent of the agency budget to 10 percent of the agency budget. Setting such a goal gives both direction and lead time to phase in the budget shifts.

Another strategy sometimes used is to build into the budget a large contingency fund and then spend any unused amounts on implementing the technology plan or other agency priorities during the last quarter of the budget cycle. Similarly, it is possible to postpone filling vacant positions and to use the salary savings from, say, a 180-day vacancy for a significant project. Of course, a third solution is simply to build a line item into the budget to pay for a planned change.

Any combination of these and other strategies can work. The main point to keep in mind is that lack of money is a common barrier to change. It is one that must be addressed by the chief executive officer and eliminated early. The other point being made is that there are numerous strategies for financing change, any combination of which may create a window of opportunity.

ACTION-BASED CONCEPT

The financing of planned change must itself be carefully planned, and financing strategies must be identified early to remove lack of funds as an excuse for not taking the planning of change seriously.

Staffing is another common source of resistance to change. Some organizations are understaffed and thus their employees are overworked. In such organizations, each position is critical, and managers need to ensure that each position is structured so as to best achieve organizational objectives. Similarly, managers need to ensure that each position is filled by a productive person.

POWER, POLITICS, AND PERSONALITIES

Power, politics, and personalities are involved in many aspects of life. They often dominate decision-making in families and in all other organizations, regardless of size.

Politics is often about winning and holding control and resources. A familiar saying has it that "politics is the art of compromise," and certainly this saying does contain an element of truth. Compromise is often important in winning and gaining control, especially where teamwork is an important part of the organization's culture.

ACTION-BASED CONCEPT

Managers must be astute and diligent in analyzing the power structure, politics, and personalities of an organization, especially when planning change. Both formal and informal power structures play a role in organizational politics, and personalities usually dominate both power and political networks.

But politics is more about power, especially the balance of power. It is about control, about making decisions, and getting things done. Power is in and of itself neutral. It is the ability to produce an effect, to make things happen, to make a difference, to be influential. Hence, it is not wrong to seek power, or to use it, or to strive to maintain it. Indeed, it is an essential part of management.

Power can be used and abused. It can corrupt. It always has to be kept in check. Power can be possessed without being expressed. That is, people can choose to use their power or not use it.

Power struggles are an inevitable part of organizational change. Individuals use power and engage in politics differently. Some individuals are dominant, extroverted, abrasive, challenging, and even confrontational. Of course, they possess these qualities in varying degrees and some are only confrontational when they judge the situation demands it. Other individuals with power are less public. They sow discontent among the staff, work to develop a consensus on opposition strategies, and generally try to exert their influence—all in private.

Regardless of how individuals react to the possibility of change, it is important to anticipate and accommodate opposition to change. Change agents always need to expect opposition, identify its source, and analyze the motives of the opponents. Only through its anticipation can opposition to change be mitigated before it is expressed.

Although influential employees can and do identify with their organizations, their ultimate concern is usually for themselves. Any change that affects their prestige or lessens their influence will be viewed as threatening. Any change that is viewed as threatening becomes a source of fear and uncertainty. Employees in an organization undergoing a major change face the prospect of having to adjust to a new organizational structure and perhaps redesigned jobs. They may question their ability to learn necessary new skills or in other ways adapt. Fears about job security and job satisfaction create powerful barriers to change and often cause employees to band together and indirectly or directly resist change.

Strategies to offset resistance to change by powerful individuals always involve anticipating the source of and nature of the resistance. Reassurance may be helpful, if it can be done honestly. For example, publicly stating that only two positions will be changed and that retraining will be available for the two employees affected will probably allay fears. Candor in explaining the need for a particular change and the logic of the plan is a good strategy. Once persuaded of its advantages, some individuals will help implement the change. However, persuasion can be time-consuming and will usually not be totally successful, especially among the staunch opposition.

Another strategy is to ask members of the organization to help design the change. Generally, people who participate in creating a plan will be committed to implementing it. Yet another strategy is to give key individuals a desirable role in designing the plan or implementing it. Disbursing personal advantages can sometimes co-opt a potential source of resistance. Unfortunately, threatening job loss, transfer, or lack of promotion will sometimes be necessary. If this strategy is used, it needs to be used early, so as to neutralize the resistance before it is expressed. It can be risky as well. In particular, it can cause the individual to bring a lawsuit and can generate opposition from friends and allies.

ACTION-BASED STRATEGY

Resistance to change must be anticipated early in the change-planning process. The source of the anticipated resistance and the reasons for it must be identified. The change-planning process must include strategies for neutralizing resistance, preferably before it is expressed.

The earlier-mentioned strategies should be used when resistance is minor. This last strategy should only be used if the resistance is anticipated to be major. Some organizations are staid and simply resistant to change. Usually in this type of organization the manager has been in place for a long time and any changes that occur are viewed as fine-tuning. Very likely, most changes are made without being debated or announced publicly.

A manager coming into such an organization will often need to change the culture of the organization into one more change-oriented. Citing suggested readings that emphasize how fast the world is changing can be helpful, as can inserting quotes in the staff newsletter. Staff development activities can focus on change in the community and how best to respond to it. One or two staff changes at the senior management level will also significantly alter the organizational culture.

MODELS OF CHANGE

There are numerous planned change strategies, but most of these are covered by two broader philosophies of change: the evolutionary approach and the revolutionary approach.

Evolutionary Change

The evolutionary approach is commonly used by organizations with leadership stability. These organizations have the luxury to plan long term and can construct

5-year goals and the incremental steps to achieve them. Planned evolutionary change usually requires a leader with a vision—someone who is persuasive and even somewhat charismatic. To successfully implement the change, the leader must often articulate his or her vision, keeping the vision and the interim steps in front of everyone else in the organization.

For example, a substance abuse treatment agency that has focused on treatment of recovering alcoholics can evolve over time into a comprehensive substance abuse treatment and prevention agency. The organization's planning team can identify completion of such a transformation as a 5-year goal, outline the requisite steps, prioritize them, and assign time frames for their accomplishment. Budget shifts, personnel shifts, revision of organizational structure, changes in the organization's board, and even a name change can all be affected. The key will be to promulgate the vision and the steps needed to realize the vision.

This is not to say that evolutionary change cannot occur without a plan. Indeed, gradual change occurs constantly, as organizations respond to pressures and opportunities. However, unless there is a goal, opportunities can be missed and some steps may need to be undone.

The approach described above involves making a series of midcourse corrections to increase the likelihood of reaching a destination not yet clearly seen. It is somewhat like piloting a plane or ship and having to adjust direction occasionally so that the ultimate destination is reached.

Revolutionary Change

The revolutionary approach to change is often used when there is new leadership, a crisis, or a major new opportunity. During a crisis, organizational survival might depend on doing a lot of things differently. If there are fiscal difficulties, the organization may have to downsize, redesign its structure, and refocus on new goals. The equivalent of martial law might be imposed, with everything re-examined and, if necessary, redesigned.

More frequently, revolutionary change occurs when new leadership assumes control, such as a newly appointed administrator or a different board of directors. A change in leadership may also result from a merger. Regardless, a new senior officer is likely to push through a lot of changes very quickly.

The new administrator has a window of opportunity to make changes more easily than will be possible in the future. The initial period after a leader comes on board is sometimes called a "honeymoon period." The employees expect change and are usually eager to support the new leader in an attempt to win favor. Thus, it makes sense for the leader to spend a few weeks or months studying the organization and the community and then devise a written plan for improving the organization. A new focus, a new structure, a new decision-making process, or a whole host of other things might be part of the plan. Needless to say, if several major revisions are made more or less at once, the change will be seen as revolutionary rather than evolutionary.

If the leader can make a compelling case in favor of change and win the commitment of employees, the implementation of the plan is likely to be successful. However, it should be noted that planned change is stressful, especially for longtime employees. There may be denial, some anger, and some depression before acceptance. Often, approximately one third of the employees will support the new order enthusiastically, one-third will not accept the changes and will actively resist them, and the remaining one-third will be more passive and will tend to go with the flow.

ACTION-BASED CONCEPT

In pushing a set of changes, managers should support the one-third of employees who are advocates for change and should focus on the one-third who are open to change but not too sure about these particular changes. While they should address, in a limited way, the concerns of the one third who resist change, they can be assured that if the other employees are persuaded of the benefits of the changes, the resisters will usually be brought along.

PLANNED CHANGE PRINCIPLES

Revolutionary change occurs quickly and requires a decisive, persuasive leader to be effective. Mandates from a new leader can be all that is required, regardless of who has been involved. But after the honeymoon period, evolutionary change and a bottom-up type of planning become standard.

There are numerous group visioning processes that can be used, as well as processes for revising mission statements, establishing long-range goals, and so on. The specific format or process selected is not critical. The ultimate object is for a plan to emerge and evolve. There are however "four cornerstones" that help to assure success: vision, focus, quality improvement, and organizational learning.[1] As stated by Tom McIlwain and James Johnson,

> Vision is essential in creating a mental model that that can be articulated and shared with others to engage their support and participation. Focus is critical to concentrate the thought, energy, and resources needed to

accomplish the mission and goals. Quality improvement assures that the plan will address operations and client satisfaction as well as facilitate the use of data in decision making. Lastly, organizational learning is important.[2]

The process usually involves the solicitation of ideas from many people and coalescing of the ideas into a plan. The administrator should write the plan, selecting those ideas that are consistent with his or her vision and synthesizing them. The plan in draft form can then be discussed and revised as needed. Getting the participation of employees in the planning process is a good way of getting the employees to buy into the plan.

It is also important that the planners or planning team have the necessary supporting data, to keep the plan realistic. A data team can be formed to generate and analyze data that the planners require.

A useful planning principle is to plan for measurable outcomes. If the outcomes are not measurable and measured, success will be impossible to document. Measuring success and reporting it widely is an important strategy to use in broadening the base of support. If there is external funding, it is likely that measurable outcomes will be required. (The *Healthy People 2010* series of reports includes excellent examples of measurable outcomes.)

There are numerous popular planning models that can be used, and no single planning model is advocated here. Most models will have a diagnostic element, a design element, and an evaluation element; there will usually be a timetable established for each phase.

ACTION-BASED CONCEPT

Any plan that is developed must have measurable objectives and a time frame for achieving each one. Other plan elements can be included as necessary.

CONCLUSION

The administrator or manager often sets the pace for change and fosters the design of a process. Of course, the process used will depend on how fast organizational change needs to occur. Revolutionary change is more likely top-down managed and mandated, while evolutionary change is more of a bottom-up planned process involving the broader organization. In any change effort, the manager must be an articulate, consistent advocate for organizational change and its envisioned goals.

IN-BASKET ASSIGNMENT

TO: Health Education and Health Promotion Specialists
FROM: The Director
RE: Planning Models

We are developing an agency planning process. I understand there are several models that are commonly used in health education and health promotion.

I have heard about PERT, Precede, Proceed, PATCH, and others. What are they? Are they appropriate for doing agency-wide planning or just for developing educational programs?

I would like a brief synopsis of these and other models, followed by a meeting to discuss them.

Thank you!

MANAGEMENT CASE STUDY

Setting

A large rural health department in a Midwestern state served 11 counties, nearly a third of the state. Budgets had to be approved by the 11 county commissions. Each commission appointed one of its commissioners to serve on the board of health.

Problem

The agency did not have a formal planning process and was struggling with technology issues, funding changes, and so on. The board of health directed the administrator to develop a formal long-range planning process and to report back on her progress in 60 days.

Alternatives Considered

The administrator decided to make a few phone calls to her counterparts in other regional rural health departments but found this to be unproductive. They were not doing formal long-range planning.

Another alternative explored was to bring in a consultant to design and facilitate a planning process. A couple more phone calls put the project price tag in the range of $10,000 to $30,000, depending on how complicated the process was and how long it took to implement it.

The final alternative considered was to read some materials on planning and develop a process that could be implemented by existing staff.

Actions Taken

The administrator asked for 3 of the 11 board members to help her design the process, thinking that the process would more likely be approved if it came from and was presented by board members.

A one-page plan for developing the process was presented to the three-member subcommittee. The steps included goal setting by the subcommittee, the development of a form to help generate suggestions from employees, the preparation of a draft to be discussed by the 11-member board of health, a mailing of the draft out to all employees for review and comment, a revision of the draft to incorporate recommendations, final review, and adoption by the board. Deadlines were established for each step 30 days or less in duration.

OUTCOME

The subcommittee modified the plan but only slightly. One of the subcommittee members presented the plan to the board of health, which adopted it without changing it.

The administrator then proceeded to implement the plan. Within a year, a fully developed, formally adopted planning process was in place, and it was used to fashion the budget requests that went to the 11 county commissions.

DISCUSSION QUESTIONS

1. What elements in the administrator's strategy were probably most responsible for the success?

2. Would this type of planning process be most likely to produce evolutionary change or revolutionary change?

3. What were the advantages of having the administrator write the plan's various drafts?

4. What were the advantages of involving all employees rather than just the members of the board of health?

5. How often would such a planning process likely need to be repeated?

6. Are there other strategies that might have been used effectively?

NOTES

1. A. O. Kilpatrick and J.A. Johnson, *Handbook of Health Administration and Policy* (New York: Marcel Dekkar, 1999).

2. T. McIlwain and J.A. Johnson, "Strategy: Planning, Management, and Critical Success Factors", in A. O. Kilpatrick and J.A. Johnson, *Handbook of Health Administration and Policy* (New York: Marcel Dekkar, 1999): 642.

CHAPTER 19

Marketing and the Media

CRITICAL ROLE OF MARKETING AND THE MEDIA

Most managers, administrators, and leaders need to understand the basics of marketing and working with the media. Indeed, entire marketing courses are commonly required in graduate-level management programs. There are numerous reasons for this. First, if an organization is not marketed adequately, it will likely run into financial difficulties. The image of the organization will also be affected, and jobs may be at stake, including the manager's.

In the case of a health education agency, there is a more basic reason than image or jobs to develop an effective marketing program. When marketers are promoting dish soap, little or no social significance is attached to customer decisions. However, when the issue is whether to control one's weight, stop smoking, reduce one's intake of fat, exercise regularly, or engage in other healthy behaviors, great benefits can accrue to the individual and society. Accordingly, marketing to increase participation becomes especially important.

The social cost of *not* marketing should not be underestimated. In a very real sense, any organization exists only by public consent. If people do not support a worthwhile organization, it will not survive. Unfortunately, it is not unusual for a small health promotion organization to be created, struggle along for a year or so, and fade away. The media will not cover the demise of the organization and the public will not mourn its passing because very few people even knew it existed. Similarly, if the public is opposed to an organization, adverse publicity can destroy it. An example is an AIDS prevention program that focuses on safe sex rather than on abstinence. For this type of program, marketing and media plans have to be carefully developed, because many in the community will choose to believe the agency is advocating premarital or extramarital sex.

The continued existence of a community health promotion agency depends on its being perceived as making a contribution to the community. If it is viewed as only serving a few people, and those not very well, or if the public's opinion is that the clients could be better served elsewhere, the issues are different. Either more people need to be served better or the agency's programs need to be better promoted so that its image improves. It is essential to pay attention to perceptions, because people act on perceptions and beliefs, even if they are wrong.

Managers, especially upper-level managers, also need to recognize that they are viewed as spokespersons for the organization by the media, various community groups, the agency's clients, and the agency's employees. Managers are always "on stage," and always represent the organization, whether at work or off work. If the managers are perceived as effective, the organization will usually be perceived as effective. Conversely, the halo surrounding a highly regarded organization will often extend to its managers.

Managers usually have "sign-off" responsibility for promotional campaigns, campaign themes, and campaign budgets. Additionally, the head administrator or another manager would typically serve as the spokesperson for a campaign. Knowledge of marketing will help the manager succeed in this role.

Managers control the budget for marketing and other agency programs, and, depending on budgetary flexibility, significant amounts of money might be able to be moved into a marketing budget at a manager's say-so. Managers need to know something about marketing, since there is always the danger that money wasted on expensive, yet ineffective, marketing programs could have been better spent elsewhere.

Finally, managers need to understand the basics of marketing because they might have to plan and implement marketing programs and campaigns. A small agency—one with a dozen or fewer employees—will not have the luxury of hiring a marketing specialist. It might decide to hire a marketing or media consultant on a part-time basis, but it more likely will assign a committee, often composed largely of volunteers, to the task of developing a marketing program. In such situations, managers often are charged with providing direction and oversight and even working with the media and writing or proofreading copy.

BASIC MARKETING AND PUBLIC RELATIONS

Marketing in a health promotion agency can occur at several levels. Obviously, the agency itself needs a public relations program. Public relations is first and foremost concerned with images and with improving people's opinion of a program or organization. Whatever the source of its funding, a health promotion agency must have a good public image.

Marketing, however, is more concerned with programs and products than with how people feel about an agency. It starts with determining what people want, need, and are willing to pay for. The goal of studying the market is to find a suitable market niche and then to tailor programs to fit that niche.

Marketing, besides being used to design programs, can also be used to promote them. A worksite program in stress management may need to be marketed. Some of its elements may need marketing as well. A workshop on conflict management or a series of lunch break meditations will likely have to be promoted if they are to attract interest.

Product marketing might even be needed. Tee shirts, water bottles, and gym bags are among the products that can be sold to provide daily reminders to clients, increase public awareness, and create opportunities for word-of-mouth advertising.

Marketing strategies for polishing an organization's image differ from the type of strategies used to market a program or program element or product. And a whole other kind of marketing is used to promote safe behaviors, such as the use of seat belts or the avoidance of drinking and driving. The purpose of social marketing is to change the public's attitude regarding a social issue, such as secondhand cigarette smoke, along with people's behavior.

Because the various kinds of marketing strategies are very different, developing a comprehensive marketing plan and implementing it is a time-consuming, expensive process. However, if done properly, marketing generates far more revenue than it costs. As advertising agencies state, advertising doesn't cost—it pays! The caveat that needs to be added is that it only pays if the marketing plan is done well and implemented carefully. A corollary to this is that, in times of budget cuts, it is usually not wise to cut advertising budgets. They should, if possible, be increased, at least if the agency has the potential to increase revenues through expanding its clientele or increasing the amount of services it provides.

Another fundamental point to keep in mind is that marketing is not done in a vacuum. Attention must be given to the environment, especially the competition. Community problems, demographics, the availability of similar services elsewhere, and other factors can affect marketing plans. A retirement community might readily support a senior aerobics program, but suppose a good one already exists. There might still be room for a water aerobics program.

Similarly, how programs are marketed is important. For example, in a retirement community, a general first-aid course might be a hard sell, but a course entitled "First Aid for Grandparents" or "What You Can Do When Someone You Love Has a Heart Attack" could pull in a large enrollment.

Keeping track of the competition is critical. The main competition for a given program is not always a similar program. The competition for a Monday night aerobics program in a retirement community may well be bingo.

It is important to know as much as possible about the price and nature of competing programs. Ideally, managers should know as much about competing programs as they do about their own programs, at least from a customer appeal perspective. They need to understand why some people choose their program and why some choose their competitors' programs. Although some things cannot be changed, it may be feasible to enhance their program's competitive advantage.

Hopefully it is obvious by now that marketing is customer (client) oriented, first, last, and always. Although marketing and public relations overlap greatly, a useful distinction is that marketing is customer focused and public relations is organization focused. The emphasis for administrators should be on marketing, finding out what the community wants and providing it.

Both public relations and marketing rely heavily on communication, and four communication-related tasks are particularly useful:

1. **Identifying and assessing the target groups**. As discussed earlier, marketing often occurs at several levels, so there will be several target groups. Public awareness campaigns may have one target group, while fund-raising may have another. Marketing for new clients likewise could be directed at multiple groups. A program for cardiac patients, for example, may target the patients themselves, their doctors and nurses, and their children. Needless to explain, the strategies for getting doctors and nurses to refer patients are very different from strategies for getting patients to self-enroll.

ACTION-BASED CONCEPT

Every marketing plan should be group specific. Identification of multiple target groups and development of group-specific marketing strategies are important.

Target groups should be as narrowly defined and as homogeneous as possible. For example, the group of cardiac patients might be subdivided based on age, gender, ethnic background, socioeconomic status, employment, or retirement status.

2. **Identifying the most effective message senders and communication channels for each target group**. Message senders or givers need to be selected with care. Generally, they need to be viewed as credible by the target group before the message is sent; otherwise it is likely to be ignored.

Who contacts whom is critical, whether the contact is in person or by way of the media. People often respond best to peers. Thus, if a doctor can be convinced to approach colleagues about referrals, success is more likely than if a manager bids for referrals.

The selection of channels is likewise important. It is preferable to use existing channels of communication. For example, cardiac patients could be reached by placing marketing materials in the waiting rooms of cardiologists and clinics and in pharmacies. Similarly, retirement center newsletters and bulletin boards could be useful for getting the message to seniors.

ACTION-BASED CONCEPT

When attempting to communicate with individuals or groups, it is usually most effective to use the communication channels they normally use, and to use peers in the process.

---

3. **Identifying specific messages for each target group**. Messages need to be carefully considered and may vary depending on the stage of the campaign. Messages designed to create interest or awareness, for example, are usually very different from those that are designed to generate action.

    Focus groups can provide an inexpensive way to generate specific messages for target groups, although other market research techniques can also be helpful.

4. **Constructing a calendar for the public relations program**. Some campaigns are season specific (e.g., "Will you be satisfied with your appearance in a swim suit next month?"). In all campaigns the critical element is timing, and the timing and repetition of messages must be carefully planned. Media representatives can help managers plan the timing of messages so as to maximize impact. Repetition is particularly important for new organizations, which need to establish name recognition.

DEVELOPING A MARKETING PLAN

Using the basic concepts presented above, it should be relatively easy to put together a public relations and/or marketing plan—one that is agency focused, program focused, or product focused or has a combination of focuses. The important thing is to develop a written plan that reflects the best thinking of key people in the agency. Although the elements or subtitles of the plan can vary, the essential pieces of the plan are those described below.

Goals and Objectives

From the outset, it is important to be very clear about what the desired outcomes are and to state them in measurable terms. For example, one goal of a public relations program might be to "increase public awareness of the family planning agency." Specific objectives might be to

(1)   increase public knowledge of the agency location,
(2)   increase public knowledge of client eligibility factors,
(3)   increase public knowledge of available family planning services, and
(4)   increase the number of clients by 10 percent.

These goals can be measured, but some form of data gathering is required to establish baseline data and, in the case of goals 1 through 3, current levels of awareness. Goal 4 is a straightforward goal, and gathering the baseline data and subsequent data would be relatively easy. Goals and objectives can be very elaborate or very simple. The key is to develop a consensus on what is to be accomplished and ensure the goals are largely measurable.

Target Groups

Specifying who a program is designed to serve is an essential step in the creation of a marketing plan. For example, is it pregnant teens who are intended to receive infant and child health services, or is it pregnant teens still in school? Or is it the teachers, counselors, doctors, or parents of pregnant teens who are to be targeted?

Messages

What is the current orientation of each of the target groups? What messages are most needed and in what sequence? Are there inaccurate beliefs that need to be dispelled? Are there obstacles to action that need to be addressed?

Channels

What communication channels are already used by the target groups? If pregnant teens are the target group, do they read the school paper, listen to an afternoon rock radio show, or periodically check the healthy teens bulletin board? Perhaps the message should be put on a billboard near the school parking lot. A story on the evening news or an article in the city newspaper will be missed by most teens, but they would likely catch the attention of parents of teens. Specifying where to advertise or promote a program is essential.

Budget

Having enough money available for the campaign will be critical—and it might seem as if there could never be enough. The difficulty of raising funds means that every available dollar must be used wisely. The budget plan should be a year long in scope, because good planning will often entail a year-long schedule of media use, perhaps with peaks and valleys. And the budget should cover the planning of research and development as well as the campaign itself, especially if it is a state or national campaign.

Tracking and Evaluation

Good marketing plans usually have a monitoring component. Perhaps the monitoring is restricted to a simple question or two asked of each new client: "How did you hear about our program," "Did our current recent radio campaign influence your decision to come to our agency," or "Have you heard our current radio ads?" If some sort of monitoring device is not built in, the organization will not know if its marketing was effective and should be repeated, or if it was a waste of time and money, and should be scrapped.

Media Selection Factors

Choosing what media to use is of course necessary. Cost is usually a consideration. Some marketing methods are free or low cost, such as the use of bulletin boards and fliers. Others can be free, such as getting an item in the newspaper, which costs nothing if the item is considered newsworthy or appropriate for a community bulletin board. Likewise, radio exposure can cost nothing if the radio station is willing to broadcast a public service announcement about the agency or program. Even television exposure can be free if a newsworthy event is scheduled and a local station is given enough time to assign a camera crew to cover it. Another strategy for gaining TV exposure is to arrange for someone from the agency to appear on a talk show.

Another important consideration is the set of media habits exhibited by the target group. If the goal is to reach senior citizens, it is necessary to find out what newsletters or newspapers they read, what radio or television programs they regularly tune in to, and so on. Obviously, it would not be appropriate to schedule a spot announcement on a hard rock radio station, but it might be appropriate to send an announcement to churches and to the local agency on aging for inclusion in its newsletters.

Yet another factor to consider is the predisposition of the target group toward the service or program. For example, if a message is simple and factual, such as the announcement of a flu shot immunization clinic, mass media may be appropriate. If the behavior being advocated is close to present practice or if the message is directed at those already predisposed to change, mass media would again be useful. For example, media announcements would have an effect on those used to getting flu shots or those who were already thinking about getting a flu shot but would probably fail to have much impact on seniors who had not had an immunization of any kind for years. Mass media also works better with more educated target groups. When working with groups lower on the socioeconomic scale, it is usually more effective to use face-to-face communication, going to group gatherings or into people's homes. Mass media also can work well if a one-time-only type action is being sought, such as "get a flu shot now," as opposed to "practice breast self examination each month." Again, the key element is to ascertain how people in the target group usually get health messages and feed the desired message into the preferred learning channel, or, better yet, use multiple methodologies.

Finally, the best type of communication channel to use depends on the familiarity of the target group with the behavior change being pushed. For example, if an agency wants to make people aware that a pneumonia immunization is now available, many types of media can be used. However, if the goal is to get senior women to schedule a Pap smear and breast examination, a face-to-face setting, where people can think about the message and have their questions answered, perhaps without even having to ask them, will be more effective. Exhibits 19–1 and 19–2 summarize the media selection criteria, and Exhibit 19–3 provides an AIDS-specific media selection guide that has been used successfully.

WORKING EFFECTIVELY WITH MEDIA PERSONNEL

A good personal working relationship with media personnel is the foundation of success. Achieving a good relationship is relatively easy, at least in small cities, because community leaders will be at common events from time to time. Making it a point to become acquainted and to converse as frequently as possible is worth the effort.

Dealing with media personnel in a professional manner is also critical, beginning with promptly returning calls and always being honest. Attempts at deception will usually be counterproductive. It is also helpful to learn what media people prefer—what formats they like, what deadlines they have, and what they consider newsworthy.

Exhibit 19–1 Communication Selection Criteria

Face-to-Face Communication

1. When message is complex
2. When behavior change is extensive
3. When target group has low educational level
4. When long-term attitude and behavior change is desired

Mass Media Communication

1. When message is simple and factual
2. When change is minor or message is directed at those already motivated to change
3. When target group has high educational level
4. When desired changes are short term

Exhibit 19–2 Matching Communication and Behavior Change Strategies

Behavior Change Strategy	*Preferred Communication Strategy*
Create awareness of a health practice	Mass media exposure
Stimulate interest in behavior change	Mass media exposure
Evaluate behavior change	Face-to-face communication
Stimulate trial of new behavior	Face-to-face communication
Stimulate adoption of behavior change	Face-to-face communication
Reinforce behavior change	Mass media exposure and face-to-face communication

Exhibit 19–3 AIDS Education Methods

Method	Target Group	Advantages	Disadvantages
Television and radio, public service announcements, news coverage, feature presentations	All	Reaches the broadest segment of the target population; can direct audience to other sources of information; radio messages can reach more specific target groups	Information may be insufficiently detailed for particular target groups
Newspapers, feature stories, news coverage, advertisements	All	Provides greater detail than radio or TV; newspapers that serve specific audiences permit targeted messages	Does not reach as many persons in each group
Posters, billboards, bus posters, public facilities	All	Can reach specific target population; can direct audience to additional sources of information and complement other methodologies by reinforcing various messages	Provides only limited amount of information
Brochures and fliers, inserts in utility bills, health care facilities, workplace	All	Messages can be individualized	May be less effective for some target groups, like prostitutes and IV drug abusers

Newsletters and journals, organization newsletters, AIDS update newsletter	Health workers, community leaders, risk population	Messages can be individualized; detailed and complex messages can be sent to segments of the public	The larger the document, the less likely it is to be read
Resource materials, guidelines, curriculum materials, reprints, resource directories	Health workers, community leaders	Provides technical information to specific target groups	The longer the document, the less likely it is to be read
Presentations, community groups, health care facilities	General public, health workers, community leaders	Specific information tailored to the group addressed; can be interactive	Labor intensive; primarily information transfer only
Workshops, drug treatment centers, safer sex workshops	Increased risk groups, health workers	Provides detailed information and emphasizes skill development	Labor intensive
Outreach activities, bars, banks, bookstores, streets	Persons at increased risk (e.g., gay and	Provides one-on-one or peer group counseling to individuals at increased risk who are most	Very labor intensive

(continues)

Exhibit 19–3 (continued)

Method	Target Group	Advantages	Disadvantages
	bisexual men, IV drug abusers, prostitutes)	difficult to reach through other means	
Counseling and testing	Persons at increased risk	Provides one-on-one counseling to individuals attempting to adopt or sustain positive health behaviors	Very labor intensive
Referral of sex and needle-sharing partners	Partners of those at increased risk due to sexual activity or IV drug use	Can offer counseling and testing for very high risk people who have shared needles and syringes or who have had unsafe sex with infected persons and may not otherwise become aware of their risk status	Very labor intensive

Source: Reprinted from *Guidelines for AIDS Prevention Program Operations*, p. 12, U.S. Department of Health and Human Services, Public Health Service, Centers for Disease Control, 1987.

Media people often want press releases to be in standard format. This typically means the structure is an inverted pyramid, with the who, what, where, when, and why described in the first two or three sentences, followed by elaboration in succeeding paragraphs. This structure permits an editor to cut the story to fit the available space.

Press conferences often are problematic for health promotion agencies, especially small ones, and should normally be reserved for major events. A press conference requires the media people to organize their schedules to accommodate the event. Coverage is usually better if phone calls are made and invitations are extended. It is embarrassing to hold a press conference and not have anyone come.

When working with the media, a few basics should be kept in mind. Blue shirts are usually preferred over white on video footage, and blouses or ties with a minimum of pattern are also more photogenic. Leaning forward a little while on camera creates a better appearance than leaning back, and projecting one's voice and speaking confidently is also important. An organization should know the message it wants to emphasize and organize relevant facts before making any contact with the media.

CONCLUSION

Using marketing and the media effectively is essential. A planned, orderly approach to program development and program marketing will pay huge dividends. The media can be used to reach great numbers of people, but just because a message is presented in the media does not mean anyone will pay attention to it. Fortunately, getting one's message across need not be a complicated process. Familiarity with the basics discussed in this chapter will usually suffice, along with judicious use of consultants when appropriate. Regardless of the background of the administrator, marketing and media strategies are too important to ignore. Reading a marketing book or two is usually worth the effort for those who feel the need for more knowledge. The newer materials on social marketing are especially helpful.

IN-BASKET ASSIGNMENT

TO: Health Education and Health Promotion Specialists
FROM: The Director
RE: Social Marketing

I have been hearing a lot about social marketing. What is it and how does it relate to health promotion?

Should we be doing some of it? If yes, what can we do for starters?

Please give me a memo with responses to these questions by Monday.

MANAGEMENT CASE STUDY

Setting

A small free-standing city health department employed about two dozen persons. They decided to conduct an employee wellness program using a modest startup budget of $1,000.

Problem

Despite an announcement placed in the newsletter, only 2 of the 24 employees came to the first activity. The manager decided that a public relations approach was not working and that they would use other more market-oriented strategies instead.

Alternatives Considered

The manager considered having representatives of the three divisions serve on a planning committee.

She also considered developing a checklist of areas and activities of interest to be used in a survey of employees.

Finally, she considered investigating how other area employee wellness programs obtained employee participation.

Actions Taken

The manager formed the planning committee, which she chaired. The committee's first task was to contact three area wellness programs and ascertain how they fostered participation.

They learned that a combination of strategies were used: involving employees in deciding what the activities would be, holding activities during work hours, making them fun, providing incentives, providing lots of choices, and publishing frequent reminders.

The steering committee decided to hold three events per year (one planned and conducted by each division). There would be a catered lunch for the staff of the division that planned and conducted the activity with the most participation.

The health department also offered to cover up to $25 in fees for employees to participate in educational or clinical events sponsored by a local hospital. The hospital agreed to place health department employees on its mailing list. (Making it easier to participate in hospital-sponsored events was viewed as one way of meeting the special needs of employees that might not warrant an in-house event.)

OUTCOME

At the end of the year, all employees had participated in at least two of the three events planned by the divisions, and most had participated in all three. The nursing division won the catered lunch. About a third of the employees participated in one or more of the hospital-sponsored events.

DISCUSSION QUESTIONS

1. What were the advantages of having each division plan an event? Was the catered lunch incentive important to the success of the program?

2. What marketing elements are evidenced in the approach used?

3. How important was the element of fun?

4. Would it likely have been as effective to subcontract the wellness program to one of the other employee wellness programs in the city?

5. Are there other strategies that might have been used effectively?

CHAPTER 20

Program Evaluation

A MANAGEMENT PERSPECTIVE

Managers are held accountable for results. They are held accountable by boards of directors, by funding agencies, by the media, and by the public.

The community that fiscally supports a health education or health promotion agency and uses its services wants to know how the services compare with those of other agencies. They also want to know if they got good value for money spent (i.e., whether extravagance and waste were prevalent).

Courts may want to know whether services were appropriate, on both an individual and collective basis. Court investigations usually arise because of a suit brought by a disgruntled patient. As a result of the focus on quality and appropriateness, most administrators and health educators no longer consider evaluation to be optional. They feel obligated to determine what has been accomplished, in part because they never know when their agency will be challenged to prove it is doing what it purports to do and is doing it well.

When a media representative is on the telephone or when a subpoena has been received or a deposition has been scheduled, it is usually too late to generate needed data. The better strategy is to anticipate what may be needed periodically and to generate it routinely and have it readily available. Of course, those who have taken courses in college or received training as a professional are usually already convinced that evaluation is essential. Additionally, the government and many foundations mandate the use of evaluation mechanisms, as does the profession's growing research agenda. Program evaluation is no longer an option or a luxury.

> ### *ACTION-BASED CONCEPT*
>
> *Managers should anticipate what questions will be posed about the adequacy of their programs, and should design evaluation plans to gather and summarize data that will readily address these concerns.*

AN EDUCATOR'S PERSPECTIVE

Professionals constantly make judgments about programs, whether their own or those of others. Such judgments are subjective opinions that may reflect personal biases. Judgments are not usually quantified. The feelings or impressions may be vague and undefined or strong and focused. The judgments may prove to be useful in future program planning or may be so biased or vague as to be useless.

When quality assurance and accountability gained ascendancy in health planning, evaluation became imperative. Judgments had to be moved from the subjective realm to the objective realm and evaluation had to become systematic so that the results would be more meaningful and therefore more useful in planning. Evaluation has always been an important planning tool, but its value increases when it is objective and systematic.

CHARACTERISTICS OF USEFUL PROGRAM EVALUATION

Evaluation should be non-threatening. Program planners should be creative, positive, and forward looking. Regardless of how well a program has been or is being done, it probably could have been more effective with more input during the planning process and indeed probably can still be improved. Learning from experience and recognizing that hindsight is better than foresight are part of the philosophy of evaluation. Stated differently, evaluation implies a willingness to change, a desire to improve. When viewed in this light, it will probably not appear threatening.

Evaluation studies can be done for reasons besides improvement. Funding agencies may want to know if funding should be continued. Administrators may want to know if a different programmatic emphasis would be more effective. Even in such circumstances, evaluation should be treated as providing an opportunity to improve a program as it develops and to measure success, not failure.

Evaluation requires sound planning skills and a commitment not to manipulate the results. Although evaluators often can manipulate the results of a study to show a desirable outcome, it is not ethical to do so. Evaluators need to use planning skills wisely in order to avoid even the appearance of duplicity.

Program directors should not cover up failures with biased, unobjective appraisals. They need to resist the temptation to select for evaluation only those program elements that appear to be successful. It is important to be comprehensive so as not to give the appearance of shifting attention from an essential part of the program that has failed to a minor part that is successful.

Evaluation also has to be timely. It can be postponed or delayed to allow concerns to dissipate over time. Also, political ends can be served by attempting to make a program look effective. Whether a program succeeds or fails, those who are involved are partisans. The evaluator and the evaluation design must show evidence of not being partisan if the results are to be credible.

Program evaluators ideally are devoid of political motives. Personal considerations sometimes do emerge. A program director may be afraid of looking ignorant about evaluation because of lack of experience. The director may be concerned that the program will be disrupted while evaluation is occurring, especially if the results are unfavorable. Another possible fear is that differing views of program objectives will be brought into the open.

An organizational climate that supports evaluation will motivate program directors to measure past success and investigate reasons for that success. Factors contributing to such a climate include organizational backing, adequate resources for evaluation, evaluation knowledge and skills, and realistic expectations.

A PROGRAM EVALUATION FOCUS

An important issue concerns who will be reading the evaluation report and what emphasis should be given to what points of view. A variety of audiences exist, with some overlap, but expectations of primary audiences are a major determinant of evaluation strategies.

In grant applications, the evaluation design usually has to be specified. The adequacy of the evaluation design may well be a primary factor in the decision to fund a project. A sophisticated evaluation plan needs to be spelled out in the grant proposal, and the plan, including the time schedule, must be adhered to completely. If money is being made available for a demonstration project, the plan should describe how the demonstration project's success will be measured and replicated on a more widespread basis.

Evaluation is also an important consideration for health promotion personnel in all situations in which others are making budgetary decisions on health education programs. In health departments, hospitals, and many other settings, health educators do not make the final decision on their budgets. Furthermore, health education budget requests usually compete for scarce resources with requests from other divisions. Administrators and budget committees respond more favorably to budget requests that are documented. Evaluation data indicating what was accomplished are impressive to such administrators and may be used to maintain a budget in an era of inadequate and shifting resources.

Even if funding is secure and evaluation data are not demanded, astute program directors should still be doing evaluation studies. The fiscal climate of any agency can change rapidly. A rapid change in the nation's inflation rates, a change in the fiscal health of an agency funding source, failure to obtain renewal of a major grant, and a change in the administrative superstructure of an agency can all result in the necessity to justify a program's existence. Unfortunately, in these cases, appropriate data cannot always be gathered quickly, and health educators who cannot document the effect of their programs may find that there is simply not enough time to do the studies. Demise of a program for lack of data would be especially tragic in such a case because more foresight in planning evaluation studies could have saved the program.

Health educators often are employed by agencies that are accountable to the public. Board members, trustees, or others representing political bodies or the public at large may demand evaluation data. It is good strategy to provide such data, whether demanded or not. Data constitute evidence that can be used to justify programmatic decisions by these bodies and may have publicity value.

Evaluation data may not be required by superiors but may be collected and made available to the media. Because people are interested in health education and in public accountability, the media is usually interested in related information. If a health educator can show a decrease in the incidence of problem pregnancies, for example, the media might be willing to base a story on this piece of information.

Educators in agencies that need public support should be especially sensitive to the news value of evaluation data. Those working in voluntary agencies or hospitals that cultivate major donors need to be concerned about informing potential donors of the impact of health education programs. Similarly, many programs depend on public awareness to increase their number of clients. Evaluation data made available to the community through the media or other sources can increase the visibility of a program and generate new clients.

In addition to the above reasons, health educators need evaluation data because they should know how they are doing and what they are accomplishing. One important element of professionalism is the desire to do the most possible and the best possible even with limited resources. Collecting evaluation data is one way of determining what has been accomplished and what changes might lead to improvement. This reasoning can be extended to argue that health educators should evaluate their efforts professionally. Indeed, many consider it unethical to fail to do so.

At least one other audience exists for evaluation data—professional colleagues. Health educators and agency managers need to learn from one another if they are to maximize their impact. A good way to increase the knowledge of other health educators is to read published evaluation studies.

Ideally, the needs of several groups can be incorporated in an evaluation design, especially if each group receives a separate report that is slanted to its particular needs. However, those planning the evaluation studies must find out who the studies are being done for, what the group or groups want to know, and what uses will be made of the data so that these needs have a reasonable chance of being met. For example, program participants might want data on program effectiveness, the governing board might want data on average program costs, program directors may want to know how the program can be improved, and funding agencies may want all the above information and more.

Once it has been determined who wants the evaluation data and what they want to know, one of several common responses can be made. Such responses are best examined in the context of a discussion of types of evaluation studies.

FORMATIVE EVALUATION

One of the main reasons for doing an evaluation study is to help develop a new program or improve an old one. Evaluation oriented toward improvement is usually built into the formative stages of a project. The process of continually performing and utilizing evaluation studies is sometimes called a feedback loop because feedback is continually provided to the program director to enable him or her to make adjustments that will improve the program. The evaluator may be the program director (or developer) or, if not, someone who must work collaboratively with the program director.

Formative evaluation is concerned with monitoring programs in their early stages. For a given program, it may include a needs assessment of the target group, the development of a consensus on goals, or an assessment of client reactions to the services that have been provided. Although formative evaluation is usually oriented toward uncovering problems that need immediate attention, it also includes retrospective review of the processes used in planning and implementing a program. For example, staff members or others could review together whether enough people were involved in planning or whether the addition of key individuals would have improved the database and the planning process. Similarly, an assessment could be made of the adequacy of media coverage, the time schedule, or any problematic areas in program implementation. Analyzing problems to determine what might have prevented them from occurring provides useful information when developing similar future programs. Because the emphasis is on data that are useful immediately, sophisticated research designs are not necessary for formative studies.

SUMMATIVE EVALUATION

Many individuals and groups are interested in knowing what was accomplished by a program, either at its end or after some interval (e.g., the end of the year). Policy makers and funding agencies are especially interested in data on achievements. Summative evaluation usually focuses on whether goals and objectives have been accomplished. Often evaluators work independently of program developers to avoid research bias. It is not usually necessary to contract with outsiders to do the evaluation. Program developers can and often do conduct credible program evaluation studies by involving several persons in the process and by making a concerted effort to avoid bias in the design of the studies and in the final reports. Summative evaluation studies require a more sophisticated research design than do formative evaluation studies. They also require more time, effort, and resources to implement.

EVALUATION QUESTIONS

An important early step in planning evaluation studies is to formulate evaluation questions. If desired, the questions may be stated as hypotheses. Hypothesis testing is an acceptable but optional method of evaluation. For beginners, it is easier and more effective to formulate questions that are to be answered. The questions should be specific and focused on the project to be evaluated. They should be written and rewritten until a consensus is reached that indeed these are the questions that need to be answered. Preferably, an evaluation committee or those involved with program design and implementation should help formulate the questions. It is important to determine if the questions to be asked are appropriate, necessary, inclusive, objectively stated, and so on.

In formative evaluation, questions can focus on effort and efficiency. For example, evaluators might want to know the following: Was there enough input from the target group to ensure the program was implemented in such a way that prospective participants were able to attend? Was there enough support from influential people? Was the timetable appropriate? Was media coverage adequate? Were locations appropriate? Were there enough dollars spent? Were time, effort, and funds expended efficiently?

Once the questions have been agreed on, the evaluation design can be finalized. Methods should be selected that will provide the needed data most efficiently. A comparison of data collection methods is presented in Table 20–1. Ease of use and cost are important variables in selecting methods. Sometimes simple, inexpensive methods are just as useful as those that are difficult and expensive.

The evaluation questions and possible methodologies for answering those questions should again be discussed by the planners to develop a useful design. For

Table 20–1 Comparison of Data Collection Methods

Method	Advantages	Disadvantages	Result Quality	State Requirements*	Costs
Person-to-person interview	High response rate Highly flexible Visual aid opportunity Community input and morale builder	High costs Raises expectations Travel expenses Possible interviewer bias Technical staff required High agency effort Possible computer needs High call-back expenses	Yields detailed and high-quality results Most representative results Quantifiable results	Technical assistance for interview construction Interviewer training Technical assistance for data analyzation processing and interpretation	High
Telephone interview	Easy to administer Low call-back expense Community input and morale builder High response rate Relatively low cost	Possible interviewer bias Possible computer needs Raises expectations Representativeness and sampling problems	Quantifiable results Relatively quality results Unless corrected, some bias in results Fairly detailed results	Interviewer training Several interviews Possible technical assistance for data analyzation Technical assistance for interview construction	Medium

(continues)

Table 20–1 (continued)

Method	Advantages	Disadvantages	Result Quality	State Requirements*	Costs
Mail-out question-naire	Low cost Minimum staff time Possible good response Larger outreach	Generally low return rate Possible bias and unrepresentative-ness	Quantifiable results Low to medium quality Possible major bias	Technical assistance for questionnaire construction If hand-processed, one or two	Low

*These were state requirements for California in 1976.

Source: Reprinted with permission from *Social Needs Assessment Handbook*, p. 115, League of California Cities, © 1976.

example, if only a few people are involved, an evaluation team may decide to interview them or send them an open-ended questionnaire. If a larger group is involved, a rating scale may be devised to quantify responses. Respondents would then check whether they agree or disagree (or strongly agree, agree, are neutral, disagree, or strongly disagree) with various statements. Other labels could be used on such a five-point scale, and frequencies, percentages, means, and ranges can all be used to summarize the data.

Formative studies are relatively easy to do and can yield useful information if done carefully. The results of a formative study should be summarized in writing, with conclusions and recommendations; distributed to appropriate individuals or groups; and filed for future use. The results should be readily accessible to facilitate their use in improving the program, which is the primary reason for doing process evaluation.

Questions focusing on outcomes are also an important part of program evaluation. A significant amount of effort can be expended on a program—and quite efficiently—with little result. Program objectives are essential to this phase of designing an evaluation study and should be stated in measurable terms. If objectives are not stated or not quantified, an important first step is to develop or rewrite them. The basic set of evaluation questions should determine whether the program objectives are being or have been accomplished and, if so, by what percentage of the participants. Questions like these should be asked: "How many clients are managing stress appropriately? How many have stopped smoking? How many are practicing breast self-examination?" Specific criteria are necessary to evaluate an outcome. For example, how many people practice breast self-examination at least every other month or, by self-report, indicate that they follow a sodium-restricted diet at least 75 percent of the time?

Inasmuch as health educators are behavior change specialists, outcome evaluation should determine whether behaviors have indeed changed. Some believe that the majority of efforts by practicing professionals should be devoted to this type of evaluation.

Impact evaluation is an especially difficult form of summative evaluation. Impact evaluation might focus on, for example, whether the incidence of disease or disorder was affected, hospitalizations were prevented, the length of stay shortened, the number of readmissions decreased, or health care costs reduced. Cost-effectiveness studies and other impact evaluation studies are relatively sophisticated and expensive and generally difficult to implement. They often are left to evaluation specialists, whether in agencies or universities. Sometimes graduate students undertake such studies as the means for getting their degrees, and a graduate student may be willing to conduct such a study for practicing professionals.

QUALITATIVE ASSESSMENT

Not all evaluation has to be quantified. Indeed, subjective opinion has always been a part of evaluation. However, qualitative evaluation can be more meaningful if it too is quantified. For example, planners' responses might vary over the question whether the planning process was effective. If they are asked to rate their opinions on a numerical scale, mean scores, ranges, and so on, can be easily computed. Qualitative assessment also can involve open-ended questions. It is possible to read all responses, list all responses in logical sequence, and assign a point value to each response. (Of course, qualitative evaluation does not need to be quantified to be useful.)

CONCLUSION

Evaluation studies can be easy or difficult to do. Some people enjoy doing such studies, whereas others dread them. Some evaluation data are useful, whereas other data seldom, if ever, get used. More and more emphasis is being placed on evaluation, and health promotion agency managers are expected to be able to do it.

No evaluation design is universally applicable, yet the principles of program evaluation must be understood and followed. If the principles are followed and the design takes into account the nature of the program and the purpose of the evaluation, the evaluation committee will usually be able to agree on a plan. Managers should be able to participate meaningfully in the process and should be able to implement the design, once formulated. But from a manager's perspective, the most important objective is to ensure that evaluation is likely to be useful and that the data will be available to answer the right questions at the right time.

IN-BASKET ASSIGNMENT

TO: Health Education and Health Promotion Specialists
FROM: The Executive Director
RE: Evaluation Instrument

Please develop a simple participant checklist that can be used in evaluating the educational component of the family planning clinic.

MANAGEMENT CASE STUDY

Setting

A coalition of community health agencies decided to do a fall educational and intervention activity blitz to get people to stop smoking. The leader of the coalition realized that the media, after spending effort promoting the events, would want to follow up on the results.

Problem

The need was to provide some immediate feedback to the media as well as some longer term data that could be used to attract funding support for a second campaign.

Alternatives Considered

One alternative considered was to subcontract with a consultant to design an evaluation plan.

Another alternative was to ask each agency to evaluate the activities they were responsible for and to report the results to coalition leaders within 48 hours after they occurred.

Another was to design a postcard-type questionnaire for a 6-month follow-up and a 1-year follow-up.

Another was to have coalition representatives conduct a staff meeting to evaluate the planning and implementation stages of the blitz.

Actions Taken

It was decided to have each of the agencies conduct an evaluation of the kind used in their own smoking cessation programs and to report the data quickly to the coalition, which would develop a summary for the media.

It was also decided to have the staff do an evaluation of the process used. A 6-month and 1-year postcard follow-up was also planned.

OUTCOME

The media reported the evaluation data, which resulted in additional media exposure. The percentage of people who attempted to stop smoking was above the national norm, although significant falloff was observed in the 6-month and 1-year evaluation data.

DISCUSSION QUESTIONS

1. Does the media have a right to report effectiveness data that make a program look ineffective?

2. How is it possible to skew the results of evaluation studies if one chooses to do so? Why is it unwise to do so?

3. Why are the 6-month or 1-year data more accurate impact indicators than data gathered on the last day of the clinic?

4. Would the evaluation scheme used be considered formative or summative or both?

5. What might the effect have been if the coalition had decided not to collect and report evaluation data?

6. How important was it to obtain and report the national norm?

7. Are there other strategies that might have been more effective?

NOTES

1. This chapter has been adapted from Chapter 25, "Evaluating Health Education Programs," in D.J. Breckon et al., *Community Health Education: Settings, Roles, and Skills for the 21st Century* (Gaithersburg, MD: Aspen Publishers, 1994).

2. A useful guide for the manager is M. Wurzbach, *Community Health Education and Promotion: A Guide to Program Design and Evaluation, 2nd ed.* (Boston: Jones and Bartlett, 2004).

CHAPTER 21

Technology and Information Systems

HISTORICAL PERSPECTIVE

Technology has played an increasingly large role in human affairs each decade since the Industrial Revolution. Indeed, technology is basically the application of scientific principles in the realm of manufacturing, and this is what spawned the Industrial Revolution. Of course, tools were used prior to the early 1800s, but the increase in the sophistication of the tools and machines since then is truly amazing.

The application of scientific principles made steam engines possible. Oil, gas, electricity, nuclear power, wind, and even the sun have now largely replaced steam as sources of energy.

The telegraph, telephone, radio, and television have changed the way people communicate. Copy machines and desktop publishing have changed the nature of printing. Eventually, digitizing pages and storing them in computers and storage devices may make printing unnecessary. E-mail and faxes are replacing ordinary mail.

Transportation, too, has changed. Automobile travel is nearly essential and air travel is commonplace. Trains and powered ships predated automobiles but now in the U.S. are largely relegated to transporting raw materials and manufactured products. Developments in the communications field, such as teleconferencing and the electronic transferring of voice, video, and data, have actually decreased the need to transport people.

In the area of computation, the abacus and slide rule have been replaced by calculators and computers. Computers have become the data analysis tool of choice, because they can process large volumes of data at ultra high speed and display the results in formats specified by the end user. Computers have also revolutionized the communications industry.

239

HOW MUCH IS ENOUGH?

Given the prevalence of technology in today's world, it of course has had a tremendous impact on management, and any book on management should discuss technology-related issues. It is not necessary, however, to get down to the level of specific equipment and applications. Unfortunately, there are still managers who need to learn how to use computers, e-mail, electronic databases, and other emerging high-tech tools.

One fundamental technology-related issue is, "How much is enough?" This is a simple question, and the simple answer is, "It depends." Managers know that times change, and that they must change, too, or be left behind. But the difficult task is to know which bridges to cross and which ones to burn.

ACTION-BASED CONCEPT

Managers should focus on how much technology is needed, how much is used by the competition, how much the staff is capable of using, and how much would be cost efficient.

An associated question is, "How much technology is needed?" The answer to that question is also, "It depends." It depends on how successful the enterprise is and what its growth pattern is likely to be. A small community-based organization has much different technology needs than a large one. An organization that has state, regional, national, and international components has still different needs. It depends on the nature of the services that are provided. An organization that provides physical therapy services has different needs than a substance abuse agency. It also depends on what the competition is doing. Most organizations compete for dollars, clients, volunteers, and so on. Whatever it takes for an organization to compete effectively is what is needed, and any amount less than this is not enough. It also depends on staffing. Some staffs are intimidated by technology, while others demand it. Some new hires will already be skilled in the use of high-tech equipment, while other staff members may refuse to learn how to operate it.

The amount of technology that is enough also depends on the budget. There is no point buying equipment that causes a financial crunch, especially if dollars are not available to train the staff in its use and otherwise support the technology. There is also a danger of purchasing equipment that is inadequate for the task or that is more sophisticated than is needed. The budget may not permit the hiring of consultants, and managers may have to rely on vendor consultants who are in reality sales representatives. Overbuying and then not using all the equipment's potential is a common management problem.

Technology can be seen as a "black hole"—more and more dollars are directed at a need that is never met. It can also be viewed as an opportunity to reduce personnel costs by doing things more efficiently. Buying high-tech equipment has seldom resulted in the reduction of personnel, but typically increases the efficiency and the productivity of employees (and ultimately can lead to the hiring of more employees as services expand).

It is obvious that there is no set answer to the question of how much is enough. Managers must consider the potential payoff of each dollar spent on technology. They should read extensively about relevant technological applications (at least one newsletter or journal that regularly discusses technological applications is a must), and they should also attend an appropriate trade show or conference each year. On top of these activities, questioning, evaluating, and thinking critically will help them determine their technology needs.

ACTION-BASED CONCEPT

Managers should read extensively about management information systems and other high-tech systems and equipment and should be conversant with the issues and the advantages and disadvantages of the various applications.

MASTER PLANNING

In small health organizations, reading, questioning, evaluating, and informal planning may be enough. However, in more complex organizations, a written technology and/or telecommunications master plan is usually recommended. Such a plan allows for incremental implementation. Moreover, it clearly specifies an end result and makes it more likely each piece will contribute to the achievement of that result.

The planning process is discussed in a previous chapter and will not be reviewed here. It will be merely noted that questions specific to technology should be addressed in the master plan (Exhibit 21–1 lists some of these questions).

Exhibit 21–1 Technology-Related Questions To Be Addressed by the Master Plan

_____ Does the organization's mission and vision statement articulate the role that information resources play in its programs and their degree of importance?

Comments:_____

_____ Does the organization address information resources in its strategic planning process or is a separate plan needed?

Comments:_____

_____ Does the organizationwide plan address voice, video, and data communication needs?

Comments:_____

_____ Does the planning process include participation by end users?

Comments:_____

_____ Does planning for facility expansion or remodeling always include discussion of telecommunication needs?

Comments:_____

_____ Do written policies adequately address access, security, copyright agreements, and client right to privacy?

Comments:_____

_____ Are sufficient staff resources and training available?

Comments:_____

_____ Are procedures and incentives in place to ensure that employees take advantage of training opportunities and utilize new technology?

Comments:_____

MANAGEMENT INFORMATION SYSTEM AND TELECOMMUNICATIONS PLANS

The technology and telecommunications master plan may in fact be referred to as a management information system (MIS) plan. Old MIS plans typically dealt with computer networks and reports, but with the advent of fiber optic cable, voice and video can flow along with data. In fact, equipment currently exists to permit video transmission on copper-based phone lines, and it is thus becoming commonplace for an MIS plan to address all forms of communication. Because many people still think of an MIS system as a data processing and reporting system, a new term, such as telecommunications master plan, may be more appropriate.

Another term increasingly used is decision support system. A decision support system is an intermediary between a management information system and telecommunications system. In a decision support system, end users are electronically provided whatever information they need to make decisions. A telecommunications system encompasses the provision of such information but also education, training, conferencing, and so on.

The process of creating a telecommunications system includes (1) a design phase, where the information needs are assessed, the objectives are established, and the plan is prepared (the essential ingredients of the plan are performance and cost factors); (2) an implementation stage, where the necessary facilities, equipment, and personnel are acquired and the staff is trained; and (3) an evaluation stage, where the system is tested. Sometimes a consultant is hired to create a plan for the agency, other times it is a staff function.

Fundamental principles of master planning include the following:

- Top management needs to be involved and supportive if the system is to be successful. Funds must be allocated, facilities might need remodeling, timetables need to be set, and so on.
- End users need to be involved in planning the system in order to get a learning head start and to gain ownership of the new system.
- Mandatory hands-on training must occur. After the new system has been implemented, it is pointless to have non-technological individuals using the old manual system.
- Keep it simple and phase it in. The system and the training must not seem so complex as to overwhelm people. Offer one-on-one help in a "mastery learning" approach to teaching.

BUDGETING FOR TECHNOLOGY

The high-tech aficionados in an organization will want the latest and best possible system, with all the "bells and whistles." They will often want to spend more than is available and may decry budget control efforts. Others may take the other extreme and argue that no new type of equipment is necessary or affordable. A realistic compromise is to establish a master plan, a realistic budget, and a time-table and to phase in the plan over more than one budget cycle, always planning for compatibility. A three-year plan will spread the cost over three budget cycles.

Another option is to lease rather than purchase equipment. This strategy not only spreads the cost but facilitates equipment upgrading. Equipment does wear out, but, more importantly, technology is changing so rapidly that a new system may be appropriate in 3 to 5 years (and sometimes less).

A question that sometimes needs to be decided early on is whether to develop software, using internal programmers or volunteers within the agency. Occasionally, internally developed software works efficiently and effectively. However, stores carry user-friendly software that can be readily adapted to all but a few applications, and free consulting help from the staff is generally available. Occasionally, training is also available.

Another budgetary issue is whether to purchase service agreements. In the case of complex systems, a service agreement is usually a mandatory, albeit expensive, element of most technological purchases or upgrades. Although not necessary for minor purchases, for large, expensive ones a service agreement is usually a good buy.

SECURITY ISSUES

The main security issues in telecommunications do not involve theft, although computers and pagers can be stolen, and the risk of theft needs to be addressed. Further, employees can tamper with the payroll or embezzle funds if they are able to access the appropriate sections of the financial software. The general method of preventing access is to use confidential passwords or unique user IDs for employees that need to get into specific sections of the software. More complex systems can be programmed to enhance security.

Most breaches of security involve unwarranted access to confidential records. There may be legal ramifications if too many people have access to a file. The need to know is usually the key factor.

Another security issue concerns e-mail. It has been established that e-mail can be subpoenaed in litigation. Obviously, managers need to be careful about what is placed in writing, electronically and otherwise, and be reasonably certain that access to confidential materials is limited.

As of this writing, cellular telephone systems are not very secure. A variety of ways exist to listen to conversations on a cell phone legally. Needless to say, managers need to be careful about discussing confidential information using a cellular telephone.

A growing security problem is inappropriate uses of organization-owned equipment. Computers might be used for personal shopping, game playing on the job, or personal business. It is also not uncommon for employees to "moonlight," that is, to use agency equipment to do paid work for others. A variety of policies can be set to address this issue.

A related issue concerns "surfing the net" for personal use or pleasure on company time. Internet access may be on a pay-per-use basis, with per minute charges. (Some contracts now provide unlimited access per contract.) Non–business-related use of the internet can be expensive, both in terms of time wasted and agency charges, and should be addressed. Policies, directives, and reminders as well as various forms of informal monitoring are appropriate for dealing with this problem.

ACTION-BASED CONCEPT

Managers must be careful to ensure the security and confidentiality of electronic files and email.

Another security issue has to do with data and information backup. If data, video, and communiqués are to be secure, they must be protected against system failure. Usually this is accomplished if backup disks are made. If paper copies are kept as backup, one advantage of an electronic system has been negated.

Management information systems have the potential to reduce paper flow but seldom do. In fact, the concept of a paperless office is still being discussed, although the potential is there. Speed of transmission and immediate access are now emphasized. In reality, there is usually more paper generated, not less. It is good, during the design phase, to specify what information is needed and what information is relevant. Data can be overwhelming, and only needed data should be generated and reported (and only when there is a demand).

ACTION-BASED CONCEPT

It is up to managers to decide what data are normally needed, when, and in what formats and to ensure that other data are only to be available on demand.

CONCLUSION

If managers neglect technology, they run the risk of allowing their organization to become noncompetitive because of inadequate information and communication systems. Technology has rapidly become indispensable, and its importance is likely to increase, not decrease.

The leadership in most organizations has the task of leading their organizations into a more technologically sophisticated age. This means the leaders must be technologically literate and must encourage employees to become technologically literate as well. In addition, the leaders of a large organization should develop a telecommunications master plan to ensure that the elements being phased in are not only compatible with future purchases but act as the necessary building blocks to help the organization achieve its goals.

IN-BASKET ASSIGNMENTS

TO: Health Education and Health Promotion Specialists
FROM: The Associate Director
RE: Innovative Telephone Applications

There are a lot of new features available on telephone systems now. Give me a list of them and brainstorm a list of possible health education and health promotion applications.

TO: Health Education and Health Promotion Specialists
FROM: The Director
RE: Training for Technology

What training opportunities are currently available that would help our staff become more technologically literate?

TO: Health Education and Health Promotion Specialists
FROM: The Director
RE: Internet Resources

I understand there are many educational and managerial resources on the internet. Go to the library or any internet connection and browse for health materials. Give me a one-page summary of the more useful ones.

TO: Health Education and Health Promotion Specialists
FROM: The Director
RE: Health Education Databases

Please find out what databases are available, how we can access them, and how they might be useful.

MANAGEMENT CASE STUDY

Setting

An urban health services clinic had five branch sites in the metropolitan area, each 20 miles or more from the headquarters clinic. The supervisors, one each in maternal and child health, communicable diseases, and chronic diseases, as well as a coordinator of health education and health promotion, were all based in the headquarters building and traveled to each site one day a week for a half day or more of supervision.

There was little or no communication between the five sites other than by telephone. The resolution of billing problems, clinical record errors, or other problems was done through phone calls, letters, and faxes.

Problem

The director of the health services clinic had read about the advantages of telecommunications and had seen features of a telecommunications system demonstrated at a recent convention. He wanted to create a telecommunications network to link the five sites but was not sure how to proceed or how much it would cost. He assumed it would be more than $100,000 and knew the budget would not be able to cover such an amount.

Alternatives Considered

One alternative considered was to ask a local vendor to design a system, with the understanding that, if the plan was accepted, the vendor would get the contract to install and manage it. Two or three telephone companies offered the requisite type of business consultation services. It was suggested that asking the clinic's telephone company and one other would ensure that competitive and comparable bids would be obtained.

Another alternative was to ask a major computer firm to design a system that included e-mail, internet access, teleconferencing, and other desirable features.

Another alternative was to hire a consultant to design a system.

It was also believed that spending a year studying systems actually in use might be wise.

If a telecommunications master planning committee was created, it could evaluate all the above options and any others that might emerge.

Actions Taken

The director decided to create a telecommunications master planning committee and charge it with evaluating computer and telecommunications options and needs and recommending a system that would meet agency needs for five to seven years. The system was also to be phased in over multiple budget cycles, and therefore the elements of the system would have to be compatible with each other.

The committee included a board member and a member from each of the five branch sites. All four divisions were represented, and an individual expected to resist such a plan was asked to join the committee. The committee met twice a month, and the meetings rotated from site to site.

Representatives from the phone companies were invited to make presentations to the group, as were representatives from the computer companies. The committee was advised to develop specific goals or a vision of what the new system should do, which it addressed in the plan.

The director (who also chaired the committee) wrote drafts of the various sections of the plan as it emerged.

OUTCOME

A phone system–based network capable of transmitting voice, video, and data was recommended. Computer terminals at each of the five sites could call up patient billing or clinical records and also be used to enter data. While the cost did exceed $100,000, it was amortized over 5 years.

A phase 2 video system that would permit teleconferencing and educational programming was designed. It was believed teleconferencing would reduce staff travel time and cost and increase supervision. The system was believed to be appropriate for employee hiring and firing conferences, consulting on difficult clinical cases, and so on. The educational television component was designed to permit both staff development and patient teaching to emanate from headquarters, and to be used at any one site or all the sites simultaneously.

DISCUSSION QUESTIONS

1. What might have prompted the director to place a board member on the telecommunications master planning committee? Why was it good strategy to have all sites represented and to rotate meetings from site to site? Similarly, why was it important to have each of the divisions represented?

2. What were the advantages and disadvantages of having the director write the report?

3. What would have been the advantages and disadvantages of using a consultant to design a telecommunications system? Of relying on the vendors to design one?

4. Were there steps missed that should have been included?

5. Were there other strategies that might have been used effectively?

CHAPTER 22

Influencing Public Policy

THE IMPORTANCE OF PUBLIC POLICY

As discussed earlier in this book, organizational policies are important to formulate and to review and revise periodically. It is especially important to have current policies and to follow them carefully during times of litigation.

Yet often public policy on matters relating to health promotion will have even more of an impact on an organization than its own policies. Public policy is usually expressed in laws, resolutions, and ordinances. It can also be expressed in funding priorities and programmatic decisions (e.g., a school board decision to implement a health education curriculum). An appropriate management function is to monitor public policy and attempt to influence it. Occasionally an agency administrator will initiate public policy proposals.

This is all part of the democratic process. As President Abraham Lincoln eloquently stated, the Constitution of the United States provides for a government "of the people, by the people and for the people." To the extent that managers allow others to govern without trying to influence the system, they are not using the system in the way it was designed to be used. Unfortunately, many people choose simply to criticize policy-making groups rather than attempt to influence policy.

Of course, it must be recognized that the responsibility is two way. The people elect representatives to local, state, and national governmental bodies, and it is the obligation of the elected representatives to stay in touch with their constituencies. Yet an elected official may represent hundreds and thousands or even millions of people and cannot personally stay in touch with each of them. All that can reasonably be expected is to provide opportunities for constituents to express their point of view. The responsibility to initiate communication thus shifts back to the citizen.

251

There are always opportunities to write letters, place phone calls, attend forums, or visit elected representatives and express an opinion. Granted, the opinion expressed by a manager of a health promotion agency is only one of many that will be considered. Yet unless it is expressed, it will likely not be considered at all, or at least the impact of that particular opinion will be lessened.

Elected officials occasionally use mailings to solicit people's views. Questionnaires, for example, are used to help determine constituent priorities. Although the response rate is often very low, questionnaires do create an opportunity for ordinary citizens to participate in the political process. (Note that a fax, e-mail message, or phone call to a legislator from a person in a high position will often outweigh the results of a questionnaire.) Similarly, constituent newsletters can help public opinion coalesce on a variety of issues.

Opportunities to influence public policy through spontaneous contact also occasionally occur. Bumping into a city or county commissioner on the sidewalk, in the supermarket, or at a social gathering may provide a chance to discuss a pressing issue. Elected state officials usually attend major gatherings, such as chamber of commerce banquets or fund-raisers, and so should health organization managers. Social contact with policy makers can enhance the effectiveness of future attempts to influence public policy. Health educators should have a budgeted allowance to attend major social functions.

ACTION-BASED CONCEPT

Health promotion agency managers should be visible at most significant gatherings, and should make a concerted effort to get to know policy makers. It is important to be seen at as many important gatherings as possible.

Managers need to also recognize that their obligation as health promoters exceeds the particular focus of their agency. For example, an American Lung Association official should be concerned about water quality and traffic safety, and someone who works in a hospice should also take positions on matters such as school-age drug prevention programs and exercise trails in the parks. Community health fairs, emergency services, public housing, smoking bans, recycling, sexual assault prevention, homeless shelters, food pantries, and bike paths are only a few of the local issues and initiatives where an opportunity to influence policy exists.

Of course, whether at the local, state, or national level, influencing the funding of prevention programs is a crucial responsibility. Changing funding priorities is a primary means of improving such programs, and if funding is not attended to, whole programs can easily be lost.

Public policy is in a sense everyone's responsibility. All too often citizens leave it to others and then complain because the policies chosen are not the ones they wanted. Clearly, the leaders of health promotion agencies have an obligation to try to bring about the selection and implementation of policies that will enhance the public's health.

ADVOCACY STRATEGIES

Advocacy is essentially the same regardless of whether it is on a local, state, or national level. It is a process of education, albeit combined with elements of power and influence. Of course, the arena in which the process takes place is not necessarily characterized by compromise.

The educational elements occur on at least two levels. Policy makers need to know what the issues are and what the various opinions on those issues are. Policy makers know that "where you stand on an issue depends on the chair in which you sit," meaning that views are affected by vested interests. If compromise is not appropriate, policy makers hope to achieve a consensus on the policy that will have the most benefits and the fewest liabilities. Again, if an opinion is not expressed, it may be missed. Of course, a manager's opinion, assuming he or she fails to express it, may be expressed by someone else.

Because multiple expressions of the same view lead elected officials to pay more attention to that view, group efforts are often initiated. A group is more visible, has more resources, and carries more political clout.

Even small groups can be influential. Several phone calls or letters on an issue create an aura of importance, especially at the local level. A leader of a health promotion agency should not find it difficult to get several people to speak out on an issue.

Managers need to be alert to the fact that taking a strong position on a public policy matter can have adverse effects as well. It is important to be sensitive to the negative potential and to think about it while preparing to take a public stance. For example, coming out strongly in favor of a particular health care reform could alienate doctors who serve on the agency's board or who serve indigent patients referred by the agency. The possibility of offending someone does not preclude taking a position on a policy issue. However, other perspectives on the issue and possible unintended side effects should be considered in advance of going public. One way to minimize the adverse consequences of taking a position is to discuss the position with an appropriate board. Indeed, some agencies require that agency positions must have board approval. Administrators in such situations must take policies to the board and must be especially careful when expressing personal opinions. The personal opinions of an administrator are often confused with the agency's positions and can get an administrator into trouble with the board.

Whether the position of an organization is determined by the administrator or the board, strategies must be developed to communicate it. As stated earlier, a letter, visit, or phone call can often be the most effective channel.

Remembering that advocacy is largely educational, it is important to have logical, persuasive documented materials. Public policy makers will not only want to know what the policy being advocated is and who is advocating it, but why. Also, it is often appropriate to acknowledge other views on the issue, and to state the reasons why the view being advocated is preferable.

Petitions can be used to generate public support for a position, but they are often discounted as poor representations of public opinion. People will often sign petitions without feeling strongly about the content. When it is a question of influencing public policy, a few letters or phone calls will usually carry more weight than a petition.

The important ingredients in an effective advocacy campaign, then, are preparation, personal contact, and continuity. It is important to clarify the issue and the effects various policies will have on society. A manager who wants to lobby for a position has a great advantage if he or she has established relationships of mutual respect with policy makers. Obviously, it is critical for managers not to "burn any bridges" over a single issue, that is, to maintain a position of influence even if the policy chosen is not the one advocated. Again, getting to know city or county managers and department heads, legislators, and their staff is essential. Frequent contact is always better than isolated contact, and managers who desire to influence public policy need to create opportunities for frequent contact. Face-to-face contact is usually most influential, a telephone conversation second most influential, followed by a letter. Of course, a conversation or phone call followed by a letter is usually even more effective, especially if the letter is a personal one.

ACTION-BASED CONCEPT

Managers should regularly monitor public opinion as it evolves into public policy and attempt to use personal or group influence to affect it.

Managers need to remember that large numbers equal power, coalitions equal power, a unified position equals power, credibility equals power, knowledge equals power, voting equals power, and money equals power.

CONCLUSION

Managers of health organizations can use politics to affect health and health education policies at the local, state, and national levels. Basic health education and community organization skills are the key tools for political action. Managers have a greater obligation to try to influence public policy than do staff health educators, especially managers in leadership positions.

Managers who use their political skills effectively can maximize their impact on the community and their value to their organization. Power, to a policy maker, is usually measured in numbers and dollars. Therefore, managers of large organizations have substantial policy-influencing power and should usually choose to use it.

IN-BASKET ASSIGNMENT

TO: The Executive Director
FROM: Chair of the Board of Directors
RE: Lobbying

I recently received a communication from a national group urging me to write a U.S. Representative about a pending health care reform bill. I thought it was illegal for personnel in not-for-profit charitable agencies to lobby.

Could we lose our ability to receive and receipt tax-free contributions if I write a legislator on this bill? What if I send it on plain white paper (minus the agency letterhead) and sign it as a concerned citizen rather than the director?

Please check it out and let me know sometime this week what my options are.

MANAGEMENT CASE STUDY

Setting

An independent university in a small university town had a health promotion major. The faculty member teaching the management course decided to engage the class in an action project so they could learn by doing.

Problem

The class decided to approach the county commissioners about starting a recycling program. They wanted to find out the most effective way to do this.

Alternatives Considered

The first alternative considered was to approach an existing community organization and offer to assist it in lobbying for a recycling program. (A variation was to try to create a coalition of such groups.)

Also considered was a class visit to a neighboring community to see a recycling program in action and to interview those who managed it about how they got started, what obstacles they had to overcome, and what advice they might offer.

The class realized it needed to perform a literature search and thoroughly explore potential costs and revenues.

The class wondered if one semester was long enough to do the project and agreed with the instructor to make it a two-semester project. The current course enrollees would do the visits, literature search, and planning, and make preliminary contact with the county officials, and next semester's students would do the lobbying for implementation.

Actions Taken

Through a literature search, the class obtained ordinances that had been adopted and chose one as the preferred model.

At a visit to a neighboring recycling program, the students were advised to try to work with the trash collection agency that had the current contract for hauling. Trash hauling vendors are often willing to work with groups who want to implement recycling.

The students detailed the problems associated with landfills and prepared a five-minute videotape of a well-run recycling program.

They worked with the trash hauler to develop a preliminary fiscal proposal.

The students' final step was to meet with the county's public works director to present their data and ask for advice and support before turning over their files to the next class.

OUTCOME

The director of public works was appreciative of the work and identified an elected county commissioner who was likely to support such a program. The director encouraged the class to arrange for this commissioner to meet with next semester's class early on to plan the campaign.

The director of public works and the elected commissioner contacted the press prior to and at the time the resolution was introduced. The students attended the public hearings and also asked some influential members of the community to attend.

The program was adopted, was modified during the first year, and remains successful.

DISCUSSION QUESTIONS

1. Why might trash haulers be interested in developing recycling programs? What does this say about organizational change?

2. How important was it to prepare a videotape of a well-run recycling program? Were there other benefits that could evolve from the visits?

3. Why was it important to work with the public works director? How might the class have proceeded if the director's response was negative?

4. Was the involvement of a commissioner important to the outcome?

5. Were there other strategies that could have been used?

CHAPTER 23

Leading and Managing into the Future

ANTICIPATING CHANGE

"The future isn't what it used to be" is more than a play on words. The rate of change has accelerated to such a degree that the future is less predictable than ever before in recorded history. Likewise, the phrase "The future is now" is hardly paradoxical. Management tools only conceptualized a few months ago are in use today. What one organizational leader is only dreaming of, another is already doing.

Leadership is more in demand than it was a few years ago. "Leadership is the art of accomplishing more than the art of management says is possible," said Colin Powell. Increasingly, that is what is required in most health promotion organizations today—accomplishing more than is thought possible. A new management style appears to be emerging, at least at the upper levels. The focus is on anticipating change and managing it effectively and engaging in entrepreneurial activity. The strategy of keeping on doing what has always been done will often lead to the same results as in previous months, not better results.

Managers are becoming change agents. To be a successful change agent, one needs to be somewhat of a futurist.

> ### ACTION-BASED CONCEPT
>
> *Managers should read materials on the future, attend conference sessions, read monthly columns devoted to new developments, read materials on trend analysis, and generally think about what is happening in health promotion, in the entire field of health care, and in the world at large.*

VISION AND VALUES

As futurist, Ian Morrison asserts, "Health care is in need of renewal, reinvigoration, and leadership."[1] We desperately need creativity and innovation, on the one hand, and pragmatic long-overdue execution of well-established ideas, on the other. All health care systems are the products of the culture and thus an organizational embodiment of societal values. Morrison identifies these core values in U.S. society as: pluralism and choice; individual accountability; ambivalence toward government; innovation; volunteerism; anti-monopoly; and competition. The manager is often faced with difficult decisions that are opposed to or consistent with these values. Some organizations even conduct a values audit to ascertain their own core values. Others establish a "values statement" that is co-equal to their mission statement. There is also an emerging trend toward values alignment for organizations to assure they are doing what they say they are and the initiatives and programs are aligned with their clients and constituents.

GLOBALIZATION

With advances in transportation and international commerce we see an ever shrinking world. In fact, the term "global village" is widely used as we perceive the interconnectedness of today's diverse societies and organizations. With globalization, new challenges emerge. Recent examples include infectious diseases like the HIV pandemic and emerging threats such as Avian Flu and West Nile Virus. Also, there continues to be the threat of terrorism and the possibility of economic upheaval.

Globalization also brings with it more immigration and thus a changing workforce. There has been a dramatic shift in U.S. demographics with the increased number of Hispanics and Asians entering the labor pool. Many bring with them education and skills that can be useful in health services organizations. Additionally, health education efforts must be culturally sensitive to be effective in reaching these populations. The manager must help the organization adapt to a more diverse workforce as well as a more diverse client base. It is strongly recommended to conduct cultural awareness training and to modify human resource planning strategies.

DISASTER PREPAREDNESS

Many recent events, and more to come, have lessons for our society as it continues to adjust to change. One of the biggest lessons involves the premium that needs to be placed on community and organizational preparedness. With the possibility of natural disaster always present and manmade ones such as acts of terrorism looming in our collective psyche, it is imperative for all organizations to have disaster plans. Additionally, education and training are necessary as are simulations and inter-organizational exercises. Preparedness requires building new partnerships with the medical community, law enforcement and public safety, emergency services, disaster management personnel, and government officials.[2]

A successful comprehensive emergency management program of preparedness, response, and recovery will help the organization through what could be its most difficult challenge. Some of the core elements of any plan or program include: how to meet client needs when the infrastructure has been damaged; how to manage volunteers and donors; how to best utilize the media; training in clinical and organizational triage; client tracking; and managing personnel shortages.

Managers will be center stage during these trying times and can expect to be pulled in many directions by board members, clients, employees, and their own families. If ever there is a time for multi-tasking, this will be it. However, those managers who have an agency-specific plan in hand will do much better. As we all know, a plan is only as good as its implementation. There will be a need to modify decisions on the ground and to adjust accordingly. This is a kind of organizational improvisation that will call upon all the skills addressed in this book—and more.

NETWORKING AND CONNECTIVITY

Successful managers who rise to leadership roles read extensively, including journals, newsletters, and columns devoted to change. Managers cannot possibly be creative enough to develop all the needed "good ideas," but they can read about what others are trying and think about what it means for the health promotion organizations they lead. There are also numerous recommended books, and, for those who do not enjoy reading, executive book summaries.

ACTION-BASED CONCEPT

Developing a network of peers willing to be consulted regularly on management issues is essential.

Reading is essential but insufficient as a way of keeping up with new developments. In urban areas, attending a monthly or quarterly breakfast or luncheon meeting is a useful way to learn what others are doing and to consult about organizational initiatives. While professional organization membership and participation is a good thing too, breakfast and luncheon meetings often include individuals from other disciplines, and a useful exchange of strategies and new initiatives can occur. Service club membership, such as membership in the Rotary Club, Lions Club, Kiwanis Club, or the Optimists, can meet some of the needs for consultation, if mealtime conversations are steered in a business direction periodically. Similarly, it is useful to network through the Chamber of Commerce.

Networking works especially well in face-to-face settings where a leisurely exploration of issues can occur, often informally and without planning. However, relationships established in such settings provide opportunities for phone conversations and consultation when needed.

Increasingly, informal consultation is occurring on computer networks, through e-mail, bulletin boards, forums, and internet "chats" or "user groups." Virtually unlimited free consultation is often available if the right network is tapped. Electronic networks have quickly equaled and perhaps surpassed face-to-face networks in importance. However, the reality is that both will be essential for the twenty-first century manager of a health promotion program.

ENTREPRENEURISM

The future orientation recommended for managers must be accompanied by a management style characterized by entrepreneurism. This involves perceiving opportunities where other managers do not and changing programs and strategies to capitalize on opportunities. Basically, entrepreneurs see an opportunity and move to take advantage of it—before anyone else. Entrepreneurs view change as healthy, search for change opportunities, and exploit them when they are located. Entrepreneurs are certainly required in new organizations or to grow small organizations. But increasingly, because of the escalating rate of change, an entrepreneurial spirit is required to manage the replacement of non–state-of-the-art, non-responsive, or even antiquated programs.

Because entrepreneurs focus on the future and on business opportunities in the external environment, they require a fluid organization, staffing and budgets that are flexible, and a leadership that rewards flexibility. Responding to opportunities typically involves organizational change.

Community organization theory and social change theory suggest that needs and wants can be created. A strong demand for wellness programs or for a specific type of screening program can be generated where no demand existed previously. Market analysis and focused marketing are important aspects of entrepreneurism.

ACTION-BASED CONCEPT

Managers must emphasize brainstorming and must tolerate risk. Always searching for multiple perspectives or asking, "How else could we do it?" or "How are others handling this?" can generate new opportunities.

Failure is more likely when risks are taken, so entrepreneurs must be prepared to tolerate partial failure or complete failure. Moreover, an entrepreneurial program must be monitored carefully and, if necessary, given midcourse revisions or be abandoned. To minimize the effects of failure on the staff, the program might be started as a pilot project, with a built-in abandonment plan if failure occurs.

Of course, entrepreneurs need to be tolerant of criticism, because even if 70 percent of the new ideas are successful, people will tend to criticize the 30 percent that are not and will forget the successes.

They also need a tolerance for uncertainty and ambiguity, because it is often difficult to anticipate all that must be done or who will do it. Many decisions must be made with incomplete or unclear information. In a sense, a tolerance for uncertainty and ambiguity is important for any leader to have, but it is critical for entrepreneurs, because they may be doing things for the first time and organizational stability and their livelihood may be at stake.

Needless to say, in such circumstances entrepreneurs must possess self-confidence, optimism, and good judgment. They also would do well to have a formal or informal group with whom to discuss decisions in order to understand the risks and likelihood of success more fully. A team approach tends to foster the entrepreneurial spirit in others and minimize criticism. However, group decision making is painfully slow, especially if a consensus is required. Thus, one common strategy is to have the group list, for each major decision, reasons for and against, advantages and disadvantages, or opportunities and barriers. With such a list in hand, an entrepreneurial manager can make the decision with a reasonable level of confidence that the option chosen is the right one.

PERSUASIVE COMMUNICATION

Persuasiveness depends on having a sound, logical plan, one rooted in fact and reason. Thus, doing a literature search, networking, or consulting with peers is helpful before putting a plan on the table. Discussing a project informally with the staff members can generate ideas for inclusion in the written proposal.

Submitting a draft to solicit comments can be a helpful strategy as well. A carefully documented written proposal is harder for the opposition to attack and is easier to implement. Most people can write a persuasive proposal if indeed the plan is logical.

> ### *ACTION-BASED CONCEPT*
>
> *Any manager headed toward a leadership position must learn how to become a good communicator. Leaders must know how to be persuasive in both informal and formal situations.*

It is harder, but equally important, to be a persuasive public speaker in large organizations. Presentations to boards or funding agencies can be critical. Written executive summaries and visuals used during presentations can make proposals more likely to be adopted.

If indeed a manager cannot effectively communicate the need for a new initiative and convince others that the plan will work, it will likely not be accepted. A manager who presents a plan that is not accepted needs to engage in introspection and ask why it was not accepted. Whether the reason was poor communication skills or the plan itself, the appropriate lessons need to be learned. Effective managers generally do not put forth plans that fail to be adopted. They learn from their failures and return with better plans that are better communicated.

INTEGRITY AND ETHICS

The management of change and the future requires trust. A leader cannot lead without the trust of potential followers. The trust required for success must be earned. That is the basis for the saying that nothing succeeds like success. And that is also why it is important for a new manager to do a few things right away that are visible to everyone and cannot miss, such as something to improve the appearance of the facility.

Starting several small projects during the first few months also establishes that a willingness to change will be the norm. Even changing the location of office furniture can contribute to that goal, as can changing standing meeting times, locations, or invitees.

Trust can grow out of success, and the goodwill that exists during a honeymoon period needs to be strengthened to form the basis of long-lasting trusting relationships. It is important not to take too many risks until a leadership team has been solidly built.

Trust generates loyalty, a quality that may be especially needed during controversial changes. But loyalty and trust both depend on integrity and ethical behavior. A manager must be dependable and must keep verbal and written agreements. Therefore, managers should be careful about making public commitments, because an inability to keep a commitment can seriously damage trust and loyalty.

A manager needs to exhibit personal and professional integrity to maximize success. Excessive partying or any behavior perceived as unethical or dishonest should be avoided. Effective leaders are perceived as role models—if not in all areas, in most. Their business activities and personal behavior must be above reproach, especially during periods of change. Opponents of change should not be allowed to target a leader's motives or morals. Loyalty based on integrity will serve the leader well. This is not to say that leaders who have questionable motives cannot be successful, but they are less likely to succeed than leaders who have consistently acted with integrity.

CONCLUSION

A new century has arrived and so has a new millennium. Even if millennium fever has not occurred, the excitement of these changing times will undoubtedly grip managers and administrators, especially leaders. Effective managers must prepare to abandon a lot of past practices, both personal and organizational. The world is changing so fast that organizations and individuals who do not also change quickly will be left behind.

Managers in the twenty-first century will have to anticipate change and create change. These two tasks are best accomplished through networking and extensive, focused reading. A willingness to try new approaches is essential, as is a willingness to take risks and multi-task during a crisis. An ability to persuade others to follow is critical. But most important of all, each manager must prove him- or herself to be someone who can be trusted—someone who is worthy of being followed.

IN-BASKET ASSIGNMENT

TO: Health Education and Health Promotion Specialists
FROM: The Executive Director
RE: Trend Analysis

The other day I saw a review of a book that analyzed future trends, *Health Care in the New Millennium,* by Ian Morrison. I would like to make it the subject of a staff meeting discussion and have you lead it.

Please construct a short bibliography on the literature of trend analysis and prepare a 15-minute review of Morrison's book.

MANAGEMENT CASE STUDY

Setting

A state health agency with national and local relationships was located in the tobacco belt of the southeastern United States. It had offered smoking cessation programs for those who wanted to stop smoking, but it had not engaged in any statewide antismoking educational activities. Yet agency planning for the twenty-first century indicated that the agency could and should play a significant role in creating a smoke-free society. Thus the agency decided to embark on an antismoking campaign.

Problem

Tobacco interests were very powerful in the state. Attacking the tobacco industry was viewed as akin to taking jobs from people, tax dollars from welfare agencies, and so on.

The tobacco companies formally offered to help support the agency's campaign with a $200,000 gift if the agency agreed to limit the campaign focus to keeping tobacco products away from children. While not formally stated, it was intimated that many individuals who benefited from the tobacco industry would likely quit financially supporting the agency, and the cut in funding would seriously jeopardize other fine programs the agency offered throughout the state.

Alternatives Considered

It was recognized that the organization's survival might be at stake and the decision whether to proceed with the campaign should be made by the board. One alternative considered was to pursue the antismoking campaign but to aggressively seek funding from non–tobacco-related companies to offset the anticipated decline in gifts from tobacco companies.

Another alternative was to build up a 1- year operating reserve to help the agency get through any fiscal crisis that might emerge.

A third alternative was to recognize the need for organizational survival and work with the tobacco industry, yet over a 10-year period, to gradually increase antitobacco activities.

Actions Taken

The board decided to work with the tobacco industry, accepting their $200,000 gift in support of a campaign to keep tobacco away from children. (The board insisted that the agency retain complete editorial control over content.)

The board also decided to increase the size of its operating reserves by 25 percent for each of the next 4 years, believing that sooner or later a funding boycott would occur.

OUTCOME

The "Keep Tobacco Away from Kids" campaign was moderately successful. The increased media exposure did help the agency increase its operating reserves. There was some increase in general antismoking educational activities, but not much.

The director believed the board had been intimidated by the tobacco industry and left to take a leadership position at a similar agency in a northern state for less salary.

DISCUSSION QUESTIONS

1. What integrity issues are involved in this situation? What ethical issues are involved? Are the issues the same for the director, the board, and the agency? What alternative would be supported by the principle that one should act to create the greatest good for the greatest number of people?

2. Should antismoking campaigns accept and use tobacco money? What would be the advantages and disadvantages of accepting tobacco money? For a health promotion agency, what would be the advantages and disadvantages of accepting money from distillers and brewers? Is good use of the money more important than its source? What circumstances might occur that would make using the money either acceptable or unacceptable?

3. What does this case study suggest about power? About politics? About leadership?

4. Are there other strategies that could have been used?

5. Are there other examples that pose similar dilemmas for managers looking ahead to the twenty-first century and the coming changes in the health promotion field?

NOTE

1. I. Morrison. *Health Care in the New Millennium: Vision, Values, and Leadership* (San Francisco: Jossey-Bass, 2000).

2. J.A. Johnson, M.H. Kennedy, and N. Delener. *Community Preparedness and Response to Terrorism, vol. 2, The Role of Community Organizations and Business* (Westport, CT: Praeger, 2005): 134.

The Fundamentals of Leadership, Management, and Administration

The action-based concepts presented in the various chapters of this book are listed here in sequence.

Chapter 1

The Evolution of Health Education, Health Promotion, and Wellness Programs

Managers should read about and be able to discuss historical milestones of their profession and their agency. An understanding of history is always important, because it is the only means of fully understanding the present and anticipating the future.

Managers must generally take quality improvement into account. Quality improvement should be an important element of virtually every decision made, whether it be improvement of the quality of life of clients, the quality of services or programs provided, the quality of staff, or the quality of decision-making processes.

Chapter 2

The Evolution of Management, Administrative, and Leadership Theories

Specialization, division of work, path of authority, and chain of command are all important elements of management.

Maximizing output efficiency and minimizing strain and waste are important elements of management.

Planning, organizing, staffing, directing, coordinating, reporting, and budgeting are important elements of management.

Management gets things done through people, and efforts to improve the working environment and worker satisfaction usually increase productivity.

No one theory will fit all situations. Managers must understand the particular circumstances and utilize appropriate elements of each major theory while maintaining flexibility.

Management is action oriented, and managers need lots of energy, the ability to be decisive, and the ability to cope with stress.

Extensive reading and informal communication are needed by managers, yet finding the time to read and communicate informally is often the most difficult task.

Leadership implies change and involves management of planned change. High-level managers will also have leadership responsibilities, and leaders often have management responsibilities.

Leaders innovate, inspire trust, make long-range plans, and motivate people to change.

Managers devote their time to solving personnel problems, financial problems, and legal problems, whereas leaders plan and manage change.

Chapter 3

Health and Quality of Life in the 21st Century

Managers need to think in terms of trends, recent changes, current shifts, and emerging issues and to read materials on trend analysis.

Managers must attend to quality, promoting it and insisting on it, for nothing can replace the impact that quality has on all an agency does.

Chapter 4

Organizational Dynamics

Managers need to study their organization's history to learn about the problems faced, the decisions made, and the accomplishments and failures.

Managers must focus on macromanagement as well as micromanagement issues.

Macromanagement requires expanding the organization's impact, which in turn requires ensuring the organization's presence in decision-making settings.

Macromanagement issues are important for a department manager whose focus includes expanding the department's influence in the organization and the community.

Chapter 5

Board Governance and Responsibility

Managers should obtain a copy of the charter, bylaws, and membership of the organization's board, study them carefully, and file them for convenient access.

Analyze who is on each board with whom you interact, why they were selected, what they bring to that board, and what their attitude is toward your program.

Prepare a list of individuals who meet the status and other board selection criteria and would likely be advocates of your program.

Scan the news reports often to ascertain who is on what board and think about what issues they are focused on. Perhaps keep a file folder of potential board members who could act as liaisons between your program and the community if placed on the board.

Minimize the use of ad hoc committees and try not to have any board member serving on more than one standing committee.

Board members should be aware of all important issues and have the opportunity to be involved in dealing with most of them.

The CEO should provide the board with an overview of the major issues facing the organization. If the board meets only quarterly, a brief written monthly report should be sent to the board members.

Seek feedback from board members on what can be done to make the board meetings more interesting, more enjoyable, and more productive.

Managers should be familiar with the procedures for changing the bylaws and charter.

All communication between the board and staff should be channeled through the chief administrator. The administrator must maintain day-to-day control of all organizational functions to keep the organization moving toward fulfillment of its mission.

Chapter 6

Organizational Charts

Always understand how the work is divided and how the specialized functions are coordinated, and look for ways to increase organizational efficiency by refining these factors.

An organizational chart should not be considered fixed or permanent. It should be reviewed periodically to determine if it offers a good foundation for accomplishing the goals of the organization.

Managers should ensure that the organization and each unit have an up-to-date organizational chart. The chart should be made available to all staff to help them understand the channels of authority and communication, information flow, status of staff members, and span of control. Because the relationships between staff and managers can change over time, the chart should be reviewed and updated every year or so.

Chapter 7

Legal and Ethical Issues

Managers need to know the laws that can apply to the organization, and emphasize the importance of practicing preventive law.

Managers need to focus on reasonable accommodations and be certain that services are provided to all regardless of ability or disability. Many inexpensive accommodations are available. A written ADA compliance plan that details how the agency will accommodate clients and employees with disabilities is usually needed.

Managers should encourage employees to call unsafe or unhealthy conditions to their attention and must always investigate such conditions immediately. If the conditions are unsafe or unhealthy, they need to be corrected as soon as is reasonable (sometimes within a day or two) because liability increases once a complaint has been filed. Even nuisance complaints should be taken seriously, and written follow-up reports need to be placed in the files.

Managers need to be certain that personnel policies and compensation systems are fair and equitably applied to all regardless of race, gender, religion, veteran status, or handicapping condition. Personnel policies must be kept current and be followed explicitly or litigation risk will increase.

Effective managers will ascertain if the diversity of an organization's staff approximates the population served and determine the extent to which programs would be enhanced by additional diversification. Effective managers know what federal or state laws apply to hiring and always comply with them.

Effective managers will generally not refer to gender, age, race, sexual orientation or physical capability with other employees in office communications unless it is in ways that will be perceived to be helpful by those whose gender, age, race, sexual orientation or physical capability differ from the manager. Effective managers will generally not refer to gender, age, race, sexual orientation, or handicapping condition with other employees in office communications unless it is in ways that will be perceived to be helpful by those of gender, age group, sexual orientation or handicapping condition different from the administrator.

Employers in nonunion settings should treat their employees equitably and should compensate them fairly. Employees are among the most valuable assets of an organization and should be treated accordingly.

Effective managers in an organization that is at best partially unionized will thoroughly understand every contractual provision and will refer to the contract often in order to follow procedures explicitly and prevent grievances.

Chapter 8

Job Descriptions

A manager should obtain a copy of the job descriptions of everyone who reports to him or her and review it periodically to ascertain if what the employee does or what the job description specifies needs to be revised.

Managers should be familiar with the requirements of and the need for certification and if appropriate should lead by example in obtaining it.

Chapter 9

Recruiting and Hiring

Before any vacancy is filled, consider carefully whether the position should be eliminated, upgraded, downgraded, revised, or combined with another to best meet shifting organizational priorities, and prepare the appropriate job description. At least as many people and as much time should normally be spent on this task as on the selection process.

It is generally desirable for organizations to have a carefully developed written internal promotion policy. The best policy is usually to hire capable people at lower levels and promote those who are effective and fully qualified. It is also wise, however, to fill some mid-level and upper-level positions with external candidates to inject new ideas into the organization.

Contact former employers any time during the search process, but only contact current employers if the committee has narrowed selection down to one or two finalists and permission has been given by the applicants.

Chapter 10

Compensation

Fringe benefits such as insurance usually involve an employee and an employer contribution. The employee contribution is usually not subject to income tax, which has the effect of increasing the value of the contribution above its face value.

Managers responsible for wages, salaries, and fringe benefits packages will always want to know what other employers are providing for similar groups.

The employee turnover rate is a good indicator of the adequacy of the compensation package and, therefore, should be monitored. If the turnover rate is too high, increases in compensation may be used to reduce it.

Managers in a collective bargaining setting should have a copy of the contract, and must abide by the requirements exactly.

A salary equity study should be done if a current one does not exist. Care must be taken not to base salaries on gender, ethnicity, age, or disability. However, experience, longevity, education, and duties can legitimately influence salary levels.

Only directory information (name, address, phone number) can generally be legally shared without the employee's permission. While there are a few exceptions, employers need to be extraordinarily careful not to divulge restricted information.

Chapter 11

Performance Incentives

It is important to monitor the productivity of each employee in both informal and formal ways. If a noticeable drop in productivity occurs, the reason for the drop should be explored informally and, if necessary, in a formal setting to determine if intervention strategies would be appropriate or helpful.

Managers must formally or informally monitor job satisfaction, employee performance, productivity, absenteeism, tardiness, and employee turnover.

Employees need opportunities for psychological and job growth, and good managers are sensitive to this need and accommodate it whenever possible.

Employees must be held accountable for productivity and need periodic feedback on their performance.

Chapter 12

Performance Appraisals

Managers should use a formal performance appraisal system for the employees they supervise. If one is already being used in the organization, this system should be selected to promote consistency and facilitate comparisons. If one is not in place, a system should be adapted or developed.

All performance appraisals should be limited to factors that directly affect performance. Job-related personal issues should be carefully addressed, and non-job-related personal issues should not be discussed unless brought up by the employee.

Because so much of a performance appraisal is subjective, it is usually appropriate for supervisors to review each performance appraisal with a superior before discussing it with the employee being evaluated to minimize the effect of rater bias.

Communication and feedback during a performance evaluation session should enhance rapport, respect, and be motivational.

Chapter 13

The Paper Trail

Supervisors must always avoid inappropriately revealing information about other employees covered by privacy laws. It is especially important not to discuss other employees in informal conversations with friends.

Other than directory data, information about an employee should not be released to other agencies without the written permission of the employee.

Personnel files and all information in them should always be treated with complete confidentiality. Access to a given employee's file should be limited to supervisors with a need to know and the employee.

Chapter 14

Career Management

Managers are advised to have a career path in mind, with a realistic plan and timetable, and to maintain flexibility in order to deal with opportunities and obstacles that occur.

Managers need to identify employees with potential for promotion and create developmental opportunities and, when appropriate, a "fast track" to move them into the next appropriate position.

When an employee is terminated, the paper trail must be extensive enough to minimize the likelihood of successful litigation. It should include documentation of poor performance or other problems, opportunities for improvement, and the reason the discharge occurred. It should also identify who was consulted or otherwise involved in making the decision.

Managers need to consult with others before forcing a job change and avoid emotional exchanges and exaggerations that might be used by the employees in future litigation.

Chapter 15

Budgeting

Effective managers thoroughly understand the organization's budget and are able to roughly determine the budget status at any future point in the fiscal year. A standing weekly meeting with the fiscal officer or a thorough reading of budget status and cash flow reports is an essential foundation of sound management practice.

Managers must understand auditor reports and respond to the issues cited in the management notes. Few if any organizations should try to get by without an annual audit of the books by a qualified firm that prepares auditor reports for other organizations.

Managers must utilize a budgeting approach that is appropriate for the agency—one that takes into account past practice, staff personalities, and agency politics.

Chapter 16

Fiscal Control and Accountability

Managers need to know the organization's traditional fiscal pressure points, especially any pressure points that are related to cash flow.

Managers must fully understand budget printouts and be able to interpret them correctly.

Managers must monitor all the accounts of the individuals they supervise, ensure that fiscal restraint is being used, and ensure that their subordinates fully understand the reports and the need for fiscal controls.

Managers need to carefully monitor receivables and payables. Their goal should be to keep receivables from extending beyond a 30-day limit and payables from extending beyond a 60-day limit.

Managers cannot assume that employees will be honest or accurate. Accuracy should be checked routinely, and spot checks should occur periodically.

Chapter 17

Grant Writing

Managers must continually monitor sources of supplementary funding and must periodically spend time and effort preparing applications or encouraging and assisting others to do so.

Grant writing involves studying application materials and guidelines, using the headings suggested, making the requested material readily apparent, and following all directions carefully and precisely. More than one person should be involved in determining what information is requested in what format and in ascertaining that all directions have been followed.

Administrators should identify what foundations with a narrow geographical focus are in the immediate area and should ascertain what their program priorities are. If it appears there may be a fit, a get-acquainted exploratory meeting is usually appropriate.

Large state or national foundations always prepare annual reports and application guidelines. Any foundation that appears to be a potential source of funding should be contacted for these items, which should be studied carefully.

Chapter 18

Planning

The financing of planned change must itself be carefully planned, and financing strategies must be identified early to remove lack of funds as an excuse for not taking the planning of change seriously.

Managers must be astute and diligent in analyzing the power structure, politics, and personalities of an organization, especially when planning change. Both formal and informal power structures play a role in organizational politics, and personalities usually dominate both power and political networks.

Resistance to change must be anticipated early in the change planning process. The source of the anticipated resistance and the reasons for it must be identified. The change planning process must include strategies for neutralizing resistance, preferably before it is expressed.

In pushing a set of changes, managers should support the one-third of employees who are advocates for change and should focus on the one-third who are open to change but not too sure about these particular changes. They should address, in a limited way, the concerns of the one-third who resist change, recognizing that if the other employees are persuaded of the benefits of the changes, the resisters will be brought along.

Any plan that is developed must have measurable objectives and a time frame for achieving each one. Other plan elements can be included as necessary.

Chapter 19

Marketing and the Media

Every marketing plan should be group specific. Identification of multiple target groups and development of group-specific marketing strategies are important.

When attempting to communicate with individuals or groups, it is usually most effective to use the communication channels they normally use, and to use peers in the process.

Chapter 20

Program Evaluation

Managers should anticipate what questions will be posed about the adequacy of their programs, and should design evaluation plans to gather and summarize data that will readily address these concerns.

Chapter 21

Technology and Information Systems

Managers should focus on how much technology is needed, how much is used by the competition, how much is the staff capable of using, and how much would be cost efficient.

Managers should read extensively about management information systems and other high-tech systems and equipment, and should be conversant with the issues and the advantages and disadvantages of the various applications.

Managers must be careful to ensure the security and confidentiality of electronic files and email.

It is up to managers to decide what data are normally needed, when, and in what formats, and to ensure that other data are only to be available on demand.

Chapter 22

Influencing Public Policy through Politics

Health promotion agency managers should be visible at most significant gatherings and should make a concerted effort to get to know policy makers. It is important to be seen at as many important gatherings as possible.

Managers should regularly monitor public opinion as it evolves into public policy and attempt to use personal or group influence to affect it.

Chapter 23

Leading and Managing in the 21st Century

Managers should read materials on the future, attend conference sessions, read monthly columns devoted to new developments, read materials on trend analysis, and generally think about what is happening in health promotion, in the entire field of health care, and in the world at large.

Developing a network of peers willing to be consulted regularly on management issues is essential.

Managers must emphasize brainstorming and must tolerate risk. Always searching for multiple perspectives or asking, "How else could we do it?" or "How are others handling this?" can generate new opportunities.

Any manager headed toward a leadership position must learn how to become a good communicator. Leaders must know how to be persuasive in both informal and formal situations.

APPENDIX B

Glossary

CONTEXTUAL TERMS

Health education takes place within the broad context of health. Certain health terms are defined to clarify how health education functions.

health. There are many definitions written for the word *health*. Three examples are provided: (1) A state of complete physical, mental, and social well-being and not merely the absence of disease and infirmity; (2) A quality of life involving dynamic interaction and independence among the individual's physical well-being, his or her mental and emotional reactions, and the social complex in which he or she exists; and (3) An integrated method of functioning which is oriented toward maximizing the potential of which the individual is capable. It requires that the individual maintain a continuum of balance and purposeful direction with the environment where he or she is functioning.

health promotion and disease prevention. Health promotion and disease prevention is the aggregate of all purposeful activities designed to improve personal and public health through a combination of strategies, including the competent implementation of behavioral change strategies, health education, health protection measures, risk factor detection, health enhancement, and health maintenance.

---

* Definitions from "health" to "accountability" are reprinted with permission from the *Journal of Health Education*. The *Journal of Health Education* is a publication of the American Alliance for Health, Physical Education, Recreation and Dance, 1900 Association Drive, Reston, VA 22091.

healthy lifestyle. A healthy lifestyle is a set of health-enhancing behaviors, shaped by internally consistent values, attitudes, beliefs, and external social and cultural forces.

official health agency. An official health agency is a publicly supported governmental organization mandated by law and/or regulation for the protection and improvement of the health of the public.

voluntary health organization. A voluntary health organization is a nonprofit association supported by contributions dedicated to conducting research and providing education and/or services related to particular health problems or concerns. (Note: *Private voluntary organization* [PVO] is the term used outside the United States to denote a voluntary health organization; in some countries and in connection with the United Nations, the term *nongovernmental organization* [NGO] is used.)

PRIMARY HEALTH EDUCATION DEFINITIONS

Certain health education terms are generic and are defined here, as follows:

certified health education specialist. A certified health education specialist (CHES) is an individual who is credentialed as a result of demonstrating competency based on criteria established by the National Commission for Health Education Credentialing (NCHEC).

health advising. Health advising is a process of informing and assisting individuals or groups in making decisions and solving problems related to health. (The Joint Commission on Health Education Terminology believes that *health counseling* is a term that should be defined by the health counseling profession.)

health education administrator. A health education administrator is a professional health educator who has the authority and responsibility to manage and coordinate all health education policies, activities, and resources within a particular setting or circumstance.

health education coordinator. A health education coordinator is a professional health educator who is responsible for the management and coordination of all health education policies, activities, and resources within a particular setting or circumstance.

health education field. The health education field is a multidisciplinary practice that is concerned with designing, implementing, and evaluating educational programs that enable individuals, families, groups, organizations, and communities to play active roles in achieving, protecting, and sustaining health.

health education process. The health education process is the continuum of learning that enables people, as individuals and as members of social structures, voluntarily to make decisions, modify behaviors, and change social conditions in ways that are health enhancing.

health education program. A health education program is a planned combination of activities developed with the involvement of specific populations and based on a needs assessment, sound principles of education, and periodic evaluation using a clear set of goals and objectives.

health educator. A health educator is a practitioner who is professionally prepared in the field of health education, who demonstrates competence in both theory and practice, and who accepts responsibility to advance the aims of the health education profession. Examples of settings for health educators and the application of health education include, but are not limited to, the following: schools, communities, postsecondary educational institutions, medical care institutions, voluntary health organizations, worksites (business and industry), rehabilitation centers, professional associations, governmental agencies, public health agencies, environmental agencies, and mental health agencies.

health information. Health information is the content of communications based on data derived from systematic and scientific methods as they relate to health issues, policies, programs, services, and other aspects of individual and public health, which can be used for informing various populations and in planning health education activities.

health literacy. Health literacy is the capacity of an individual to obtain, interpret, and understand basic health information and services and the competence to use such information and services in ways that are health enhancing.

DEFINITIONS RELATED TO COMMUNITY SETTINGS

The terms that relate more specifically to community or public health education are defined here.

community health education. Community health education is the application of a variety of methods that result in the education and mobilization of community members in actions for resolving health issues and problems that affect the community. These methods include, but are not limited to, group process, mass media, communication, community organization, organization development, strategic planning, skills training, legislation, policy making, and advocacy.

community health educator. A community health educator is a practitioner who is professionally prepared in the field of community/public health education, who demonstrates competence in the planning, implementation, and evaluation of a broad range of health promoting or health-enhancing programs for community groups.

DEFINITIONS RELATED TO EDUCATIONAL SETTINGS

The terms that relate more specifically to school health education are defined here.

comprehensive school health instruction. Comprehensive school health instruction refers to the development, delivery, and evaluation of a planned curriculum, preschool through grade 12, with goals, objectives, content sequence, and specific classroom lessons that include, but are not limited to, the following major content areas: community health, consumer health, environmental health, family life, mental and emotional health, injury prevention and safety, nutrition, personal health, prevention and control of disease, and substance use and abuse.

comprehensive school health program. A comprehensive school health program is an organized set of policies, procedures, and activities designed to protect and promote the health and well-being of students and staff, which has traditionally included health services, healthful school environment, and health education. It should also include, but not be limited to, guidance and counseling, physical education, food service, social work, psychological services, and employee health promotion.

postsecondary health education program. A postsecondary health education program is a planned set of health education policies, procedures, activities, and services that are directed to students, faculty, and/or staff of colleges, universities, and other higher education institutions. This includes, but is not limited to, the following: general health courses for students, employee and student health promotion activities, health services, professional preparation of health educators and other professionals, self-help groups, and student life.

school health education. School health education is one component of the comprehensive school health program. It includes the development, delivery, and evaluation of a planned instructional program and other activities for students, preschool through grade 12, for parents, and for school staff, and is designed to positively influence the health knowledge, attitudes, and skills of individuals.

school health educator. A school health educator is a practitioner who is professionally prepared in the field of school health education, meets state teaching requirements, and demonstrates competence in the development, delivery, and evaluation of curricula for students and adults in the school setting that enhance health knowledge, attitudes, and problem-solving skills.

school health services. School health services are that part of the school health program provided by physicians, nurses, dentists, health educators, other allied health personnel, social workers, teachers, and others to appraise, protect, and promote the health of students and school personnel. These services are designed to ensure access to and the appropriate use of primary health care services, prevent and control communicable disease, provide emergency care for injury or sudden illness, promote and provide optimum sanitary conditions in a safe school facility and environment, and provide concurrent learning opportunities that are conducive to the maintenance and promotion of individual and community health.

GENERAL MANAGEMENT TERMS

accountability. Obligations created by acceptance of responsibilities; being answerable for the results of one's actions.

action plan. A listing of specific steps to be taken in order to accomplish a specified goal. An action plan is usually accompanied by a timetable for each step.

ad hoc committee. A temporary group convened for the accomplishment of a specific task, after which it is disbanded.

administration. Actions taken to achieve organizational goals.

affiliation needs. The human need to belong to a group and be highly regarded by members of that group.

affirmative action. A program implemented by an employer that includes specific steps to increase minority representation in the workplace; positive actions taken to eliminate job discrimination in all phases of employment.

Americans with Disabilities Act (ADA). Federal legislation that requires that facilities and services be accessible to persons with temporary or permanent disabilities; also ensures that disabled persons are not discriminated against in employment practices.

applicant pool. The group of individuals seeking to be appointed to a vacant position.

audit. An independent review and confirmation that financial reports are accurate and that standard accounting procedures were used to prepare the reports. *See also* **internal audit**.

authority. The power and responsibility to make decisions or control the behaviors of others; the right to make decisions.

autocratic leadership. A leadership style based on authority and issuing of orders. Autocratic leadership involves little or no consultation in pure form and is more task oriented than people oriented. *See also* **charismatic leadership** *and* **democratic leadership**.

balance sheet budget. Expected or actual financial status at the end of the fiscal year.

baseline measures. Preintervention data; collected data used for comparison purposes to determine the effect of a new program.

bottom-up management. Management style that encourages delegation of authority and participation of all employees.

brainstorming. A group procedure used to solve problems by generating many possible solutions before any solution is evaluated.

budget. A fiscal plan that estimates projected revenues and how they will be spent.

bureaucracy. A form of organization where regulations and controls predominate; a form of organization based on logic, systems, and rules.

burnout. A condition in which formerly conscientious workers have ceased being effective, usually as a result of cumulative stress. Work is no longer meaningful.

bylaws. A legal document formulated by the board of a not-for-profit organization. The bylaws govern the structure and function of the organization.

cash budget. A type of budget that projects cash availability and cash utilization rather than the year-end balance.

CD/ROM. A computer device (a *c*ompact *d*isc in *r*ead *o*nly *m*emory format) that electronically stores and makes available on demand educational, music, video, and other types of information.

centralization. Retention of decision making by top management. *See* **decentralization**.

chain of command. The supervisor-supervisee flow of authority that specifies who reports to whom.

change agent. A person who views creating change as an important part of his or her responsibility. A change agent can be an employee or an external consultant.

charismatic leadership. A leadership style that is based upon energetic, highly personal management traits. *See also* **autocratic leadership** *and* **democratic leadership**.

chief executive officer (CEO). The top paid administrator. The CEO of a company is often the president, although many other titles are used.

chief financial officer (CFO). The person whose responsibility for the budget is exceeded only by the responsibility of the chief executive officer. The CFO is often a vice-president or controller, although other titles are commonly used.

coalition. A group of organizations that have created an alliance in order to enhance the members' power and influence.

collective bargaining. The formal process of negotiating and administering a written signed agreement between labor and management. Collective bargaining usually covers wages, working conditions, and fringe benefits, and the agreement, once signed, has the force of law.

compensation. Wages and salaries paid to employees and other benefits such as insurance coverage.

contingency planning. The incorporation of a margin of error into plans in order to accommodate unforeseen events.

cost-benefit analysis. A method of evaluating alternatives by comparing the costs of an action and its benefits.

criterion. A measurable indicator of job performance.

database. A collection of information. A computer database may be a small personal database stored in a microcomputer or a very large database stored in a mainframe computer.

decentralization. Delegation of a great deal of authority to lower levels of management. *See* **centralization**.

delegation. The downward transfer of authority from one position to another.

democratic leadership. A leadership style that emphasizes group decision making. *See also* **autocratic leadership** *and* **charismatic leadership**.

division of labor. Use of narrow job descriptions and repetition to increase efficiency and effectiveness.

e-mail. Electronic mail distributed over a computer network.

employee assistance program (EAP). A workplace program that focuses on employee problems such as substance abuse, burnout, fiscal problems, emotional problems, and marital problems.

entrepreneurism. A leadership style that emphasizes new initiatives.

Environmental Protection Agency (EPA). The federal agency that monitors compliance with and enforces water, air, noise, and toxic waste pollution rules.

Equal Employment Opportunity Commission (EEOC). The federal agency responsible for enforcing antidiscrimination rules in the workplace. Discrimination on the basis of race, national origin, gender, religion, sexual orientation, disability, or veteran status is prohibited.

esteem needs. The human need to feel competent and to have one's achievements recognized by others. Esteem needs are included in Maslow's hierarchy of needs.

ethics. A system or code that lays out what is good, right, and honorable.

exit interview. Brief structured interview required of employees who are leaving a company.

extrinsic rewards. Payoffs granted to an individual by other people, such as incentives in motivation program. *See* **intrinsic reward**.

fax machine. An electronic device that sends and receives facsimiles of documents over phone lines.

first-line manager. A supervisor who is responsible for workers but not for other managers. *See also* **mid-level manager** *and* **top management**.

fixed costs. Ongoing costs that change little from year to year, such as personnel, insurance, lease, utility, and debt service costs.

flat organizational structure. An organizational structure characterized by wide spans of control and few hierarchy levels.

flex time. An employee scheduling system that permits employees to vary their work schedule to accommodate personal needs such as child care and transportation.

formative evaluation. Assessment during a project's development and early implementation for the purpose of improving the project in later stages. *See also* **summative evaluation**.

fringe benefits. Elements of an employee's compensation package other than wage or salary. Fringe benefits typically include vacation time, a retirement pension, and insurance coverage.

grapevine. Informal channels of communication.

halo effect. The tendency to rate an employee well, based on past performance rather than on current performance. *See* **horns effect**.

Hawthorne effect. The tendency of individuals who receive special attention to perform up to expectations. Employees who are being monitored work better than those who are not, because employees desire to meet expectations.

horns effect. The tendency to rate an employee poorly, based on past performance rather than current performance. *See* **halo effect**.

humanistic approach. A management style based on the belief that managers get things done through people. This approach emphasizes worker participation and worker satisfaction.

incremental changes. Minor adjustments to keep the organization moving toward its goals.

information overload. A condition that occurs when managers have so much information available that they have difficulty making decisions and determining what information to disregard.

internal audit. A review of financial records by a financial division employee to check for accuracy and adherence to procedures. The main purpose of an internal audit is to determine if fraud or other undesirable practices are occurring. *See also* **audit**.

internet. A term used to describe the interconnection of hundreds of computer networks in such a way that allows them to communicate with each other and allows the user to search them all simultaneously—sometimes called the Information Superhighway.

interpersonal communication. Verbal and nonverbal transmission of messages, usually in a face-to-face setting.

intrinsic rewards. Self-granted and internally experienced payoffs. *See* **extrinsic rewards**.

job enrichment. The addition of responsibilities to a position so that the work is more meaningful to the position holder. It is often used to increase satisfaction with jobs that are monotonous.

job specifications. Requirements of a position, including education, work experience, certifications, and skills.

leadership. The process of influencing an organization and its employees to move toward goals and objectives.

letter of transmittal. Cover memo that accompanies documents being mailed, such as grant applications.

liability. Vulnerability to legal action because of alleged bad judgment or bad practice. The risk associated with liability can be reduced by purchasing liability insurance.

line authority. Direct supervisory authority.

litigation. Lawsuits and other legally filed complaints that claim violation of laws and regulations.

lobbying. An organized attempt to influence the outcome of a political process. Lobbying usually includes letters, phone calls, and visits—sometimes referred to as advocacy.

management. The process of achieving results through controlling human, financial, and technical resources.

management information system (MIS). A system, typically computer based, that provides managers with information needed for decision making.

marketing. Determination of what programs are wanted or needed by target groups, determination of what the attributes of these programs are, and promotion of such programs. Marketing includes but is not limited to public relations. *See also* **public relations**.

Maslow's hierarchy of needs. A motivational theory according to which workers naturally want to meet low- and high-level needs. *See also* **physiological needs, safety needs, social needs, esteem needs,** *and* **self-actualization needs**.

mentor. A person who has accepted the role of introducing a new employee to the organization and the complexities of the position; an experienced employee who has agreed to guide an inexperienced employee. Mentors are frequently used to prepare individuals for career advancement.

merit pay. A form of performance incentive; a salary or wage increase granted for outstanding achievement. Merit pay may be a permanent increase or only for the period it was granted (a one-time-only bonus).

mid-level manager. A manager below the level of vice-president who supervises other managers. *See also* **first-line manager** *and* **top management**.

mission statement. A carefully formulated statement that defines the purpose of an organization. It may be a sentence or two in length or several pages. It is the beginning point for most planning procedures.

motivators. Factors such as achievement, recognition, responsibility, and advancement that act as incentives to improve job performance. *See also* **intrinsic incentives** *and* **extrinsic incentives**.

not-for-profit organization. An organization not created for the purpose of generating profit. Such organizations must meet legal requirements for designation as a not-for-profit. While all organizations can receive gifts, not-for-profit organizations are generally able to receipt charitable gifts that the donors can deduct for tax purposes.

nuisance complaints. Minor legal actions. Nuisance complaints are sometimes filed by disgruntled former employees or clients.

organizational chart. A visual presentation of how the parts of an organization fit together.

organizing. The process of coordinating the efforts of employees to accomplish managerial goals.

participative management. A management style that emphasizes democratic decision making.

performance appraisal. A written evaluation and employee feedback process used in the workplace. Performance appraisals form an important part of the paper trail used in job actions.

perks. Informal job benefits, such as a private office and a company car.

PERT chart. A type of planning chart (PERT stands for *p*rogram *e*valuation and *r*eview *t*echnique). A PERT chart includes a timetable and diagram for each step.

Peter principle. The notion that individuals will be promoted to or otherwise rise to their levels of incompetence.

physiological needs. Needs that must be met if an organism is to survive. Human physiological needs include the need for food, water, sleep, shelter, and clothing. These needs compose the lowest level of Maslow's hierarchy of needs.

planning. The process by which an organization's staff decide on goals, objectives, and strategies.

policies. Formally approved rules, regulations, and guidelines for action.

power. The ability to get others to perform or refrain from certain actions. In an organization, power usually involves influence over human and fiscal resources, and it can be possessed without necessarily being expressed.

privacy laws. Federal laws that prohibit discussion or release of information about employees without their permission, other than name, address, phone number, and dates of employment.

pro bono services. Free professional services. Pro bono services are often donated to organizations serving the general public by attorneys, accountants, and others.

promotion. Moving an employee to a position with more responsibilities, more status, and better compensation.

public relations. Efforts to promote a program or organization. It usually involves but is not limited to media campaigns. *See also* **marketing**.

recruitment. The process of seeking, locating, and hiring acceptable employees.

reduction in force (RIF). A layoff of employees accompanied by elimination of positions; downsizing.

resources. Human, fiscal, or technical assets available to be used in achieving goals and objectives.

reverse discrimination. Preferential treatment of a protected class that has the effect of discriminating against unprotected classes. Caucasian males are sometimes claimed to be the victims of reverse discrimination because of efforts to overcome the effects of past discrimination against women and racial minority groups.

role. A set of duties and activities assigned to a person. A position may involve more than one role, which can lead to role ambiguity or even role conflict.

safety needs. The need for security, need for order, need for freedom from fear, and so on. Safety needs are included in Maslow's hierarchy of needs.

salary range. The difference between the lowest salary level (sometimes referred to as "the floor") and the highest salary level (sometimes referred to as "the ceiling") for a comparable group of employees. The range permits differences based on seniority, merit, and the market.

self-actualization needs. The need felt by humans to be or do whatever is most meaningful to them. Self-actualization needs are at the apex of Maslow's hierarchy of needs.

sexual harassment. Unwanted sexual attention that creates an offensive or intimidating work environment.

social needs. The human need to associate with and be accepted by others. Social needs compose one level of Maslow's hierarchy of needs.

staffing. The process of providing needed human resources in an organization.

standing committee. A permanent group with a relatively permanent function, such as a finance committee.

strategic planning. A process through which senior staff decide on goals, objectives, and strategies to accomplish the mission of the organization.

summative evaluation. Evaluation at the end of a program (or at specified intervals) to determine whether goals or objectives have been accomplished. *See also* **formative evaluation**.

support staff. Secretarial, clerical, technical, and other staff who are essential to the smooth operation of an organization.

systems approach. Breaking the whole into logical parts that interrelate in an orderly fashion; studying the component parts to better understand the whole.

telecommunications. Transmission of voice, video, or data via telephone lines.

time management. That body of knowledge that emphasizes efficient use of time.

top management. Managers at the vice-presidential level and above who are responsible for the overall management of the organization. *See* **mid-level manager** *and* **first-line manager**.

trend analysis. Projection of future events based on analysis of past events. Trend analysis is often based on newspaper-clipping analysis.

tuition reimbursement. Payment of college tuition as a staff development strategy. A typical requirement for reimbursement is that the course grade is a C or better.

union. A legally constituted organization that represents an employee group and negotiates compensation and working conditions for the employees.

unity of command. An attribute of some organizational structures. Unity of command exists if each employee is responsible to only one supervisor.

zero-base budgeting. A budgeting method that requires the manager to justify the entire budget.

APPENDIX C

Bibliography

HEALTH EDUCATION AND HEALTH PROMOTION

American College Health Association, 2002. Healthy campus 2010: making it happen. Baltimore: ACHA.

Altschuld, J.W. and Witkin, B.R. 2000. From needs assessment to action. Thousand Oaks, CA: Sage

Bartholomew, L.K., et.al. 2001 Intervention Mapping: Designing Health Evidence-based Health Promotion Programs. Mountain View, CA: Mayfield Publishing

Bellingham, R., et al. 1993. Designing effective health promotion programs. Amherst, MA: Human Resources Development Press.

Bensley, R.J. and Brookins-Fisher, J. 2003. Community health education methods. 2nd ed. Boston: Jones and Bartlett.

Blonna, R and D. Watter 2005 Health Counseling Sudbury, MA: Jones and Bartlett

Breckon, D.J. 1982. Hospital health education: A guide to program development. Gaithersburg, MD: Aspen Publishers.

Breckon, D.J., et al. 1994. Community health education: Settings, roles and skills for the 21st century. 3d ed. Gaithersburg, MD: Aspen Publishers.

Burton, R., and G. MacDonald. 1992. Health promotion: Disciplines and diversity. New York, Routledge.

Cottrell, R.R. and McKenzie, J.F 2005. Health Promotion and Education Research Methods. Sudbury, MA: Jones and Bartlett

DiClemente, R. Kegler, M.C., and Crosby, R.A. 2002. Emerging theories in health promotion practice and research. San Francisco: Jossey-Bass.

Deeds, S.G. 1992. The health education specialist: Self-study for professional competence. Los Alamitos, CA: Loose Canon Publications.

Dignan, M.B., and C.P. Carr. 1992. Program planning for health education and health promotion. 2d ed. Malvern, PA: Lea and Febiger.

Downs, S., and L. Murphy. 1994. Healthy communities resource guide. Denver, CO: National Civic League.

Gilbert, G.S., and R.G. Sawyer. 2000. Health education: Creating strategies for school and community health. Boston: Jones and Bartlett.

Gilmore, G., and M. Campbell. 2005. Needs and Capacity Assessment Strategies for Health Education and Promotion, 3rd ed. Sudbury, MA: Jones and Bartlett

Glanz, K., et al., eds. 2002. Health behavior and health education: Theory, research and practice. San Francisco: Jossey-Bass.

Glaros, T., and B. Wilson. 1995. Managing health promotion programs: Student workbook and case studies. Champaign: IL: Human Kinetics.

Gold, R.S. 1991. Microcomputer applications in health education. Dubuque, IA: William C. Brown Publishers.

Green, L.W., and M.W. Kreuter. 1991. Health promotion planning: An educational and environmental approach. 2d ed. Mountain View, CA: Mayfield Publishing.

Green, L.W., and J.M. Ottoson. 1994. Community health. 7th ed. London: Chapman and Hall.

Healthy Communities 2000: Model Standards. 1991. Washington, DC: U.S. Government Printing Office.

Healthy People 2000: National Health Promotion and Disease Prevention Objectives. 1991. Washington, DC: U.S. Government Printing Office.

Healthy People 2010: A Systematic Approach to Health Improvement. 2001. Washington, DC: U.S. Government Printing Office.

Hodges, B. 2005 Assessment and Planning in Health Programs. Sudbury, MA: Jones and Bartlett

Issel, L.M. 2004. Health Program Planning and Evaluation: A Practical, Systematic Approach for Community Health. Boston, Jones and Bartlett.

Kotch, J. 2005. Maternal and Child Health: Programs, Problems and Policy. Boston: Jones and Bartlett.Kreuter, M.W., et al. 1996. Community health promotion ideas that work: A field-book for practitioners. Atlanta, GA: Health 2000.

Kreuter, M.W., et al. 2000. Tailoring Health Messages. Hillsdale, NJ: Erlbaum.

Lorig, K., et al. 1996. Outcome measures for health education and other health care interventions. New York: Sage.

McKenzie, J.F., R.R. Pinger and J.E. Kotecki 2005 An Introduction to Community Health, 5th ed. Boston: Jones and Bartlett

McKenzie, J.F., et.al. 2005. Planning, implementing, and evaluating health promotion programs. 4th ed. San Francisco: Pearson.

Minkler, M. and N. Wallerstein 2003. Community-based Participatory Research for Health. San Francisco: Jossey-Bass.

O'Donnell, M.P., and S.S. Harris. 1994. Health promotion in the workplace. Albany, NY: Delmar Publishers.

Opatz, J.P. 1993. Economic impact of worksite health promotion. Champaign, IL: Human Kinetics.

Patton, R., and W. Cissell. 1990. Community organization: Traditional principles and modern applications. Johnson City, TN: Latchpins Press.

Petersen, D.J. and G.R. Alexander. 2001. Needs Assessment in Public Health New York: Plenum

Rogers, E.M. 2001. Diffusion of innovations. 5th ed. New York: The Free Press.

Sarvela, P., and R.S. McDermott. 1993. Health education and measurement: A practitioner's perspectives. Madison, WI: Brown and Benchmark.

Shield, J., et al. 1992. Developing health education materials for special audiences. Chicago: American Dietetic Association.

Tones, K., and S. Eilford. 1994. Effectiveness, efficiency and equity. 2nd ed London: Chapman and Hall.

Valente, T.W. 2002. Evaluating Health Promotion Programs. New York: Oxford University Press

Wallack, L., et al. 1992. Media advocacy and public health. Newbury Park, CA: Sage.

Ward, W.B., and F. Lewis, eds. 1991. Advances in health education and health promotion. Baltimore, MD: P.H. Brooks Publishing Co.

Wendel, S., ed. 1993. Healthy, wealthy and wise. Omaha, NE: Wellness Council of America.

Wilson, B., and T. Glaros. 1994. Managing health promotion programs. Champaign, IL: Human Kinetics.

Windsor, R. 1994. Evaluation of health promotion, health education, and disease prevention programs. Mountain View, CA: Mayfield Publishers.

Wurzbach, M. 2004. Community Health education and Promotion: A Guide for Program design and Evaluation, 2nd ed. Boston: Jones and Bartlett

MANAGEMENT, LEADERSHIP, AND ADMINISTRATION

Baldridge National Quality Program 2004 Health Care Criteria for Performance Excellence. Gaithersburg, MD: BNQP

Bell, A. and Smith D. 2003 Learning Team Skills. Upper saddle River, NJ: Prentice Hall

Bass, B. 1994. Improving organizational effectiveness through transformational leadership. New York: Sage.

———. 1990. Becoming a master manager: A competency framework. New York: Wiley.

Bellman, G.M. 1993. Getting things done when you are not in charge: How to succeed in a support position. New York: Simon & Schuster.

Bennis, W.G. 1993. An invented life: Reflections on leadership and change. Reading, MA: Addison-Wesley.

———. 1994. On becoming a leader. Reading, MA: Addison-Wesley.

Bethel, S. 1990. Making a difference: 12 qualities that make you a leader. Berkeley, CA: Berkeley Books.

Boland, D. 1991. Let me speak to the manager: Selling from the buyer's point of view. Miami, FL: Avant Books.

Bolman, L.G. 1991. Reframing organizations: Artistry, choice, and leadership. San Francisco: Jossey-Bass.

Bouvee, C.B., et al. 2003. Management. New York: McGraw-Hill.

Bryson, J. 1992. Leadership for the common good: Tackling public problems in a shared-power world. San Francisco: Jossey-Bass.

Caroselli, M. 1990. The language of leadership. Amherst, MA: Human Resource Development Press.

Cleary, T. 1994. The human element: A course in resourceful thinking. New York: Random House.

Cohen, W. 1990. The art of the leader. Englewood Cliffs, NJ: Prentice Hall.

Collins, J. 2005. Good to Great and the Social Sectors. Boulder, CO: Collins.

Conger, J. 2002. Learning to lead: The art of transforming managers into leaders. San Francisco: Jossey-Bass.

Covey, S.R. 1991. Principle-centered leadership. New York: Summit Books.

Cox, S., J. manion, and D. Miller 2005. Nature's Wisdom in the Workplace: Managing in Today's Health Care Organizations. Bloomington, MN: Synergy Press.

De Pree, M. 1990. Leadership is an art. New York: Dell.

————. 1992. Leadership jazz. New York: Doubleday.

Donnithorne, L. 1993. The West Point way of leadership: From learning principled leadership to practicing it. New York: Doubleday.

Drucker, P. 1990. Managing the nonprofit organization: Principles and practices. New York: HarperCollins.

Duke, B. 1991. Education and leadership for the twenty-first century. Brooklyn, NY: Praeger.

Egan, G. 1993. Adding value: A systematic guide to business-driven management and leadership. San Francisco: Jossey-Bass.

Fisher, K. 1993. Leading self-directed work teams: A guide to developing new team leadership skills. New York: McGraw-Hill.

Fisher, C.D., Schoenfeldt, and Saw, J.B. 2003. Human Resources Management, 5th ed., Boston: Houghton Mifflin

Fitzenz, J and Davison, B. 2002. How to Measure Human Resources. New York: McGraw Hill

Foege, W.H.; Daulaire, N.M.P.; Black, R.E.; and Pearson, C.E. 2005. Global Health Leadership and Management. San Francisco, CA: Jossey-Bass.

Fried, B. and Johnson, J.A. 2001. Human Resources in Healthcare. Chicago: Health Administration Press.

Fried, B.J., Fottler, M.D., and Johnson, J.A. 2005, Human Resources in Healthcare: Managing for Success. Chicago, Health Administration Press

Friesen, M.E. and J.A. Johnson. 1995. The Success Paradigm: Creating Organizational Effectiveness through Quality and Strategy. Westport, CT: Quorum Books

Heneman, H.G. and Judge, T.A. 2003. Staffing Organizations. Middleton, WI: Mendota House.

Gelinas L and C. Bohlen. 2002. Tomorrow's Workforce. Irving TX: Voluntary Hospitals Association.

Gibson, J.L., et al. 2003. Fundamentals of management. 10th ed. Boston: Richard D. Irwin.

Greenleaf, R.K. 1996. On becoming a servant leader. San Francisco: Jossey-Bass.

Hackman, M. and C. Johnson. 2004. Leadership: A Communication Perspective. Long Grove, IL: Waveland.

Hellriegel, D., and J.W. Slocum. 1996. Management. Dallas, TX: Southwestern Publishers.

Hersey, P. 1993. Management of organizational behavior: Utilizing human resources. Englewood Cliffs, NJ: Prentice Hall.

Hesselbein, F., et al. 1996. The leader of the future. San Francisco: Jossey-Bass.

Hickman, C. 1990. Mind of a manager, soul of a leader. New York: Wiley.

Horton, T.R. 1991. Beyond the trust gap: Forging a new partnership between managers and their employers. Bluc Ridge, IL: Business One Irwin.

Hutton, D.W. 1994. The change agents' handbook. Milwaukee, WI: ASQC Quality Press.

Johnson, J.A., M. H. Kennedy, and N. Delener. 2005. Community Prparedness: The Role of Community Organizations and Business. New York: Preager.

Kaplan, R.E. 1991. Beyond ambition: How driven managers can lead better and live better. San Francisco: Jossey-Bass.

Katzenbach, J. and D. Smith. 2003. The Wisdom of Teams. Boston: Harvard Press

Kilpatrick, A. O. and J.A. Johnson. 1999. Handbook of Health Administration and Policy. New York: Marcel-Dekker.

Koestenbaum, P. 1991. Leadership: The inner side of greatness: A philosophy for leaders. San Francisco: Jossey-Bass.

Kotter, J. 1990. A force for change: How leadership differs from management. New York: The Free Press.

Kouzes, J.M. 2003. Credibility: How leaders gain and lose it, why people demand it. San Francisco: Jossey-Bass.

Kouzes, J.M. and B.Z. Posner 2002. The Leadership Challenge: How to Get Extraordinary Things Done in Organizations 3rd ed San Francisco: Jossy-Bass.

Kouzes, J.M. and B.Z. Posner 2003. Encouraging the Heart: A Ledaers Guide to Rewarding and Recognizing Others. San Francisco: Jossey-Bass

Kreitner, R. 2002. Management. 6th ed. Boston: Houghton Mifflin.

Lang, A. 1996. A practical guide to nonprofit financial management. Gaithersburg, MD: Aspen Publishers.

Lencioni, P. 2002. The Five Dysfunctions of a Team. San Francisco: Jossey-Bass.

Levin, H.M. and P.J. McEwan. 2001. Cost Effectiveness Analysis. Thousand Oaks, CA: Sage

Lundy, J.L. 1993. Lead, follow, or get out of the way: Invaluable insights into leadership style. San Diego, CA: Pfeiffer.

Manion, J. 2005. From Management to Leadership. San Francisco: Jossy-Bass

Morrison, A.W. 1992. The new leaders: Guidelines on leadership diversity in America. San Francisco: Jossey-Bass.

Nanus, B. 1992. Visionary leadership: Creating a compelling sense of direction for your organization. San Francisco: Jossey-Bass.

Novick, L. and G. Mays. 2005 Public Health Administration: Principles for Population-Based Management. Boston: Joes and Bartlett.

Oakley, E. 1993. Enlightened leadership: Getting to the heart of change. New York: Simon & Schuster.

O'Neil, J.R. 1993. The paradox of success: When winning at work means losing at life: A book of renewal for leaders. New York: G.P. Putnam's Sons.

Osborn, C. 1994. How would Confucius ask for a raise? 100 solutions for tough business problems. New York: William Morrow.

Peck, M.S., et al. 1996. Reflections on leadership. Indianapolis, IN: Greenleaf Center for Servant Leadership.

Pegg, M. 1994. Positive leadership: How to build a winning team. San Diego, CA: Pfeiffer.

Porter-O'Grady, T and K. Malloch. 2003. Quantum Leadership. Boston: Jones and Bartlett

Powell, G. 2003. Women and Men in Management, 3rd ed. Newbury Park, CA: Sage.

Reynolds, J. 1994. Out front leadership: Discovering, developing, and delivering your potential. Austin, TX: Mott & Carlisle.

Rothwell, W. J. 2001. Executive Succession Planning. New York: AMACOM.

Rue, L.W., and L.L. Byars. 1992. Management: Skills and applications. Boston: Richard D. Irwin.

Schein, E.H. 1992. Organizational culture and leadership. San Francisco: Jossey-Bass.

Sims, H.P. 1992. The new leadership paradigm: Social learning and cognition in organizations. Thousand Oaks, CA: Sage.

Snyder, N.H. 1994. Vision, values, and courage: Leadership for quality management. Old Tappan, NJ: Maxwell MacMillan.

Spears, L. and M. Lawrence. 2002. Focus on Leadership: Servant Leadership for the 21st Century. New York: Wiley and Sons

Stoner, J.A., and R. Freeman. 2002. Management. 6th ed. Englewoods Cliffs, NJ: Prentice Hall.

Author Bios

James A. Johnson, Ph.D. is a medical social scientist and a Professor in the Dow College of Health Professions at Central Michigan University. He was previously Chair of the Department of Health Administration and Policy at the Medical University of South Carolina. He teaches courses in organizational behavior and development, international health, systems thinking, and community health. Dr. Johnson's publications include 100 articles and 10 books on a wide range of health care issues. He is past editor of the *Journal of Healthcare Management* published by the American College of Healthcare Executives (ACHE) and past editor of the *Journal of Management Practice*. He has served on the Board of Directors for the Association of University Programs in Health Administration (AUPHA) and currently serves on the scientific advisory board of the National Diabetes Trust Foundation. Dr Johnson has traveled to and worked in 21 different countries. He also works with the World Health Organization in Geneva, Switzerland and has involved many students in this activity. He completed his masters degree at Auburn University and Ph.D. at Florida State University.

Donald J. Breckon, MA, MPH, PhD, is president emeritus of Park University in Parkville, Missouri, a suburb of Kansas City. He served as President for 14 years before retiring. He was born, raised, and educated in Michigan. His degrees are from Central Michigan University, The University of Michigan, and Michigan State University.

Dr. Breckon served in a variety of faculty and administrative positions at Central Michigan University over a 24-year period. He was a professor of health education and health science while holding consecutive appointments as Assistant Dean of Health, Physical Education, Recreation, and Athletics; Associate Dean of Education, Health, and Human Services; and Acting Dean of Graduate Studies/

Associate Vice Provost for Research. He also spent a year as a postdoctoral Academic Administration Fellow with the American Council on Education, prior to assuming the presidency of what was then Park College.

While at Central Michigan University, Dr. Breckon developed the under-graduate and graduate degree programs in public health education and health promotion, hospital health education and health promotion, and allied health edu-cation. He was also instrumental in developing the Master of Science in Health Administration, and taught in the program for many years. He has published approximately 150 articles in more than 30 professional journals, along with 12 chapters in various books of readings, 15 monographs, and 3 nationally used col-lege textbooks, one of which was the first edition of this book

Dr. Breckon's retirement as a university president provided him the opportunity to return to occasional teaching of Health Science/Health Administration courses via the internet and in evening programs. He developed a Health Administration program within an existing MBA program, and taught courses in that program, both online and in face-to face settings. . He enjoys writing and still writes peri-odic opinion pieces for the local newspaper.

Dr. Breckon has been active in state and national professional health educa-tion and health administration organizations. He has also been active in local and state government, serving as mayor of Mt. Pleasant, Michigan, on governor's task forces, and in various appointed positions in Michigan and Missouri. He recently completed a term on the Board of the American Red Cross of Greater Kansas City. He currently serves on the Saint Luke's Hospital Board of Directors, as well as its Executive Committee and Long Range Planning Committee. He also serves on the Council of Governors of the American Hospital Association. .

Dr Breckon has received more than three dozen awards, commendations, and recognitions, including a listing in *Who's Who in America* and an Honorary Doctorate in Public Service from Central Michigan University.

Dr. Breckon is married and has four daughters and seven grandchildren. He views his position as university president and his political involvement as evi-dence that health education and health administration skills are applicable to a wide range of positions and settings. . He especially enjoys lobbying on national and state legislative health care issues, and does so frequently as a hospital trustee, and on behalf of the American Hospital Association.

Don's primary interests now that he has fully retired are his wife of 47 years, Sandy, their children and grand children, as well as international travel. Together they have completed more than three dozen cruises on the most of the major oceans and rivers of the world, They have traveled as People to People Health Care Delegates to South Africa, and have been on four African Safaris.

Dr Breckon is very grateful to Dr Johnson for revising and updating this book, and continues to wish the very best to all students preparing to enter the health care/health services professions.

Index